Wayward Women

Wayward Women

Sexuality and Agency in a New Guinea Society

Holly Wardlow

UNIVERSITY OF CALIFORNIA PRESS

Berkeley / Los Angeles / London

University of California Press
Berkeley and Los Angeles, California

University of California Press, Ltd.
London, England

© 2006 by The Regents of the University of California

Library of Congress Cataloging-in-Publication Data

Wardlow, Holly.
    Wayward women : sexuality and agency in a New Guinea society / Holly
Wardlow.
        p. cm.
    Includes bibliographical references and index.
    ISBN 0-520-24559-8 (alk. paper).—ISBN 0-520-24560-1 (pbk. : alk. paper)
    1. Women, Huli—Papua New Guinea—Tari District—Sexual Behavior.
2. Women, Huli—Papua New Guinea—Tari District—Social conditions.
3. Women, Huli—Papua New Guinea—Tari District—Economic conditions.   4. Bride price—Papua New Guinea—Tari District.   5. Courtship—
Papua New Guinea—Tari District.   6. Tari District (Papua New Guinea)—
Social conditions.   7. Tari District (Papua New Guinea)—Economic conditions.   I. Title.

DU740.42.W354   2006
305.409956'1—dc22   2005028155

15   14   13   12   11   10   09   08   07   06
10   9   8   7   6   5   4   3   2   1

Contents

Illustrations

Maps

Figures

All photos were taken by the author.

Tables

Acknowledgments

Many people provided help and support during my fieldwork in Papua New Guinea and during the writing of this book. In Tari, Mary Michael was a particularly good friend—funny, insightful, loyal, and affectionate. Jacinta Haiyabe and other women at the Tari District Women's Association—Janet Magabe, Betty Tom, Alison, and Regina—were also good friends and helpful informants. The Tari Hospital staff, and especially Pauline Agilo, were consistently obliging. Thanks also to Peter Ekopia and his wife Margaret, to James Samkul and his family, to Maria Kati, and to Jenny Yaliya for their help with this project.

I had a number of field assistants along the way, but Henry Hariki Pagana was the most perspicacious and steadfast, and made the transcription, translation, and analysis of village court cases particularly fun since he also was driven to understand the aims, strategies, and rhetorical artistry of the various actors. I learned recently that his older brother, Ato Louis Pagana, died. For a brief period of time near the end of my fieldwork Ato hosted me and helped me to interview men who attended *dawe anda*. At that time I wished that I had met him far earlier since he was such an intelligent and thoughtful man. I am terribly sorry about his death. My condolences also to the family of Nancy Tapili, who also briefly worked as my field assistant. Special thanks go to the Papua New Guinea Institute of Medical Research and especially Michael Alpers, Deborah Lehman, Carol Jenkins, Travis Jenkins, John Vail, James Marabe, and all of the staff of what was then the Tari Research Unit. Travis Jenkins patiently helped me take still photographs of the video

Bobby Teardrops for one of the first articles I published. I was very sorry to hear that he died; my condolences to his family.

Special thanks also go to Tom Wagner, who at that time worked in the Department of Geology at the University of Papua New Guinea. When I came to Port Moresby for field breaks, he was always happy to hear about my observations, insights, and experiences, and only once complained that "all I could talk about was the Huli." That Tom was genuinely interested in all I had to say, and usually even wanted to hear more, made all the difference in the world. Thanks also go to Richard and Jeannie Teare, who generously took good care of me upon my arrival in Papua New Guinea and then again after I had to abandon my second field site. Geoff Hiatt and his father, Ron Hiatt, both of whom worked in Tari at various points in time and both of whom have worked for Porgera Joint Venture, provided very useful information regarding Tari during the early colonial period, the political histories of various clans in the Tari Basin, and what it is like to work as a community relations officer for a gold mine.

Outside of Papua New Guinea, my deepest thanks go to my graduate advisor, Bruce Knauft. During my fieldwork Bruce assiduously read the field notes I mailed home and faxed me helpful comments and questions. Later he read multiple drafts of dissertation chapters and article manuscripts, as well as the manuscript for this book. I cannot thank him enough for his enthusiasm, intellectual engagement, and all the time he has been willing to give for reading my work and talking about it. I do not think there could be a better advisor. At Emory University I would also like to thank Peter Brown, Corinne Kratz, and Donald Donham for their insights, challenging questions, and useful advice. For their deep friendship and intellectual companionship during graduate school and after, special thanks go Wynne Maggi, Gayatri Reddy, Dan Smith, Jessica Gregg, Jennifer Hirsch, and Donna Murdock. Since graduating from Emory, I have been especially lucky to have Joel Robbins as a colleague. Many thanks for his very close reading of the manuscript for this book, as well as for the always interesting and fun conversation. Shirley Lindenbaum and Janice Boddy also provided insightful questions and comments about the manuscript, and I am very grateful for their input.

The University of Iowa and the University generously gave me time to write as well as supportive and collegial faculty and graduate students. Research for this book was made possible by grants from Fulbright-Hays (#PO22A40008), Wenner-Gren (#5848), the National Science Foundation (#9412381), the Harry Frank Guggenheim Foundation, the Association for Women in Science, and the National Women's Studies Association.

I would also like to thank my family. My sister, Katherine, came to visit me in Tari during the first year of my fieldwork, and my parents came the next year. I thank them for wanting to share the fieldwork experience, as well as for taking me away from it for short periods of time. I am particularly grateful to my sister for being willing to hike down slippery mountains, through deep Huli trenches, and across precarious bridges. That she needed so much help doing these things reminded my Huli friends of how pathetically clumsy I had been at first, and thus how much I had improved (though I often still needed someone's helping hand). So, for making me look good, many thanks to you, Kat.

Finally, for his patience, good humor, and love during the writing of this book, I thank my partner, Ken MacDonald. I look forward to the day when I can share Tari with him.

Introduction

Pugume Mangobe's grave was an obvious thing to ask about when I settled into my first rural field site north of Tari town.[1] I walked past it almost every day on the way from the house where I was staying to the
trade store that had been converted into an office for me. The sky blue
concrete marker drew one's attention, and yet care for it seemed desul-
tory; the paint was starting to chip and fade, spiky grass grew high
around it. Pugume had been the third of five sisters, I was told, the
middle child of Mangobe's third and last wife. As the story went, Mangobe had been a well-respected local leader; known for his eloquence, he
was one of the few men who could deftly use the cryptic metaphors,
double entendres, and other aphoristic elements of traditional Huli oratory. And he was hardworking: his gardens and pigs thrived, and he had
healthy, adult children from all three of his marriages.[2] However, Mangobe was quite old by the time of the Mt. Kare gold rush in the late 1980s,
and he was very angry when Pugume and her mother abandoned him to
go look for gold, flagrantly disobeying his orders. Or at least this was one
reason given for why he struck her down with an axe one morning as she
was bent over a stream washing clothes.

Other people said no, it had nothing to do with the gold rush. Mangobe was angry about getting old and sick, incensed that he would not
live to see his three youngest daughters marry and that his wife and her
brothers would thus claim the young women's bridewealth. He decided
that if he couldn't have his daughters' bridewealth, then no one else
would either, and so he set out to kill the youngest three, but only man-

aged to get one. That was what the four remaining daughters believed. Still others just thought he had lost his mind in his old age, and there was no knowing what he was thinking or feeling when he killed Pugume. Many men turned odd in their old age, they said—some went off and lived alone in the bush; one was known to have gone mute for years, and when he started talking again he was suddenly as sweet tempered as he had been irascible in the past. But other people retorted that at the time of the murder Mangobe was already too disabled by respiratory illness to have been able to carry it out himself, and that he had hired someone else to do it, suggesting that it was not an insane or impulsive act. Whatever Mangobe's reasons, he confessed to the murder and died in prison of pneumonia not long after.

The story of Pugume Mangobe's murder took on mythic qualities for me. "Once there were five sisters . . .," I found myself murmuring when we passed her grave, putting her history into the (Western) language and cadence of legend. For a time I was preoccupied with why: why did he do it, what was he so angry about, what had his wife and daughters done, or what did he think they had done? And I was not the only one to think about Pugume in an almost allegorical way; other people seemed to see her that way too. Her story—its ghastly and extraordinary nature—lent itself to morality tales about troublesome aspects of contemporary Huli sociality: the chaos and disruption caused by the Mt. Kare gold rush, the supposed unruliness of women in the contemporary context, people's sometimes disconcertingly single-minded preoccupation with bride-wealth transactions. Pugume's tale could be used in a kind of knowing, admonitory way to pass judgment on all these things. So perhaps it isn't surprising that I found myself believing that if I could understand Pugume's murder I would have "the key" to Huli gender relations in the contemporary context.

However, one anomalous case does not an ethnography make, and while violence against women, sometimes fatal, is very high among the Huli (Barss 1991; see also Counts 1992; Toft 1985), in fact the murder of women by their own natal family members is quite rare. The narrative and analytical track I ultimately followed was that of the remaining Mangobe sisters, for their stories did not end with Pugume's death, of course. I knew all four sisters quite well, particularly the youngest two, and kept track of their tumultuous lives during my twenty-six months of field-work, from April 1995 to June 1997. I was also painfully aware of what others said about them, as people tried to convince me not to talk to them, give them gifts, or be seen walking in public with them. They were *pasinja meri* (literally, passenger women), people warned me—defiant, too independent, too peripatetic, and believed to exchange sex for money. "They have no brothers to beat them," I heard time and again, and since their father had died, they were not "under the legs" of any man. Without the disciplinary influence of male kin, they had become wayward, promiscuous, and untrustworthy—as likely to steal from me and betray me as to be my friends, people claimed.

Only one of the Mangobe sisters actually came close to self-identifying as a passenger woman over the course of my fieldwork, and even she seemed only to be trying it on for size, at some moments impishly enacting some of the behaviors associated with passenger women—lingering near trade stores to flirt openly with men, using slightly provocative language in public—and at other moments trying to scramble out from under the weight of the stigma attached to the category. Nevertheless, in part because of what I witnessed of the lives of the Mangobe sisters—their seemingly contradictory attempts to both defy and conform to what is expected of *wali ore* (literally, women really; good women)—I became interested in how self-identified Huli passenger women come to inhabit that subject position; the kinds of agency that they and other Huli women exercise in the contemporary context; how and why sexuality becomes an effective resource for female agency; and the ways in which passenger women's actions are both a response to and a materialization of what is sometimes referred to by scholars of Melanesia as "incipient individualism."

The category *pasinja meri* is protean and difficult to pin down. From one angle the term seems to have no consistent referent and exists only as a discourse mobilized by men, other women, hospital employees, the police, and religious authorities to categorize women—stigmatizing some for their behavior and controlling others with the fear that they might be so labeled. And yet there are women who call themselves *pasinja meri,* embracing this label with gleeful impudence, angry defiance, or shame. In a sense, then, the ontological status of *pasinja meri* is dual: it is a discourse used to control women's behavior, and it is an identity category or subject position that some women enter through complex trajectories that are not fully captured by simple notions of "choice" or "force" (see also Law 1997). To provide a preliminary, simplified description, self-identified *pasinja meri* are women—often married and with children—who run away from their husbands or natal families and engage in extramarital sex, often in exchange for money (Wardlow 2002a). This description may make them sound like prostitutes or sex workers, but this book is not—or at least not only—an ethnography of prostitution. Rather, it is an analysis of female agency in a particular postcolonial context—a context of high male out-migration for wage labor; a context where roads and markets and the absence of men have enabled women to be more mobile and less monitored than they were in the past; and a context where bridewealth transactions are both fundamental to the social meaning and value of women and an important means by which rural, unemployed people gain access to cash.

In addition to their transgressive sexuality, a number of other characteristics are also associated with passenger women. People often say that they are "greedy for money" (why else would they exchange sex for money?) and too lazy to work hard at gardening or raising pigs, as other women do. Also, according to many passenger women themselves, they use vulgar language in public—conduct that is highly improper and potentially polluting (Goldman 1983)—and are always on the move, never "under the legs of men," as women should be. Finally, and most damning, they are often described as *"bighed,"* a Melanesian Pidgin word that means impertinent or obstinate, but, when used by Huli people to describe women, implies conceit, defiance, and "self-importance"—both in the sense of arrogance and in the sense of making one's individual self the final arbiter of one's choices (cf. Leavitt 1998). In order to theorize the broader cultural and historical significance of passenger women for the Huli, it is necessary to discuss the three conceptual frameworks that underpin my analysis: agency, sexuality, and incipient individualism.

Agency and Melanesia

This project, at its heart, is an exploration of female agency—the way female agency is shaped by both cultural and economic context, and the reasons why sexuality becomes an important instrument of this agency, particularly when women feel betrayed, neglected, or commoditized by their kin. In my analysis of Huli passenger women, and Huli female agency more generally, I take an approach informed by "practice theory," which, as Karp observes, "provides an analytic frame which allows ethnographers to describe the complex relations among the agents' strategies, the symbolic forms they invoke in their actions, and the distribution of power in society" (1986: 1321; see also Bourdieu 1977; Bourdieu and Wacquant 1992). Similarly, Ortner asserts that an orientation informed by practice theory involves "seeking the configuration of cultural forms, social relations, and historical processes that move people to act in ways that produce the effects in question" (1989: 12; see also Sahlins 1981). For the purposes of the present analysis, then, in order to understand why some Huli women act in ways that have come to be reified in the category "passenger woman," it is necessary to understand the sociocultural structures that produce and constrain particular modes of agency among Huli women, as well as the ways in which these "structures" are changing in the context of wage labor and the commoditization of social relations.

According to Ortner, actor-oriented analyses emerged in opposition to paradigms that prioritized social structure, "hypercoherent studies of symbolic systems" (1984: 144), and a conception of the human subject as simply enacting the roles and norms of whatever culture s/he was in. However, she notes, the conceptual orientations and modes of analysis that are loosely grouped together under the term "practice theory" differ from earlier actor-oriented analyses—such as transactionalism—in three ways. First, ideally they do not oppose the human actor to "the system," but instead acknowledge that the system powerfully shapes and is shaped by human action: "Human action considered apart from its structural contexts and its structural implications is not 'practice' " (1989: 12). Second, approaches informed by practice theory focus on asymmetrical relationships of power. As Ortner flatly states, "Human activity regarded as taking place in a world of politically neutral relations is not 'practice' " (1989: 12). Finally, practice theory conceptualizes the actors' desires, goals, and imagined possibilities as thoroughly cultural. That is to say, actors may be "rational" and "strategic," but their rationality proceeds according to specific cultural logics and values, and their strategies are generated and constrained, both imaginatively and materially, by sociocultural context. In sum, practice-oriented approaches try to theorize how and why social systems and structures of inequality are reproduced and/or changed through the actions of persons who are importantly shaped by these very systems.

In accord with this approach, I analyze certain Huli social institutions and interpersonal relations—such as the practice of bridewealth marriage or the brother-sister relationship—as "structures" that generate specific modes of female agency. Importantly, as Ortner notes, the notion of structure includes "emotional and moral configurations, and not just abstract ordering principles" (1989:14). In other words, bridewealth marriage or brother-sister relationships are not just about social roles or categories of kinship, but also about "structures of feeling" (Williams 1977). For example, that Huli women learn to be *wali ore* (good women) in the context of brother-sister relationships saturates the formative experience of proper femininity with a sense of intimacy and attachment, and these feelings shape the imaginable possibilities for action. Nevertheless, such "structures" are not static: that men are absent for wage labor changes what it means to be a sister; that bridewealth is increasingly monetized and used as a means to gain cash changes what it means to be a wife. It is in this nexus of robust but changing structures that passenger women's actions become think-able in the contemporary context.

However, before any scholar of Melanesia can proceed with an actor-oriented analysis, he or she is faced with the fact that the concepts of "actor," "agency," and "structure"—all key, if heuristic, symbols for a practice theory approach—have been theorized otherwise in the Melanesian context. Most theorizations of agency tend to assume an individual actor as the locus of desire and action. This singular actor is not fully autonomous and does not enact some sort of abstract, voluntaristic "free will"—in the sense of being completely disembedded from social context; indeed, unmediated, free-floating will is impossible in anthropological understandings of practice (Ahearn 2001; Maggi 2001). Moreover, the individual actor may—according to more poststructuralist renditions—be conceptualized as "emerging from the uneasy suturing of incommensurable discursive positions" (McNay 2000: 17) or be adversely positioned within intersecting hierarchies (Ortner 1995). In sum, the actor or agent of practice theory does not necessarily correspond to the "peculiar" (Geertz 1984) individual of "the West": bounded, self-authoring, and "ontologically . . . prior to the relations in which it ultimately finds itself thrown in life" (Weiner 1999: 236). Nevertheless, even with all these caveats and complexities, most theorizations of agency do rely conceptually and methodologically on an actor characterized by self-reflection and an individual capacity to act.

Contrasting with such accounts is the theorization of Melanesian agency, put forward most notably by Marilyn Strathern (1988), as emerging from a relationally constituted person—a "dividual," not an "individual." Persons, in this perspective, are "constructed as the plural and composite site of the relationships that produced them" (13), or as Biersack puts it, the "dividual" is "a s/he who is multiply authored or caused and who is complexly positioned within a network of consanguines and affines . . . born of others and dependent and interdependent rather than autonomous" (1991: 148). According to Strathern, as well as many scholars of Melanesia who don't necessarily subscribe wholeheartedly to the concept of the "dividual," the archetypical Melanesian person is gradually and continually "made" through the various substances contributed to them during conception, nurture, initiation, and other ritual events (Knauft 1989), and is thus "a living commemoration of the actions which produced it" (Strathern 1988: 302). Even physical objects—shells, bodily ornaments, or pigs—are potentially generative "substances," for gifts embody the giver and are "partible" aspects of them—they "circulate as parts of persons" (178)—creating others by enmeshing them in relationality. As Busby notes, "The flow of internal substances such as semen or blood is no different from the flow of valuables: both are objectifications of relations, and both must be detached from the person before they can be transacted" (1997: 275). Persons are thus only fleetingly and provisionally unitary actors, for they are always oriented toward and moved by the relationships in which they are embedded and of which they are made. This conceptualization of personhood clearly implies a different notion of agency than that generally found in practice theory. And, as Kratz notes, "Ideas about personhood and agency are always intimately entwined" (2000: 137); thus, the agency associated with the Melanesian relational or "dividual" person consists of "externalizing" or "activating" aspects of the composite self through participating in gift exchange and other practices that put one's "partible" aspects into social circulation. As Mallett says, "a person's actions in any given context are evoked, generated, or caused by the particular relations that constitute him/her" (2003: 21).

Strathern's and others' (Geertz 1984; Shweder and Bourne 1984) exegeses of relational personhood and agency act as a useful brake on the potentially runaway train of individual voluntarism in actor-oriented theories. Nevertheless, they have been critiqued from a range of perspectives. Many scholars find fault with the "radical alterity" attributed to Melanesia, India, Bali, and other geographies associated with sociocentric personhood. As Sökefeld argues, by privileging culturally distinctive idioms of personhood, anthropologists imply that "anthropology's subjects have an identity (shared with others, derived from a culture) *instead of* a self" (1999: 418). In other words, the individual/dividual, egocentric/sociocentric opposition is an insidious "us"/"them" orientalism that dehumanizes non-Western others. Other critics suggest that the wholly sociocentric person—particularly in its Strathernian rendition—logically precludes the possibility of agency, leaving only the enactment of social patterns (Josephides 1991); thus, oppositional or resistant agency is rendered conceptually impossible. Relatedly, many scholars have reacted strongly to Strathern's seemingly static and ahistorical representation of Melanesian personhood, as if Melanesians had somehow missed the boats of colonialism, governmentality, and globalization (Thomas 1991; Carrier 1992).

Another perspective sees the value in acknowledging and explicating indigenous modes of relationality and social action, but suggests that taking an actor-oriented and/or ethnohistorical approach can enable the ethnographer to discern multiple and shifting modes of personhood and agency more complex than those revealed by terms like "individual" or "dividual" (Foster 1995; Stewart and Strathern 2000a; Ewing 1990; Shaw 2000). Along these lines, Mattison Mines has challenged received notions of Indian sociocentrism by using life history narratives to identify critical junctures in actors' lives when they think and act in quite individualistic ways (1988). Jacobson-Widding similarly complicates understandings of Congolese personhood by showing that the ideologically privileged values of sociocentrism are offset by those of individualism, often referred to through the metaphor of "the shadow" (1990). In the Melanesian context, a number of scholars have pointed out that Melanesians, while relationally oriented, also value self-assertion and individual accomplishment (Stewart and Strathern 2000b). And, in the North American context, feminist scholars have long been skeptical of the American "autonomy obsession" (Code 1991), arguing that dominant constructions of the Western individual are a masculinist "illusion of the Enlightenment conception of the subject" (Mackenzie and Stoljar 2000: 11). Indeed feminist philosopher Annette Baier has tried to complicate notions of Western individualism by introducing the concept of "second persons"—a concept disconcertingly similar to that of the Indian or Melanesian "dividual"—which refers to the relational basis for personhood: "Persons are essentially successors, heirs to other persons who formed and cared for them, and their personality is revealed both in their relations to others and in their response to their own recognized genesis" (1985: 85; see also Code 1991: 71–109).

Perhaps, then, it is prudent to bear in mind LiPuma's assertion that "in all cultures . . . there exist both individual and dividual modalities or aspects of personhood . . . [But] cultures differ critically in the ontological status, visibility, and force granted individual/relational aspects of persons" (1998: 56–57). It is this more complex and contingent notion of personhood—one that is compatible with practice theory in its attention to experience and history, but that also makes space for the possibility of "radical alterity"—that I try to operationalize in my analysis of Huli women's agency. LiPuma adds that "the progress of modernity in Melanesia simultaneously create[s] and capitalize[s] on the foregrounding, affirmation, and promotion of the individual aspect of this tension, thus leading to a greater visibility and public presence of persons as individuals" (57). In other words there is something about modernity—and just what will be discussed later in this chapter—that elicits and accentuates the individualistic modality of personhood.

Female Agency

The already knotty issue of how to conceptualize the relationship between culturally constituted personhood and historically situated agency becomes yet more complicated when one asserts, as I do for the Huli, that agency is gendered—in other words, that there are particular modes of exerting power or producing effects that are particular to women as women or men as men. Both Melanesian ethnography and recent feminist theory question the idea that gender is a stable category or experience, albeit in somewhat different ways. From the Melanesianist perspective, gender is a contingent and achieved quality that consists, at least in part, of the bodily substances that go into and out of a person over the course of the life cycle. To take the classic example, among a number of cultural groups, in order for boys to become more male, female substance must be removed—sometimes through nose-bleeding—and male substance must be added—sometimes through the ingestion of semen or semen-like fluids (Herdt 1999; Knauft 1989). Conversely, a woman may become less female and more male—acquiring in the process some of the perquisites and costs of maleness—as she gradually expels her female substances through pregnancy, birth, and lactation (Meigs 1990; cf. Wood 1999). And, putting a somewhat different twist on the idea of shifting male and female substances, Strathern (1988) asserts that both male and female aspects are contained within each composite person, and thus a singular or unitary gender—being male *or* female—is provisional and only emerges, or is elicited by others, in particular social contexts in order to achieve particular ends. In short, it may be difficult to talk about something called "female agency" if Melanesian persons are situationally gendered or if femaleness ebbs and flows over time.

From the perspective of feminist theory, a concept of "female agency" is equally problematic in that "femaleness" may be only one among a person's range of identifications, which can include kinship relations, class, race, sexuality, religion, and so on. Moreover, gender itself has come to be seen as a kind of agency or practice—the act of doing or performing maleness or femaleness. Since gender is a kind of doing—an action, not an essence; a process, not a category—then there is always at least the possibility that one could "do" or "perform" otherwise, again making gender seem provisional and unstable—not fixed enough to engender its own habitual modes of social action.

A number of responses can be made to these challenges to the notion of a stable gendered agency, and these responses can be made on both ethnographic and conceptual levels. First, most Huli people seem to have a fairly rigid and dichotomous notion of gender, what constitutes proper male and female behavior, how girls should be socialized differently than boys, and so on (Goldman 1983). Huli *mana*—traditional lore or cultural knowledge—about gender is quite elaborate, taught at a very young age, and reinforced by daily discourse, practice, and disciplinary measures; thus, any child can recite, "women are for bridewealth" or "women raise pigs, make gardens, and have babies."[3] This is not to say that gendered expectations are not contested; it is only to confirm that, as Lois McNay says, "gender identities are not free-floating: they involve deep-rooted investments on the part of individuals and historically sedimented practices which severely limit their . . . transformability" (2000: 18; see also Moore 1994, 1999).

Butler's and others' theorizations of the "somatization of power relations" (McNay 2000: 36) are especially useful in countering both feminist and Melanesianist misgivings about the durability of gender. As McNay summarizes,

> Butler's formulation of the idea of the performative attempts to move beyond understanding the construction of gender identity as a one-sided process of imposition or determination by thinking of it in terms of the temporally more open process of repetition. Repetition denotes both a process of profound corporeal inscription and also a fundamental instability at the heart of dominant gender norms . . . the idea of the performative expresses both the cultural arbitrariness or "performed" nature of gender identity and also its deep inculcation in that every performance serves to reinscribe it upon the body. Performance does not refer to a voluntarist process of performance so much as a "forced reiteration of norms." (33)

Among the Huli, bodily and spatial practices repeatedly enact a rigid duality of gender (Goldman 1983; Clark 1997). In the past—and to a large extent today—men and women lived in separate houses and maintained separate gardens; as Glasse writes, "Huli men are domestically independent of their women—virtually all men prepare and cook their own food.

Only young boys and senile men would eat food cooked by a woman"
(1968: 64). In many areas there were separate walking paths for men and
women, and where there were not, men would carefully walk just to the
side of paths to avoid stepping in women's footprints. Women, it is often
said, should be "under the legs of men," which symbolically conveys the
expectation that they be subordinate in male-female interactions, as well
as indicating a general spatial rule in which women should never be
higher than men—for example, in any conversation between brother and
sister or husband and wife, men physically locate themselves on the
higher piece of ground; in any family compound, men's houses are up the
hill from women's houses; in areas of land where there are separate walking paths for men and women, the higher paths are for men. Much as
Bourdieu (1977) has pointed out, the ideologies of gender hierarchy are
repeatedly instantiated in spatial arrangements and bodily comportment.

Regular, everyday bodily practice for women—taking care not to step
over people's legs, firewood, pots and pans, or other objects that might
indirectly transfer potentially dangerous female substances to another
person—also works to install in female bodies a particular gender regimentation. Bodily practices during menstruation—arising before dawn
to wash and not cooking for, talking to, or handing objects to men—ac-
centuate this regimentation. The significance of these practices are, to
some degree, open to personal interpretation. Some women, for example, speak of them as oppressive, while others think of them as acts of
familial care or as a kind of marital intimacy from afar (see also Biersack
1987, 1998). Nevertheless, whatever meanings any individual woman
might bring to these practices, that women as women do them reinforces
the duality of gender.

Buttressing or complementing such bodily practices are an array of discourses about women that depict them and their bodies as impulsive,
ngubi (smelly), without *mana* (that is, without cultural knowledge or the
ability to fully internalize social rules), without *hongo* (without strength,
which refers to both physical and moral strength), and as moved by hidden, sometimes inscrutable intentions. Women are also considered emotionally deficient. During my fieldwork, it was impressed on me that one
thing I needed to understand about the Huli was, as one college-educated
friend put it, "emotions *bilong mipela* fluctuate" (our emotions fluctuate),
and Huli men expressed pride in what they described as their ability to
explode into a fierce rage one minute and laugh the next. However,
women are said to be less capable of these mercurial changes of temper,
and in particular hold on to anger for too long (with good reason, I often

thought).[4] Even male bodies are said to be more aesthetically pleasing than female bodies; for example, it is said that men are naturally able to attract women, while women must resort to love magic. Similarly, many Huli myths praise the beauty of the female protagonist by likening her to a man: "Her daughter was very beautiful. Her daughter had arms and thighs like a young man" *(Ibu wane wandari mbiria paya ore. Ibu wane nde ki bi igiri ale ke bi igiri ale)*. In the Melanesian context, outward beauty indexes internal potency, so to say that men are more beautiful than women is to also say that they "naturally" have more social charisma and efficacy.

Gender can be seen, then, as "the effect of a set of regulatory practices that seek to render gender identity uniform" (Moore 1999: 155), and it is in this sense that one can talk about "female agency" as gendered modes of action that stem from (1) culturally specific constructions of personhood that among the Huli can be described as both "dividual" and "individual"; (2) women's social position as "under the legs of men" and needing to be "fenced in," idioms for expressing a particular kind of disciplinary but protective male dominance; and (3) institutionalized practices that effectively exclude women from modes of agency to which men have access, such as being easily able to bring conflicts into the public sphere (see also MacLeod 1992). Below I sketch out a few dimensions of Huli female agency (discussed in more detail in chapter 2) in order to show the ways in which they are connected to personhood and social structure.

Perhaps most important to an understanding of Huli female agency is the notion that women must be "fenced in" or "under the legs of men." These very common phrases—and other linguistic patterns that also indicate women's symbolic association with stasis and enclosure (Goldman 1983)—indicate that women are meant to be subordinate, but subordinate in a particular way; that is, women, their bodily energies, and their agency are meant to be encompassed. Their capacities for acting on the social order are always already contained within and mobilized for plans larger than themselves—whether it is bringing in bridewealth for one's natal family, reproducing one's affinal family, or raising pigs for others' transactions. Moreover, while the phrase "under the legs of men" refers to women's proper position vis-à-vis men, it can also refer to the more general expectation that women subordinate their desires to the needs of their families or clans. To "fence women in" indicates that women, like pigs or crops, need to be controlled, but also that they require nurture and protection. In order to bring forth and make use of women's most valuable and efficacious qualities, they should be subordinate to and dis-

FIGURE 1. Young woman inside her brother's fence.

ciplined by others, men in particular. The other salient dimension of the "fence" analogy is that pigs or crops are never "for themselves" — they are always for human purposes; similarly, women too are for, and therefore encompassed by, transactions beyond themselves.

Arguably, men too, in their "dividual" or relational mode, are never "for themselves" and always for transactions beyond themselves; however, men are symbolically configured as being able to formulate, initiate, carry out, represent, and take responsibility for these transactions, and thus they are more often positioned as encompassing others, not being encompassed by them, as women are. Thus, one mode of female agency among the Huli is what I call "encompassed agency"—action that produces effects, but effects whose ends are beyond the individual's actions and for a wider purpose. Thus, I follow Jolly's assertion that "the value of women's work is *not* erased, but it is *encompassed,* rendered inferior to the superior value of male work" (1992: 143). By using the term "encompassed" I deliberately avoid concepts like "exploitation" and try to stay closer to Huli idioms for women's social action and women's own understanding of their acts as being necessary to and part of collective action. In more concrete and experiential terms, women are usually invested in and do not feel excluded from collective action, even if they are not its initiators, public representatives, or immediate beneficiaries. Men may be the public orators and recipients in bridewealth or homicide compensation payments — or, these days, Christian holidays and celebrations for visiting politicians — but women do not necessarily feel marginalized by the gendered structure of these events because they have worked to make the event possible and as clan or family members they have a stake in the outcome.

At the same time, life history interviews with women show that they do have their own individual goals and that these goals can differ from or oppose those of husband, brothers, family, or clan. However, women are constrained in the kinds of social action they can exert. For example, women are structurally impeded in forming the kin-based corporate groups that men do, and marriage practices and gender ideologies — virilocality, limits on women's mobility, male control over who may live in a woman's house — work to prevent female solidarity. Thus, female agency is often atomistic rather than a collective activity.[5] Relatedly, hegemonic discourses assert that women are less capable of being effective speaking subjects, and so women's words — in both public and domestic spaces — are easily dismissed. This is not to say that women are never recognized as persuasive speakers, only that dominant discourses make it is easy for others to trivialize what women say.

Perhaps not surprisingly, then, another important mode of female action, particularly more resistant action, is what I call, after Corrine Kratz (2000), "negative agency" — that is, the refusal to cooperate with others' projects, the refusal to be encompassed. Kratz has demonstrated that in some contexts, marriage in particular, Okiek women's interests are subsumed or encompassed by others; thus, for example, they can exert agency only by complying with arranged marriages, which are then lauded as the achievement of other actors, or by refusing designated partners, in which case they are blamed. Similarly, Huli women's agency consists primarily of either deploying their energies and skills for others' social endeavors or withdrawing their energies and capacities from these endeavors. In other words, an important means available to women of influencing the social field is the refusal to cooperate, and particularly the refusal to commit their bodies to projects of social reproduction. This refusal can take a variety of forms: the refusal to garden; the sullen refusal to speak when directly addressed; the refusal to have sex (which women usually frame as refusing to "let him give me more children," even if this is not a husband's motivation); the refusal to carry out tasks often demanded by men, such as doing laundry or fetching things; and, in the case of passenger women, the refusal to participate in bridewealth transactions or to stay in a marriage.

It is important to be clear about why Huli women engage in negative agency. As Ortner has pointed out, "the absence of agency"—and, I would add, the exercise of negative agency—"must be seen very critically as effects of power" (1996: 10). Huli women exercise negative agency precisely because they are positioned as encompassed by the projects of others—whether men, their clans, or their families—and thus less able to initiate their own projects. As will be seen, such acts of refusal are often self-destructive. The withdrawal or excision of bodily capacities from the social body can entail the elimination of these capacities altogether, as in cases where women commit suicide or cut off the tips of their fingers (discussed in chapter 2). Indeed, I argue that the decision to act as a *pasinja meri* is another form of this negative agency in which a woman severs from the social group that which should most be encompassed by it—her sexuality.

Sexuality and Agency

What, one might wonder, makes passenger women's "amputation," or withdrawal, of their reproductive energies from the social body so transgressive—an act that can lead their kin, particularly their male kin, to regard them as nonpersons; an act that some passenger women themselves liken to a kind of suicide? In other world areas—particularly the Mediterranean or Latin America—one might think immediately of the "honor/shame" dynamic, in which the honor of a woman's family rests on her sexual propriety. However, while Huli brothers and husbands are certainly ashamed by passenger women's behavior, and while they may be vulnerable to gossip about how they are not "strong" enough to control their women, it is not their honor that is at the heart of men's anger. To understand why passenger women's behavior is so subversive, one must understand the construction of Huli female sexuality in the context of bridewealth and social reproduction.

Women's sexuality in the context of the bridewealth system is largely thought of as reproductive capacity, and while it may be located in a woman's body, it does not belong to her. It is not a "thing" possessed by her to be deployed as she sees fit. Rather, as an energy or potency created by her family and clan, her sexuality/reproductive capacity is meant to be deployed by them as a "partible" aspect of their identities. It is tempting to say that a woman's reproductive capacity is *socially* owned rather than *individually* owned, and such a formulation would not be entirely wrong; however, it falls prey to what Strathern (1988) has called the commodity "root metaphor"—a metaphor so dominant in Western cultural logics that it is difficult to conceptualize human relationships with nonhuman objects or with abstract qualities in terms other than "active subjects *own-ing* passive objects" (Jolly 1992: 142, my emphasis): one "has" a person-ality, one "has" tastes or dislikes; one should "take ownership" of one's own problems, responsibilities, and so on. Thus, it is not quite accurate to understand Huli women's sexuality as "owned" by their kin. (Indeed, I argue that it is precisely the emergent power of the commodity root metaphor, and Huli women's sense that they *are* becoming socially "owned," that motivates some to become *pasinja meri*). Rather, women's sexuality is understood as socially constituted and encompassed: in bridewealth transactions a woman "belongs" to her clan because she is an aspect or part of them. If a woman uses her sexuality autonomously—in premarital sex, in extramarital sex—it is considered a "theft" of the woman by the other (male) party, and thus a theft of clan potency and po-tential clan wealth.

As is explained in chapter 3, the cooperation of women in their role as embodied wealth, embodied clan potency, and transacted person is indispensable to Huli social reproduction and can be thought of as a kind of "compulsory heterosexuality" (Rubin 1975). The nature of this com-pulsory quality can be seen in the one village court case I knew of con-cerning a sexual liaison between two young women. Everyone agreed that something improper had taken place, and the owner of the house in which they were discovered argued successfully that he should receive compensation for the "pollution" of his land, standard practice when young heterosexual couples are caught having sex on other people's property. However, since sex is defined as the male use of female sexual-ity, and since neither offending participant was male, neither party could be designated as "stealing" the other, and neither party could demand marriage or compensation from the other, the standard ways of resolv-ing premarital sex cases. The two parties were in a quandary: what the two women had been up to was of a sexual nature, but by definition was not sex and could not be structurally resolved through the remedies at hand. Ultimately neither family gave compensation to the other, and it seemed to be assumed by all that both women would eventually marry; the incident was considered an anomaly, not an indication of sexual pref-erence or identity. Thus, compulsory heterosexuality in this context is about marriage, reproduction, and the delicate web of debts and social re-lations that are kept in balance through the continual circulation of bridewealth. What most defines women as women, then, is the subordination of their sexuality to the larger project of social reproduction. Women are expected to exercise "encompassed agency" in the arena of bridewealth transactions, and thus what is notable about *pasinja meri* is their refusal to be encompassed in the very arena where it matters most.

Another way of conceptualizing Huli women's encompassment (or its refusal) in the arena of sexuality is to observe that women's normative sexuality corresponds to what Foucault (1990a) calls "the deployment of alliance," while that of passenger women seems akin to, although not precisely like, what he calls "the deployment of sexuality." It should be noted that Foucault, like Lévi-Strauss before him, is not particularly attuned to the acutely gendered nature of "the deployment of alliance" (Rubin 1975); nevertheless, his model seems apt for the Huli case:

> It will be granted no doubt that relations of sex gave rise, in every society, to a *deployment of alliance:* a system of marriage, of fixation and development of kinship ties. . . . Western societies created and deployed a new apparatus which was superimposed on the previous one, and which, without completely supplanting the latter, helped to reduce its importance. I am speaking of the *deployment of sexuality* . . . if the deployment of alliance is firmly tied to the economy due to the role it can play in the transmission or circulation of wealth, the deployment of sexuality is linked to the economy through numerous and subtle relays, the main one of which, however, is the body—the body that produces and consumes. In a word, the deployment of alliance is attuned to a homeostasis of the social body, which it has the function of maintaining. . . . The deployment of sexuality has its reason for being, not in reproducing itself, but in proliferating, innovating, annexing, creating, and penetrating bodies in an increasingly detailed way, and in controlling populations in an increasingly comprehensive way. (1990a:105–7)

Putting this model into more gendered and concrete terms, one can observe that Huli women are expected to cooperate with bridewealth marriage in order to ensure "the transmission or circulation of wealth" and that they thereby work to sustain "the homeostasis of the social body." Huli *pasinja meri,* on the other hand, by refusing marriage, running away from existing marriages, and exchanging sex for money clearly do not correspond to a properly functioning "deployment of alliance." Moreover, theirs is a sexuality that is more about bodily sensations than procreation, more about sex as analogous to commodity consumption than sex as a force of reproduction. Indeed, many passenger women deliberately liken themselves to other items of consumption, such as Pepsi, a topic taken up in chapters 4 and 5.

And yet, passenger women also do not quite correspond to Foucault's "deployment of sexuality." Sexuality, for Foucault, is a "set of effects produced in bodies" (1990a: 127) by the various discourses of medicine, psychiatry, epidemiology, and demography, and such discourses are not—or at least not yet—an important component of passenger women's social identity or personal experience. What can be called "sexuality," according to Foucault, seems very specific to the West's history of Christian confession and the rise of health sciences; sexuality is not sexuality until it can be talked about, counted, and categorized.[6] Admittedly, Huli passenger women seem to be increasingly reified or constituted by Christian and medical discourses; however, these discourses do not by any means explain why the women who come to inhabit this category act in the ways that they do. An analysis of *pasinja meri* thus suggests that Foucault's history of sexuality may privilege institutional and discursive mechanisms, and that it is equally important to analyze moments of agency on the part of actors, particularly as they find themselves ever more embedded in capitalist social relations (Clark 1997; Nihill 1994).

In other words, what remains undeveloped in Foucault's history is a theorization of sexual subjectivity and its relationship to agency. As Joseph Bristow points out, "Foucault rarely construes the subject in relation to affective or emotional response. His research has little or no interest in the subject's inner life. . . . By refusing the subject the interiority familiar to both humanist, psychoanalytic, as well as certain Marxist orthodoxies, *The History of Sexuality* fashions the subject exclusively in terms of pleasures that rest on a somatic surface" (1997: 196). Lynn Hunt similarly, though less caustically, notes that Foucault had, in the introduction to volume 2 of *The History of Sexuality*, intended to provide a history of subjectivity:

> He outlines the three axes that constitute sexuality: (1) the formation of sciences *(savoirs)* that refer to it, (2) the systems of power that regulate its practice, and (3) the forms within which individuals are able, are obliged, to recognize themselves as subjects of this sexuality. Foucault goes on to recognize that the third of these was much harder for him to investigate . . . Foucault's methods of approach were much better suited to the analysis of sciences and systems of power than they were to the analysis of the development of forms of subjectivity. (1992: 85)

One of the aims of this book, then, is to provide a culturally nuanced sense of passenger women's sexual subjectivity, as it informs and is potentially changed by the modes of agency that they exercise. *Pasinja meri* become who they are not through discourses about them in which their sexuality is "solidified in them . . . revealed, isolated, intensified, incorporated," (Foucault 1990a: 48), but in the first instance through resisting and refusing to participate in a "deployment of alliance" (that is, bridewealth marriage). The existing discourses about them will likely intensify and become more elaborate, eventually making the category of *pasinja meri* "a personage, a past, a case history, and a childhood" (43). That there is a name for them demonstrates that exactly this process is occurring. Arguably, in fact, this book is a part of the scientific and discursive processes that will eventually confer on passenger women "analytical, visible, and permanent reality" (44)—thus, the importance, to my mind, of (1) showing the variability of *pasinja meri* histories, practices, and experiences, or, in other words, the ways in which they always exceed and elude categorization; (2) privileging their words and their understandings over the discourses about them; and (3) showing the ways in which their practices both emerge from and are a response to structural contradictions in the context of commoditization.

Incipient Individualism

As discussed above, representations of personhood as "individual," "dividual," "relational," "sociocentric," or "egocentric" have been complicated by findings that dominant notions of personhood are often crosscut by other, often more muted or devalued, dimensions. Indeed, as an ethnographer it is possible to witness moments of confusion or contestation, when actors are unsure of, or in disagreement about, whether one should be acting relationally or individually. A simple example that occurred near the end of my fieldwork concerns the very public murder of a Tari Hospital employee. Not long before this murder, a woman and her brother had been killed by the woman's husband. Some of their kin retaliated by waylaying the hospital employee just outside the hospital entrance and stabbing him to death simply because he belonged to the same clan as the woman's husband. The hospital worker had not known this woman or her brother, and, since clans can number 500 people or more, he only vaguely knew her husband (his fellow clan member). People's reactions to the logic of this retaliatory murder were quite mixed. Some asserted that his clan affiliation—his relational identity, as it were—made him a legitimate target. He belonged to that clan, and as a member, he or any other member could be killed for revenge. Moreover, the people in this camp asserted that since he had a salary—in an area where so few people do—he should have realized that he was vulnerable, since a clan seeking revenge will deliberately target the powerful resources of another clan. Further, they said that "this is always how we have done things"; in other words, everyone should know that we still think relationally when it comes to interclan disputes and revenge homicide. Others were appalled at this act and argued that the hospital employee had done nothing to warrant the brutal attack; he, as an individual, had had nothing to do with the precipitating conflict. Perhaps not surprisingly it was primarily government workers who took the latter position: as people with salaries, many of them feel beleaguered by demands that they act relationally when they themselves want to act as individuals, and thus they may be particularly predisposed to supporting a more individualistic logic. Moreover, hospital workers in particular often feel that they should be immune from interclan violence because as public servants they themselves are expected to transcend their relational identities and provide assistance to any patient regardless of clan affiliation. That they save the lives of members of enemy clans and are still vulnerable to attacks by these clans strikes them as quite unjust.

If one accepts that these dual modes of personhood can coexist, if in highly contested ways, then a variety of questions emerge. For one, might a transformation be occurring, with more individualistic expressions of agency coming to the fore (LiPuma 1998), or, conceptualized somewhat differently, are the contexts that elicit more autonomous modes of agency becoming predominant in the contemporary context? And if "modernity" has something to do with an increase in individualism, what is it about modernity that has this effect? Further, how might the expression of a more individualized sensibility be gendered?

While theorizations of the individual are myriad in Western social theory (Shanahan 1992; Heller et al. 1986), in the literature about personhood and individualism in Melanesia it is "possessive individualism" (MacPherson 1962)—that is, the proprietorship of one's own capacities, or being the owner of one's self—that has been emphasized and contrasted with more relational notions. As McElhinny puts it, rephrasing Strathern, "It is idiosyncratic to a Western bourgeois way of understanding property to suggest that singular items are attached to singular owners, with the fact of possession constructing the possessor as a unitary social unity (McElhinny 1998: 181; Strathern 1988: 104). From an ontological perspective, then, the possessive individual comes about at the exact moment that private property constructs the person as a singu-

lar owner of that property. While private property has been key to theorizations of Western possessive individualism, three other factors have
been causally emphasized as eliciting a more individualistic mode of
being in the Melanesian context: Christianity ("owning" one's own belief), commodity consumption (owning things), and wage labor (own-
ing one's own bodily energies for the purpose of selling them to others).

Joel Robbins, for example, observes that Christianity, "with its focus
on the individual as the unit of salvation and the emphasis it places of self-
examination" (2002: 189), worries the Urapmin as they struggle to retain
an important role for relationality in this scheme. He tells of a friend's
troubled meditation on the gospel of Matthew: "The Bible says each person has their own belief. My wife can't break off part of her belief and give
it to me . . . a man can't give a piece of belief to his wife or children. Each
has their own" (193). As Robbins observes, "The image of the person at
once wholly responsible for himself or herself and utterly unable mean-
ingfully to help others squares poorly with the Urapmin social understanding and experience" (196). Thus, Christianity contributes to increasing individualism at the same time as it is creatively transformed by
the Urapmin into something more relational.

Robert Foster, in contrast, has written extensively on the way in which
commodity consumption and mass media work to promote possessive
individualism in Papua New Guinea (2002). He points out that a vast
marketing array has been established, with companies sponsoring sports
teams, giving out free samples at cultural shows, and even hiring small
theater groups to perform skits about the use of various products in geographic areas with little access to television or radio.[7] Analyzing a series
of advertisements, Foster points out that the ads often depict a sole and
generic "consumer citizen," standing alone and not easily identified with
any particular cultural group, implying that "individuals distinguish
themselves from each other through the work of consuming or appropriating particular objects . . . 'Ownership' or 'having' is the means for at-
taching specific qualities to an otherwise generic person" (75; see also
LiPuma 1999). And deftly bringing together the impacts of both Christianity and consumerism, Gewertz and Errington (1996) juxtapose a
Pepsi ad and a Christian youth crusade to show that while employing
quite different, even opposed, rhetorics, both emphasize individualistic
self-crafting.

Focusing less on consumption—of religious ideologies or of commodities—and more on the mode of production, LiPuma (1998) notes
that capitalist wage labor also promotes individualism by changing the

meaning of labor. Labor in the Melanesian relational economy is always embedded in social reproduction, and is thus always for others. As Biersack puts it, "The life cycle is actually a cycle of work in which a person takes up or retires from a succession of projects as he or she first matures, then ages. . . . work-as-transaction is the primary mode of sociality. . . . one lives in service to others, as an expenditure, a sacrifice, of life—but under a condition of reciprocity" (1995b: 241–43). In contrast, labor in a capitalist economy is assumed to belong to the individual, who then has the right—or the necessity—to sell it. As Beck and Beck-Gernsheim put it, "The ideal image conveyed by the labor market is that of a completely mobile individual regarding him/herself as a functioning flexible work unit . . . prepared to disregard the social commitment linked to his/her existence and identity" (1995: 6). The practices of commoditized labor reinforce the sense that one's bodily capacities are one's own to sell: having to apply for a job as an individual; individual paychecks; the obligation, as an individual, to be on the job during specific hours; being evaluated, promoted, or fired on the basis of one's individual performance; and the penalties for making the mistake of thinking that the products of one's labor are relational (by taking them or giving them to kin and friends). Moreover, the wage one receives further facilitates removing one's self from, or transcending, the relational economy by giving one access to commodities, services, and pleasures that one cannot get through the relational economy (LiPuma 1999).

An analysis of Huli *pasinja meri* contributes to the theorization of possessive individualism in Melanesia by demonstrating another, highly gendered, means through which persons become the "proprietors of their own capacities"—that is, by deliberately removing these capacities from the social body through acts of resistance or negative agency. What most defines *pasinja meri* as a category is their treatment of "their own" sexuality as an individual possession, rather than as a socially embedded capacity. Passenger women step outside the bridewealth system, and instead use their sexuality for their own desires, whether those desires are physical, emotional, fiscal, or for revenge. This should not be taken to mean that engaging in sex with multiple partners and exchanging sex for money somehow thoroughly transforms passenger women into full-fledged possessive individuals. Most *pasinja meri* attempt to keep one foot in the relational economy, working in the gardens of their female kin and often using some of their money to contribute to kin's children's school fees. Moreover, many eventually attempt to reintegrate themselves into family and clan, since, having stepped out of the relational economy, they worry that they will have "no one to build a house for them, no one to give them land, no one to help make their gardens—all they have to eat is their own vaginas"—a phrase commonly used to condemn the costs of *pasinja meri's* individualism. Nevertheless, while *pasinja meri* should not be seen as wholly autonomous, self-authoring persons, they can be seen as enacting individualism in the very contexts—sexuality and reproduction—where women are expected to temper or suppress individualistic modes of agency.

Importantly, becoming a *pasinja meri* is causally connected to other individualizing processes. For one, working men's withdrawal from relationality—because of obligations to be on the job or because of declining interest in extended relations—often leaves married women feeling that they are no longer "in between" (Strathern 1972) their natal relations and their affinal relations.[8] Men's increasing desire to use bridewealth transactions to acquire cash, and men's assertions that they have "bought" their wives and thus have rights of authority over them (Jolly 1994), similarly instill in women the sense that they are commodities rather than important actors in the work of social reproduction. It is precisely this growing sense of "declining dividuality" that spurs some women to take steps to deny their kin the possibility of bridewealth or deny their husbands their "services" as wives by withdrawing their sexual capacities from the relational economy by exchanging sex for money.

Plan of Chapters

The title of this ethnography, *Wayward Women,* has multiple meanings. On the one hand, this is one of the first book-length treatments of prostitution in Melanesia—that is, it is an analysis of how and why some women become sexually "wayward"—embarking on an illicit and stigmatized path. As such, this book challenges conventional academic wisdom about why women exchange sex for money, arguing that Huli passenger women are not driven by economic desperation. While it is certainly capitalist economic structures that are ultimately responsible for putting women on this path, women choose this path not because of economic marginalization but because of the broader commoditization of social relations and the consequent decline of relationally embedded personhood. And yet my goal is not to bracket Huli passenger women off as essentially different from other Huli women; indeed, dominant Huli discourses describe *all* women as potentially wayward in one way or another. And in the contemporary context, it is likely that all Huli women engage at one time or another in struggles over autonomy, social reproduction, and the encompassment of female agency. Thus, "wayward" in the title refers to the fact that many women describe incidents in which they "broke the fence" *(brukim banis)* or "jumped over the fence" *(kalapim banis)* — that is, took actions to escape or resist social encompassment, if only momentarily. And finally, that one must choose a "way" or "road" is a prominent idiom in contemporary Papua New Guinea. Men are often told that they must decide what road to follow — *we bilong tumbuna* or *rot bilong tumbuna* (the ancestors' way or road), *"we bilong lotu"* (the religious path), *"we bilong ol rascal"* (the criminal path), and so on. The *"way*ward" of this title, then, refers to the fact that no longer solely "under the legs of men," Huli women also are put in the position of "choosing" different ways or paths, not always knowing the social repercussions that may result, and not always able to backtrack if the path they follow or forge becomes untenable.

The book begins as a walk through the Huli landscape, starting in Tari, the only town in Huli territory, and expanding out to the rural areas where I first lived. It is also a walk through a cartography of desire, for the Huli talk about the current era as a problematic of desire, and symbols of desire — and efforts to constrain and limit it — can be seen throughout the environment, from the groups of men gambling at the marketplace for hours on end to the weekly church sermons on the evils of jealousy and covetousness. The "fencing in" of women is also discussed in this chapter, for the encompassment of female agency is seen as one of the most important, and yet increasingly difficult, ways to constrain the dangers of desire.

If chapter 1 explicates what it means to "fence in" women, then chapter 2 examines the ways in which women *"brukim banis"* (break the fence). I analyze modes of Huli female agency, focusing on the way their agency is often expressed bodily, is conceptualized as normatively encompassed, and takes the form of what I call "negative agency" when women want to resist this encompassment. In this chapter I explicate the concept of negative agency as the refusal to cooperate with others' plans and expectations, as well as a kind of excision of a woman's individual energies and skills from the social body. I also focus on women's physical aggression as a mode of agency that women highly value, despite the fact that in conflicts with men they often lose. Through case studies and hospital injury data I show that women are actively socialized to be aggressive and, for the most part, embrace this aggression as an important means of influencing social relations.

Chapter 3 discusses bridewealth marriage both as central to the reproduction of Huli sociality and as the "structure" that most shapes female
agency. Women's sense of self-value is shaped by bridewealth, and it is difficult for most women to imagine legitimate female personhood outside
of the bridewealth system. Nevertheless, largely because of male out-
migration and monetization of the economy, women's roles in the
bridewealth system are both shifting and becoming more contradictory.
As mothers, women are increasingly in a position to demand a greater
proportion of bridewealth, while as wives they often feel commoditized
by it.

It is precisely because women are so defined by bridewealth that their
sexuality becomes an important instrument of retaliation when they feel
betrayed or exploited by kin. In chapter 4, I discuss how "becoming" a
pasinja meri is an act of negative agency—that is, the removal of their sex-
ual/reproductive powers from encompassment by the social body. What
looks like prostitution, then, can also be seen as the refusal to subordinate
their most socially valuable energies to the will of their families, husbands, and clans. In this chapter I also step back for a moment to consider
methods and analysis—specifically the dilemmas of understanding
"agency" using the tools of the anthropology trade, interviews and participant observation. In chapter 5, I continue my analysis of passenger
women by discussing how their sexual practices are understood by them
and others, and how their motivations and desires change over time.

In chapter 6, I conclude my discussion of passenger women by examining the Huli *dawe anda,* traditional courtship party houses that are now
somewhat like brothels. Women who go to *dawe anda* can be seen as a
subset of the *pasinja meri* category: they are motivated to abandon their
marriages for the same reasons other *pasinja meri* do, but they have fewer
options since they tend to be older, less educated, and less well traveled.
Thus, while women who are more sophisticated may rebel against their
families or husband by hopping on a bus and engaging in sex work or serial relationships in another town, less sophisticated women have few options but to remain in a marriage or flee to the somewhat safe haven of a
dawe anda.

A Note on Fieldwork

Doing fieldwork among the Huli was quite difficult. For one, property
crime was common—*rascals* (criminals) frequently held up buses and

sometimes stores at gunpoint—and as a white outsider I was a target for theft. The houses of two families I lived with were broken into, one at night while we were there, and I came to feel that it might not be ethical for me to live with rural families since I seemed to be putting them at risk. On the other hand, because people wanted to be generous and protective hosts, they quickly quashed any ideas I might have had about having my own house. Indeed, while living in rural areas, I was never permitted to be alone, expressly because of fears for my safety. After living for almost a year in two different rural households, I moved to Tari town for my second year of fieldwork and lived in a household on the Tari Hospital compound, a situation that was safer and that enabled me to conduct private interviews with a wide range of women. During the last couple months of my fieldwork I moved to a third rural household, but again decided to leave after another incident of theft.

When doing fieldwork in rural areas, I lived with women and their children and was accompanied everywhere by them or my field assistants.[9] The men in these households were either already living in nearby clan men's houses or moved to these houses for the duration of my stay, occasionally joining us for meals and checking in on us a couple times a day. While I sometimes found the lack of solitary time suffocating—I savored the times I woke up in the middle of the night needing to pee and was able to sneak outside without waking anyone—my situation enabled me to gain an intense and intimate view of Huli women's lives. My participant observation and later interviews showed that women experience a high degree of surveillance. In particular most women tried to avoid getting the reputation of being *bighed,* which, as mentioned earlier, is a Tok Pisin (also known as Melanesian Pidgin) term that, when applied to women, implies defiance, vanity, and self-importance. When people spoke of women who had been raped or killed, they almost invariably described them as having been *bighed,* a label that served to blame them and that effectively worked to make women monitor their own and other women's behavior. Since white women were also often described as *bighed,* I took pains to present myself as a *wali ore* (good woman) as one means of trying to ensure my safety. Being labeled as *bighed* was so explicitly linked to punitive violence against women that at one point a couple of my friends took it upon themselves to pretend they didn't know me and to ask various people in town about me, cheerfully reporting back that I had no cause for worry because I was not considered *bighed,* knowledge I received with both relief (I personally felt less vulnerable) and dismay (that a woman's reputation was so candidly linked to potential violence).

While rates of violence in general, and specifically against women, are quite high among the Huli (Barss 1991), talk about violence was even more pervasive—sometimes in the form of news about people seen at the hospital or police station, and sometimes in the more moralistic and cautionary registers of gossip and storytelling. Of course over the span of two years I realized that many of the stories I heard were recycled again and again, didn't represent separate incidents, and had, over time, taken on myth-like qualities (Wardlow 2002a). Nevertheless, the pervasive discourse about violence, reinforced by interviews which often concerned physical fights and punctuated by actual occurrences of violence to women I knew, made for fieldwork that was often draining.

My fieldwork was also difficult because I found myself inadvertently engaging in the "participant" side of participant observation more than I planned for or wanted, usually through the venue of village court cases. For example, I was evicted from my first field site and then taken to village court because of an accusation of menstrual pollution (discussed in the next chapter), and was forced to abandon my second field site after testifying against my male host in a domestic violence dispute. I discuss this latter incident here in part for the sake of candor about fieldwork occurrences that likely shape one's ethnographic lens, and in part as an example of the fact that I often learned most at those times when I really did not want to be participating, or even observing, at all.

This couple had a history of physical altercation: when I examined Yerime's clinic book—a book used by health-care workers to record illnesses, injuries, and treatments—I noted that she had previously been hospitalized two times after fights with her husband. Moreover, they had no children after five years of marriage, and Yerime often asserted, both privately and in public, that Alembo was a *"gonolia man"* (had a sexually transmitted disease; Wardlow 2002c). Indeed, Yerime took advantage of my presence to avoid sex with Alembo (something her natal kin told her to do), to invite her younger sister to live with us against his wishes, and to be more defiant than she might otherwise have been. Indeed, from the moment I arrived, Yerime stated to me (somewhat incautiously, I thought— I knew I could be trusted, but she didn't) that she wanted to leave Alembo.

Because Yerime had no children of her own and because with my resources we could support a larger household, Yerime invited two young neighboring boys to live with us. After witnessing a few minor fights between Yerime and Alembo, Angi, the older boy, about eleven years old, promised Yerime that if her kin ever took Alembo to village court for injuring her he would testify on her behalf. Already by age eleven Angi knew that a village court case was a likely eventuality in this marriage, and he was trying to prepare himself for his role as witness. (The younger boy soon left our household because he and his family were afraid of this likely eventuality). As it turned out, Angi was unable to keep his promise: he was a member of Alembo's clan, Alembo had at one point contributed to his school fees, and Alembo had agreed to take him in because Angi's own father was neglecting him, believing him to be the result of his wife's adultery. In short, Angi was not in a position to act independently. Thus, when the fateful day came, Angi, in tears, lied about the fight and said that the large, ugly bruise on Yerime's side was due to a fall, not to Alembo's kicking her. Since Alembo was officially my host, and Yerime's relationship with me was "encompassed" by his larger project of hosting me, I also should have lied or modified my testimony or made up an excuse to avoid testifying altogether—or at least these would have been acceptable courses of action. As the only adult witness to this incident—and knowing that I could extricate myself from this situation if need be (as turned out to be the case)—I felt my only option was to tell things as I had seen them. What many people seemed to find remarkable about the case was that I had *"tok stret"* (talk straight)—that is, I testified that Yerime had lunged at Alembo with a knife *and* that he had kicked her, not shaping my testimony in allegiance with one party or the other. That I contradicted Angi's testimony only made things worse for him—not only was he a "Judas," as Yerime publicly shrieked at him, he was a liar.

This incident raises a number of questions: What is ethical practice in situations like these? How did these experiences usefully inform or negatively bias my understanding of Huli marital relations and the way I conducted and interpreted later interviews with other women? Certainly, by living with this couple and then testifying at their village court case, I gained a very particular view of Huli domestic relations—a snapshot in time of a marriage that some people characterized as worse than most, and others characterized as typical. And, although witnessing this fight, testifying at the subsequent court case, and fleeing this field site for fear of Alembo's retaliation were far and away the most frightening and painful of my "inadvertent participant" experiences, it was through living with this couple that I was able to gain specific insights about the range of factors that contribute to marital strife in the contemporary context, the social dynamics of Huli court cases, women's strategies for trying to leave their husbands, and the way in which bridewealth exigencies constrain these strategies. (It was from this court case too, and especially witnessing the untenable role that Angi was forced to play, that I gained a better sense of the harsh realities of "relational" personhood, particularly when one is in a structurally weak position.)

Although the local dispute mediators had warned Alembo (and promised Yerime) that they would grant Yerime her divorce without the return of bridewealth should he put her in the hospital again, in fact many men in the community—including these mediators—had given or received bridewealth for this marriage and were not at all willing to grant a divorce. Thus, this case turned into a compensation case, and Yerime went to live with her brothers until Alembo could make the required payment.[10] Yerime, although disappointed by the mediators' decision and angry that her brothers had not more strenuously supported her request for divorce (as they had said they would), abided by the decision. Other women I interviewed, however, took their initial steps to become passenger women when faced with similar circumstances.

CHAPTER I

"Tari is a *jelas* place"

The Fieldwork Setting

We were sitting high up on a craggy ledge from where we could just see Tari town in the distance—the sudden bare stretch of land that was the airstrip, corrugated metal roofs glinting in the sun. Tai Bayabe was telling me—somewhat boastfully, somewhat matter-of-factly—of how he had orchestrated the armed holdups of a convoy of politicians' trucks, and, on a separate occasion, of the local luxury hotel. He himself had not actually participated, but he had given the young men in his clan tacit permission to carry out these thefts. When I asked him why he had done these things, he flatly stated, "Tari is a covetous place. Resentment did it" (Tari *em jelas ples, ya. Madane piyita*). Indeed, whenever something went wrong in Tari—when an expatriate store manager was killed by an employee he had fired, when the small bank was held up by an armed gang, when people were robbed—someone was sure to comment darkly that "Tari *em jelas ples*," or, as the younger, more hip (and literate) generation says, a "J place."

Although clearly derived from the English word, *jelas* does not refer to jealousy—that is, a feeling of hostility toward a rival or toward someone who is perceived to have an advantage. In fact, there is a Huli word, *"pono,"* or *"ponana,"* which means exactly that. Rather, *jelas* means something more like covetousness or an inordinate and dangerous feeling of desire—for money, for things, and sometimes for people. Huli people often say that this is the fundamental difference between the past (variously defined as either before colonialism or before the arrival of the road in 1981) and the present: everyone is *"jelas"* now; everyone is plagued by desire (also see Robbins 1998; LiPuma 1999; Gewertz and Errington 1998). Indeed, some Huli say they have no word for the way desire is experienced now, their own word for desire, *hame,* being inadequate.

Madane, the second part of Tai Bayabe's terse explanation of his behavior, means something like resentment at having been disappointed or betrayed, and it refers to a situation in which one's sense of entitlement to something—a sum of cash, a job, a pig—is violated by the giver's refusal or failure to abide by a promise or obligation. Thus, when Tai Bayabe said that he had acted out of *madane,* he was implying that the politicians and the hotel managers had reneged on some implicit or explicit promise. The politicians had promised the development of roads and the use of their discretionary funds to subsidize school fees, but they had failed to keep these promises. The hotel managers had not hired the number of local people they had promised, the wages were too low, and they didn't provide meals for their employees. They too had failed in their obligations. (Tai Bayabe was also likely giving me a pointed message: he had arranged for young men in his clan to assist a geologist friend of mine in collecting samples of volcanic rock, and through these stories he was probably cautioning us to treat these workers well.) It is disconcerting to arrive as an inexperienced anthropologist, with little sense of what one's social obligations might be, and to be told repeatedly that bad things have happened to people—particularly those who have more wealth or power than others—because they failed in their social obligations. And, it is difficult after the fact to write about people who often characterize themselves as covetous and resentful. But I begin my representation of my field site with these charged affective descriptors—rather than with more material or demographic facts—because this was the way Tari was often narrated to me, both by Huli people and others.

When I first arrived in Tari, it did not appear to me as a place that would inspire unmanageable feelings of desire. Tari consists of an airstrip with a hospital and primary school on one side, and government buildings, the main market, and a few stores on the other. Walking on any of the few dirt roads leading out of town brings one immediately to sweet potato fields. And yet, the longer I was there, and particularly the more time I spent in rural areas where people owned very few things, the more I myself was intoxicated by the one big store in town that displayed knock-off Levi jeans from Thailand; shiny, lacy little girls' dresses from the Philippines; CD players from Japan; thick soft acrylic blankets in tiger-print patterns from China; and steel-toed leather work boots from Australia. And the longer I was there the more I noticed the way in which

FIGURE 2. Along the Tari airstrip fence.

desire is materialized in Tari: the long line of dart boards set up adjacent to the main market where men can pay 10 toeia per dart for a chance to win a can of Coke (1 Papua New Guinea kina was worth approximately 80 cents US at that time, so each dart cost about 8 cents); the circles of people squatting in the dust to play high-stakes card games; the crowds of people who gathered whenever a plane landed, straining to see what kinds of cargo passengers had brought back from the capital city; the women milling through the biggest store in town, frisked on their way out by security guards to see if they had tucked packets of instant noodle soup or bars of soap into their babies' diapers. I quickly came to feel the acute palpability of commodity hunger in Tari.

There are probably many places in the world that have developed a discourse about desire in the wake of global economic restructuring, so perhaps Huli discourses about *jelas* are not unique. But to claim that one's society is *madane* (resentful, angrily disappointed) may be less common, and the fact that *jelas* and *madane* are so inextricably bound in Huli discourse may also seem curious. *Madane* is an emotion term that encompasses a complex social scenario: it is about feeling entitled to a particular thing because of another person's explicit promise or implicit social obligation, the failure of that person to follow through, the consequent

FIGURE 3. The long line of dartboards at the edge of the main market in Tari. Men pay 10 toeia per dart to play, and receive a can of Coke if they win.

sense of having been let down or betrayed, and the potentially destructive acts one does in response to these feelings. In contrast to Western conceptualizations of emotion as individualized, internal feeling states, *madane* is very socially engaged: it arises in response to others' acts (or failures to act), and it necessarily entails consequent actions toward those others. *Madane* always refers outward to specific others, and at the center of *madane* is social obligation, particularly the failure or refusal of social obligation. When salaried workers refuse to contribute to kin's compensation payments and then find their gardens dug up, this is attributed to *madane*. When the owners of PMVs (public motor vehicles, public buses) refuse to let relatives ride for free and then find the tires slashed, this too is attributed to *madane*.

Although it is awkward to discuss an "epidemiology of emotions," Huli people assert that *madane* has increased and that this is because *jelas* has also increased: people have become more selfishly desirous, and this causes them to lose sight of others and to fail them more often, which, in turn, leads to increased feelings of dashed expectations and resentment. Aletta Biersack has discussed a similar predicament among the neighboring Paiela:

> Property is an asset its owner deploys to meet obligations . . . If the word
> "right" is applicable at all, it is something that the would-be recipients of
> property (kinsmen and affines) rather than its owners have. Rights are in
> the first instance rights of request, and owners have not so much rights of
> consumption, but obligations to respond morally to such requests . . .
> Someone who has a right of request and is denied is justifiably angry and
> may seek justice in litigation, withdraw his or her support, even resort to
> violence. (1992: 2)

This description might overstate the case for the Huli, who recognize
"rights to keep" as much as "rights of request." Nevertheless, the Huli
value and actively socialize reciprocity: among the first few words taught
to children are *"ngi"* (give me) and *"ma"* (here, take it), and children are
regularly told that if they aren't generous or don't show appreciation for
others' generosity then they will "only have their own shit to eat," a
graphic and repugnant representation of pure individualism.

People's attempts to maneuver between the poles of selfish desire and
social obligation can make for unexpected contradictions. The morning
I arrived in Tari I was met by a young Huli man who had been assigned
to pick me up at the airstrip and take me to the flat on the hospital compound where I would stay until I decided on a rural field site. He had important business to take care of first, however. He quickly explained that
there was a liquor ban in Tari, but not in Tabubil, where the plane was
headed next. The plane would go to Tabubil, then turn around and go
back exactly the way it had come, stopping in Tari a second time. We
therefore needed to go to the post office to wire money to friends in
Tabubil so that they could buy a case of Gold Cup (cheap whiskey), box
it up and label it "paint," and then send it on the return flight. He had already bribed the Tari police so that they wouldn't scrutinize the "paint"
cartons as they were off-loaded, but we did have to meet his teenage
cousin, who was going to buy the liquor from him at the wholesale price,
and who would then sell the liquor at three times this price to men in Tari.
His cousin needed the money to pay his school fees at a Seventh Day Ad-
ventist (SDA) high school located in another town. If we didn't take care
of this business immediately, his cousin would be unable to attend school
the next year.

Wasn't there a high school in Tari? I asked. Yes, but it was a Catholic
school, and SDA students needed to attend their own school so as to
avoid being corrupted by non-SDA students who had *"pasin nogut"* (literally, no-good ways, immoral behavior). Wondering if he saw any irony
in this Byzantine scheme, I teasingly asked whether bribing the police and

illegally selling alcohol might count as *pasin nogut,* and wasn't alcohol forbidden to SDA people anyway? He laughed. And, I persisted (lurching immediately into the gadfly mode of ethnographic inquiry), if these didn't count as *pasin nogut,* what sorts of *pasin nogut* was he so worried about in non-SDA students? They would teach his young cousin to steal, write love letters, smoke, *frenim meri* (literally, to befriend women, which can mean anything from flirting to having sex), go to "bush discos," and be *"jelas tumas"* (to be overly desirous and covetous), he replied. (Bush discos, a recent innovation among the Huli, are controversial late night dance parties, where a local string band plays and fees are charged for entrance and food.) Selling something banned by the provincial government was not wrong, he asserted, because the Southern Highlands provincial government, based in Mendi town and headed at that time by a Mendi premier, blatantly favored the Mendi cultural group. Disobeying laws legislated by a government that deliberately marginalized the Huli people could not be considered wrong. Theft and illicit sex, on the other hand, were *pasin nogut,* he explained, as were the behaviors which promoted them, such as smoking in mixed-sex groups, writing love letters, and being *jelas tumas.* In this complicated scenario, and its rationale, one sees a preoccupation with desire, both the need to control it through the cultivation of particular moral selves (SDA in this case) and the impulse to exploit it (by selling alcohol) in order finance the possibility of controlling it.

Of course one should not take Huli assertions of *"jelas"* and *"madane"* at face value. It is important to ask why Huli people engage in this brand of "auto-orientalism" — representing themselves as excessively desirous, too easily failing each other, and too easily embittered by others' similar failures. First, one should note that this discourse always has a temporal dimension — Tari is a *jelas* place *now;* the past is portrayed as a more disciplined, orderly, and relational era. Second, self, place, and material environment are imbricated in this discourse: the desiring self has become more difficult to manage, but this change has occurred as Tari itself has changed. Tari is said to be a place where commodities are on display, eliciting desire within people; thus, the emotional terrain has changed in synchrony with the material lifeworld. If there is a new episteme of desire instantiated within people's selves, it cannot be disentangled from the external environment which provokes and sustains this desire; in other words, the discourse of *jelas* and *madane* is not one of an essentialized, timeless Huli identity.

Perhaps most important, the pervasive discourse about *madane* and *jelas* can be interpreted as an expression of the tensions the Huli are experiencing between relational and more individualistic modes of social interaction, particularly in a context of increasing economic disparities. Many narratives I heard in which *jelas* or *madane* featured prominently were stories in which one person expected another, more powerful person to act relationally—by giving a gift or fulfilling a presumed obligation—only to find that the other had acted in a fashion interpreted as selfish, individualistic, or antisocial. Such tensions are exacerbated in a contemporary context in which there are more things to want, in which money is increasingly needed for everyday life, and in which some people have money and others do not. And since *madane* exists primarily in its material manifestations, it is a means of punishing those who are perceived to be selfish and reminding others to be attuned to the demands of reciprocity. Moreover, as will be seen, concerns about greed, individualism, and the failure of reciprocity are projected onto the figure of the *pasinja meri,* who is said to epitomize a perverse mobilization of selfish desire. *Pasinja meri* are said to be *jelas tumas* (overly desirous)—for money, for sex, and for autonomy—and they therefore "treat their vaginas like market goods" *(putim tau olsem maket).*

In the remainder of this chapter, I describe my fieldwork settings—both Tari town and the more rural areas I lived in—but I do so through the problematic or "compelling concern" (Wikan 1989) of desire. I first provide a brief history of the area, and then take the reader on a walk through the Tari area, pointing out the ways in which the problem of desire is instantiated and managed in the social landscape.

Historical Context

With a population of approximately 90,000, the Huli are one of the largest cultural groups in Papua New Guinea and are generally considered "fringe" highlanders (Biersack 1995a). Like other groups of the New Guinea highlands, they are primarily subsistence horticulturalists who raise pigs; however, departing somewhat dramatically from "core" highland groups—the groups first "discovered," settled, and studied by (respectively) prospectors, plantation owners, and anthropologists—they do not engage in elaborate cycles of competitive exchange.

The Huli practice a flexible system of land tenure and residence that allows individuals to claim rights to land through connections to both male and female ancestors (discussed in greater depth later in this

MAP 1. Map of Papua New Guinea. Tari town is west of Mendi, the capital of Southern Highlands Province. (University of Toronto, Cartography Department)

chapter). This practice has facilitated the redistribution of people during times of famine or warfare, or in response to increasing population pressures. However, as Ballard (2002) points out, this complex and highly negotiable system also engenders conflicting claims, which may in part explain the impressive generational depth of Huli *dindi malu*—literally, land genealogies—a genre of knowledge about lineage and land usage employed to resolve territorial disputes (Allen 1995). Extrapolating from *dindi malu* and oral histories, Ballard (1995, 2002) hypothesizes that during the nineteenth and early twentieth centuries,

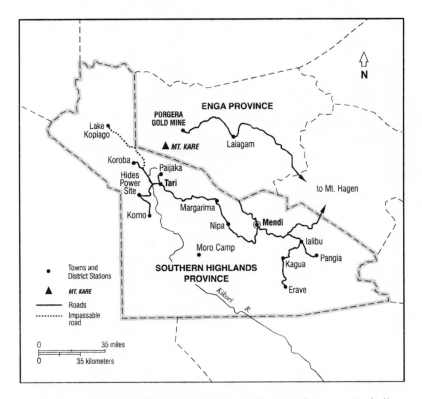

MAP 2. Map of Southern Highlands Province and surrounding areas, including the Porgera gold mine, located north of Tari in Enga Province. (University of Toronto, Cartography Department)

there was a pattern of Huli expansion, often aggressive in nature, out from the fertile valley where Tari town is now located into more marginal valleys and the mountainous areas north of Tari. Ballard also suggests that there was a gradual but dramatic change in the structure of Huli society associated with the adoption of the sweet potato during the seventeenth century (see also Modjeska 1982; Watson 1977): prior to the adoption of sweet potato, Huli society appears to have been dominated by hereditary leaders who were the eldest sons of eldest sons in a clan's senior lineage, a genealogical strategy still used today to assert superior claims to land (Wardlow 2001). Over time, perhaps spurred by increases in food and pig production made possible by sweet potato, leadership among the Huli shifted from being ascribed to achieved, and was, moreover, decentralized into a wide range of prestigious male roles (military leaders, ritual experts, orators, traders, mediators, and men of wealth).

The first contact between Huli people and Europeans took place in 1934 when two mining prospectors, Jack and Tom Fox, killed approximately fifty Huli as they attempted to pass through Huli territory. A few Australian patrols traveled across Huli land in the late 1930s, but a permanent colonial post, Tari, was not established until 1952. Missionaries from a range of Christian denominations were quick to arrive, and by 1956 the Evangelical Church of Papua New Guinea, the Catholic Church, the United Church, and the Seventh Day Adventists had all established missions in the area. In the mid-1990s, the Assembly of God Church and Jehovah's Witnesses also had a significant presence. Not until 1981, however, was the Highlands Highway, the one all-weather road stretching from east to west across the center of Papua New Guinea, extended to Tari; not surprisingly, the number of Huli out-migrations increased dramatically in the early 1980s (Lehman 2002). Also contributing to long-standing high levels of out-migration, particularly by men, were colonial economic policies designed to shape Southern Highlands Province into a labor pool for coffee and other plantations located in other provinces (Harris 1972).

Opportunities for acquiring cash remain meager in the Tari area, with government services such as schools, health centers, the post office, and the legal system providing the bulk of salaried employment, and a couple national stores with branches in Tari offering wage employment for clerks and security guards. Other important means of obtaining cash are selling produce, secondhand clothing, or wholesale goods, such as soap, at the main market; selling parchment coffee to the buyers who periodically come to town; and getting remittances from kin who have jobs at mine sites or in Port Moresby, the capital city of Papua New Guinea. Those people who manage to save enough money from remittances or from the sale of goods at market often establish small trade stores, buying foodstuffs wholesale in Tari or further afield, and then selling them for a small profit.

The Instantiation of Desire in Tari Town

Huli people often told me, again comparing the present with some imagined scene of the orderly past, "Before we just desired with our eyes, but now, where the eyes go first, the hand quickly follows." Desire—whether for things or for people—is ontologically tied to the visual, and according to Huli *mana* (traditional custom, wisdom), it should be made an explicit object of management through various precepts and injunctions, many of which are designed to limit the visibility of potentially coveted items. Thus, for example, one should not display food or money in front of others unless one intends to give them away because to display some object is to make it an object of desire. As Frankel notes in his taxonomy of Huli illnesses, "The combination of a hungry glance and the act of swallowing are sufficient to cause illness in the person whose food it is. This is known as *lingi,* which means literally 'give me what is there' " (Frankel 1986: 140). A woman who is menstruating should keep herself out of sight of her husband because the sight of her could inspire his desire, making it more likely that he will find himself in a situation where he is at risk for "menstrual pollution." People's homes should be surrounded by stands of thick bushes and trees, both for privacy and for protection against the desire that one's flourishing sweet potato gardens or coffee trees might inspire in others. Desire should be managed through self-control, but it should also be managed socially by making potentially coveted items less visible.

Desire is thus tied to visibility, but visibility is tied to spatiality. What one can see (and covet) depends on where one is able to go and how desirable items are situated in space. Thus, according to many Huli people, one reason why desire has become more problematic is that the social organization of space, and people's movements within space, have changed. The colonial-enforced cessation of tribal fighting, the construction of roads, and the development of markets has made for increased mobility, and increased mobility augments the possibility that one will see desirable things. Fundamental to this change has been the creation of "town." In the past, Huli men were quite mobile for the purposes of ritual (Ballard 1994; Glasse 1995), extensive trade (Ballard 1994), and the maintenance of multiple households (Glasse 1968; Allen 1995). But now the dominant motivation for mobility, for both men and women, is to go to town. Town is where intoxicating commodities can be seen; where one might run into a relative who has money; and where young people might spy *lawini* (romantic interests) who can be stealthily followed or flirted with in the main market. Town is also where gambling is far more public and visible. In addition to the long line of dart boards near the main market, there are a few shack-like *haus snooker* (snooker houses) scattered around the edges of town, and one cannot make one's way around the airstrip without seeing numerous small circles of card players sitting in the dust, flinging their toiea pieces and the occasional 2-kina note to and fro after every hand.[1] A few times a year, usually on a Friday—when Tari is so packed that people murmur there must be ghosts roaming the town and blending into the crowds—the police will decide they need to cut down on public gambling, and they will suddenly zoom up in their white four-wheel drive, double-cab Land Cruisers and fire off smoke bombs near the groups of gamblers clustered around trade stores.

The trade stores themselves always have their goods stacked away on shelves behind a long counter, and there is often thick wire mesh stretching from the counter to the ceiling—all measures to prevent theft. You can see what the store has in stock, but you must ask for items, and the clerk will fetch them and put them on the counter. Only one store—the largest one in town and the only one that caters to the expatriate missionaries in the area—allows people to walk through and take things off the shelf. However, upon leaving the store, one must show one's receipt to a security guard, who matches the purchases against this receipt and pats down bodies for possible stolen goods. If one is white or a wage-earning regular customer, such as a hospital employee, this search is cursory. If not, it can be quite scrupulous. Across from this store is one of the few two-story buildings in town, where the bank used to be before it was held up by armed gangs one too many times and the national branch closed it.

Continuing around the Tari airstrip one might pass a few coffee buyers who have established makeshift business sites along the airstrip fence by hanging sets of scales from thick wooden sticks jammed into the dirt. The bags of parchment coffee that people bring to be weighed often seem pathetically small, particularly if one has walked through the coffee buyer areas of Goroka or Mt. Hagen, other highlands towns. And when one spends some time out in a rural area one finds that, unlike other areas of the highlands, where people have established large coffee gardens, most Huli maintain around ten to twenty trees right next to their houses which they only bother with if they are sorely pressed for cash. Those families who have invested more intensely in coffee production bypass the buyers who come to town, knowing they can get much better prices in Mt. Hagen, and believing it is worth the day-long ride and the risk of being held up by armed gangs of *"rascals"* (criminals). Public buses are often stopped at roadblocks and robbed, so almost everyone who has traveled back and forth between Tari and Mendi or Mt. Hagen has a story to tell of when *"ol rascal ensapim mi"* (when the rascals "hands-up!"-ed me; Wardlow 2002b). People have developed ingenious ways to outwit *ras-*

cals. My field assistant's brother, for example, boasted of the time when he stitched his cash into the collar of his shirt, leaving only a few kina in his pocket so that the *rascals* believed they had taken all he had.

In sum, Tari town is a site and symbol of desire. However, Tari also sometimes feels as if it only has a tentative, evanescent status. All Huli land belongs to specific clans, and people from the landowning clans at the edges of town often assert that they have never been adequately compensated by the government for ceding the land on which Tari is built. At any moment, people sometimes declare, they could decide to reclaim this land; indeed, not long before I arrived, there was a fierce tribal war between the two clans on either side of the airstrip. Fighting with bows and arrows and homemade guns occurred on the airstrip, on the hospital grounds, and between store buildings, shutting down all government services and stores. For all practical purposes Tari town ceased to exist for a brief period of time. And, when a store manager was killed by *rascals* soon after my arrival, the government workers, most of them Huli themselves, threatened to quit: they were tired of feeling that every store they walked into could be held up at any moment. Moreover, because the bank in Tari was closed, they had to go all the way to Mendi, a five- to seven-hour ride by public bus, to cash their paychecks, risking holdups on the road. Something had to be done about crime, they asserted, or they were perfectly willing to let Tari "go back to ground zero" *(kamap graun zero)*, "burn to the ground" *(paia olgeta)*, and "revert to jungle" *(kamap bush stret)*. Additional highway patrol police were promised, as were eventual banking services, and things soon returned to the edgy but functional norm.

Mining and Desire

Any map of desire in the contemporary Huli landscape would be incomplete without mention of the daily buzz of helicopters flying overhead, circulating between Tari town, the Hides power station to the south, and the Mt. Kare and Porgera gold mines to the north. While many people point to the coming of the Highlands Highway as the time when *jelas* became less manageable, others assert that it was the Mt. Kare gold rush, and other interactions with mining companies, that shaped the new episteme of desire. Huli people have been intimately involved in the discovery and development of two mine sites: some receive yearly payments from the Porgera gold mine for use of their land, and many of them participated in the gold rush at Mt. Kare during the late 1980s (Ryan 1991;

Vail 1995). Below I briefly discuss these two mine sites and the ways in which they have shaped the social landscape.

PORGERA

Somewhat surprisingly, the giant Porgera gold mine, located in Enga Province, depends on the Hides power station, a natural gas plant located 30 miles south in Huli territory, to generate the electricity for its mining operation. There is no road between Hides and Porgera, but there is a stretch of giant pylons stringing miles and miles of power lines through people's sweet potato gardens and then through the mountainous unin-habited wilderness (Ballard 1994). Each pylon has a designated number, and Porgera pays yearly "land occupation fees" to those families who own land on which the pylons are erected (but does not supply electricity to them or to Tari town). The weeks when occupation fees are paid is an exciting time. The "lands officer" and a couple of "community liaison officers," along with a band of heavily armed police, rent out a trade store in a particular area for a few days, and simply go pylon by pylon, calling out the names of landowners from a previously assembled list, while everyone watches individuals go up to the counter of the trade store to collect their allotment of money. Payments can range from a few kina into the thousands per individual per year, and it is the responsibility of community liaison officers to meet with individuals and families ahead of time to decide just who is going to be "on the list" for the year. Most of these payments are straightforward, although sometimes contentious within a family, especially when members have gone to live elsewhere but suddenly show up to demand a portion of the payment.

Gender is also important to community debates about compensation from mining companies. During the year that I observed these payments being made, at least half of the people walking up to the trade store counter to collect money were women. A few of these were sisters collecting on behalf of absent brothers, who were the officially named recipients, but many were collecting "in their own names" as agnates of the clans involved. This pattern was a deliberate break from the past, I was told. In previous years only men received the land occupation fees, but they had gambled or drunk it all away, and many women complained that as agnates, and as women who had families to take care of, they should also receive money. Both of these arguments were considered legitimate by the local leaders, who set a firm example by including their daughters and sisters on their lists.[2]

FIGURE 4. One in the chain of pylons that threads up and down mountains and through people's gardens, carrying electricity from the Hides power station south of Tari to the Porgera gold mine in Enga Province. Disgruntled landowners occasionally topple these pylons, shutting down Porgera for days or even weeks at a time.

MT. KARE

The history of gold mining at Mt. Kare has been quite conflict ridden: there have been conflicts between landowners and "the company," conflicts among the various groups that claim to be landowners, and complex litigation over the exploration license (Vail 1995). A short version of the history of mining at Mt. Kare is that Conzinc Rio Tinto (CRA), a powerful company with mines throughout Papua New Guinea as well as elsewhere in the world, was granted the exploration license in the area, but was prevented from proceeding by a massive gold rush in the late 1980s. At that time it is estimated that at least AU$100 million worth of gold, mostly in the form of nuggets lying on or near the surface of the earth, was extracted, primarily by Huli and Paiela people (Ryan 1991). Mt. Kare is at an altitude that precludes settlement and gardening, and during the gold rush, all food was brought in by helicopter and sold at exorbitantly inflated prices. Moreover, there were inadequate health and sanitation facilities for the thousands of people who came to pan for gold, and typhoid and pneumonia were rife.

Nevertheless, the sudden wealth also facilitated easy generosity and the intensification of social relations. Huli men and women reminisce about the gold rush as a time when "money poured through our hands like water"; "Air Niugini (the national airline) was our PMV (public bus)"; and "we were all *millionaire man na meri*" (millionaire men and women). Men would make grand entrances by helicopter onto the land of their future in-laws, pay bridewealth in cash, and fly off again; and women could be "like men" and "go forward," as people say, in publicly contributing to relatives' bridewealth payments, school fees, and pig feasts. Many people believed that the gold would never end and that a new era had begun in which both duty and desire could be satisfied. This optimism was grounded in a cosmologically legitimated sense of entitlement: Mt. Kare was the traditional home to an important sacred site, and the gold deposit there is often said to be the skin or feces of the powerful serpent ancestor, Tai Yundiga, who inhabits and guards the site (Wardlow 2001; Biersack 1999; Clark 1993). How could the gold come to an end, people asked, if it was constantly being produced by Tai Yundiga? However, the surface gold did come to an end, abruptly curtailing the period of exuberant prodigality. When CRA was finally able to proceed, they ran into conflicts with local landowner groups and, after an armed attack on the mine site, eventually gave up their lease. Another company won the right to conduct mineral exploration, but was challenged in court and only recently has been able to proceed with exploration (see Vail 1995 for a more detailed description of the legal history of the Mt. Kare license).

When Huli people discuss the recent history of Mt. Kare, they often say that they were only living out what their ancestors predicted. Traditional myths and place-names are often said to be "prophecies" or "parables" (Huli people use the English words) that people never understand until it is too late. In this case, the name of the mountain, Kare, people say, is derived from the Huli word *"karere,"* which means to fight frantically over a desired item. It is what happens when someone puts out some food and tells people to help themselves instead of dividing up and distributing the portions for them. So, people say, the ancestors who named Mt. Kare knew that in the future it would be a site of greed, dissension, and turmoil.

MINERAL WEALTH AND "LAND GENEALOGIES"

Just who has the right to collect mining company payments is deeply embedded in notions of kinship and social organization; conversely, notions of social organization are increasingly becoming embedded in mineral extraction operations. Indeed, when I asked the meanings of *tene* and *yamuwini*—two important kinship terms explicated below—I was often told that *tene* were the ones who could go up to the counter and collect money, while *yamuwini* were those who had a right to ask their *tene* for some of the money but who could not themselves collect money from mining companies. This is certainly not how *tene* and *yamuwini* have been explained to ethnographers in the past (Goldman 1983).

Huli social organization has long intrigued and frustrated ethnographers as a system which resists easy categorization as agnatic or cognatic (Glasse 1968; Goldman 1983, 1988; Ballard 1995; Allen 1995). It is not my intention here to review this debate, but some background is necessary for understanding the social context of mining operations. The Huli are organized into *hameigini* (literally, fathers-sons), groups that I call clans, and each clan is associated with a specific territory (*dindi hameigini,* literally, land of fathers-sons) named after the clan and often called a "parish" in the ethnographic literature. The agnates of a clan are the clan's *tene* (root or source), but they do not necessarily live on the clan's territory. Those residents on a clan territory who are non-agnatic cognates of the clan are called *yamuwini* (literally, placed by a woman). Everyone is an agnate or *tene* of only one clan (one's F, FF, FFF, etc.), but a potential *yamuwini* of multiple clans (through one's mother's father or mother, through one's father's mother, etc.). *Tene,* as agnates, always have rights to clan land, but non-agnatic cognates can only acquire and maintain rights to land through the cultivation of relationships with agnates of the clan. In other words, a non-agnatic cognate cannot claim rights to land or become *yamuwini* simply by virtue of having a female genealogical link to a particular clan—this is a necessary but not sufficient condition—one must also work at cementing the relationship with one's *tene.*

What has made this "system" somewhat confusing for ethnographers (and for colonial administrators in the past and mining administrators in the present) is that many men do actualize their potential rights to residence on land belonging to a clan in which they are not *tene,* so a clan's agnates are often widely dispersed. Repeated surveys of parish composition have shown that they often consist of more *yamuwini* than *tene* (Glasse 1968; Goldman 1983; Frankel 1986; Ballard 1995; cf. Biersack 1995b). This happens for a variety of reasons: a family may have moved to a cross-cousin's area because of warfare or famine, and the descendents remained; a woman may have been given land by her father or brothers and then passed it on to her children; or a man might simply get along with his mother's relatives better than his father's. In the past, in fact, certain clan rituals required the presence of *yamuwini,* and an important piece of *mana* (customary knowledge) still passed on from fathers to sons is that brothers should not live together on contiguous areas of land, but should spread out and cultivate different areas.[3] Thus, ethnographers have found themselves in communities where people talk of the importance of agnates, but in which there is a minority of agnates to be found.[4]

This already complicated and potentially contentious system has been made even more so by mining company methods of determining who is eligible for profits and land occupation fees. Mining companies generally use *dindi malu* (land genealogies) to ascertain current "ownership" of land. Establishing a legitimate status with the mining company requires that one's ancestors have lived on the land in question and that one be knowledgeable of the appropriate genealogy that connects one to these ancestors. Huli men tend to be quite proud of their deep genealogical knowledge and consider it a potent cosmological instrument as well as a means for settling land disputes. In this respect, then, they wholeheartedly agree with mining companies' fetishization of genealogy. However, the Huli definition of *dindi malu* differs from that of mining companies: just as important as the genealogical information are the secret myths associated with various ancestors, and mining officials' failure to treat ancestral myths as powerful and important has been a source of consternation.

The following text is a brief excerpt of a document given to Mt. Kare mining company officials in order to establish rights to compensation money for a particular clan. Accompanied by maps, diagrams, and even a glossary, and typed painstakingly in halting English, this text is an example of how claimants do their best to present ancestral myths in ways that they hope will convince mining officials of their importance. (My explanatory comments are in brackets.)

•   •   •

In this text to read the names of places, caves, mountains that their names used in the stories still exist today at Mt. Kare, where the gold deposit is. In this occurrence there is somebody who used to give gifts, who used to show miracles and tested on people [the author is referring to the clan's founding ancestor, who, as is typical in *dindi malu*, was human-like, but also capable of supernatural acts]. Those people who are tested and never fulfilled are punished, and those who fulfilled the testing are given some gifts. From the story, the people who passed their testing were the real landowners of Mt. Kare and also the relatives of the tester. It is our custom that the names of those persons are kept secret, that their names should not be mentioned also . . .

It all happened when Mr. Tara A__ was traveling from Paiela territory to Huli territory. On his way he was given a tree branch (Haroli Kepage Tebohe) with three nuts on that stem. He did not know what was that and he continue his journey to Huli. On his return journey, it was Habobo river that got flooded on a dry day and it crushed him and washed him ashore. For the second time he did not know what was happening and he continue his journey. Now it was his second journey back to Huli and on his way on that same place of the incidents when he was hang by a rope called Neparabu and tied him to a pandanus tree roots. He did not even figure out the third occurrence on his journey . . . So all those tested and have not fulfilled were caught with leprosy. [In other words, the apical ancestor attempted to make his presence known to particular descendents through extraordinary occurrences, such as a river that floods for no reason or an ensnaring vine that seems to come out of nowhere, but the above protagonist failed to understand the significance of these incidents and was therefore afflicted with leprosy.]

So now it was tested on another clansman, Mr. M__. While M__ was at Kolepa when two cuscus *(haguanda)* was killed and thrown down from the top of the pandanus leaf *(kuku hini mane)*. While he was operating the cuscus he found a gift *(alu hibiri)* in the cuscus pouch . . . a man appear and told him, "previously I gave you a gift. So now I will give you another gifts." . . . Early in the morning M___ woke up and saw . . . that there had been three person who spent the night there. Because there were two human waste and the third one was bird's excreta. Where the two men had slept he found three things. They were a human killing machine propeller *(mirilini)* a bow *(tabagua)* and a lighter *(kilakila)*. Where the bird had slept he found an Engan wig *(manda wagaroro)*, an Engan spear, a pair of cooking tongs, and an Engan human organ of generation coverer *(khaki tambale)*. By looking at the properties left, they were from two different tribes, one from the south, a Bosavian (Duguba), and one from the north, an Engan (Obena). They were left so that the man from the centre could use it, actually it was left for M__, a Hulian . . . All those properties or gifts were for himself and for his future generations. [In other words, this protagonist successfully recognized unnatural occurrences as a kind of "test," and he was therefore rewarded with a special stone he found in the pouch of a marsupial he had killed (the cuscus). Later, he woke to find signs that other beings had been present while he had slept and that they had left him particular objects symbolic of their cultural origins to either the south or the north of the Huli.]

• • •

What the author is attempting to communicate is that the mythic founder of this clan made contact with his descendants through unusual and significant objects or events, and those individuals who recognized these incidents as signs of ancestral presence were rewarded with magical gifts which tied them and their lineages to the land at Mt. Kare. The bow, "lighter" (torch), and "killing machine propeller" are all objects associated with cultural groups south of Tari, evidence that the ancestor had established ritual ties with these groups. Similarly, the wig, spear, and "human organ of generation coverer" (pubic apron) are all objects belonging to cultural groups to the north of the Huli. This narrative thus articulates a theme of long-standing significance to Huli cultural identity—the assertion that the Huli are the cosmologically mandated center of the regional universe, and have the duty of mediating contact between the cultural groups to the south and north of them, in the realms of both ritual and trade (Frankel 1986; Ballard 1994). The gifts from the

ancestor demonstrate that he traveled to these far-off cultural areas, obtained their respective emblematic objects, but did not allow these two
peoples to meet. That he fulfilled the central ritual mission of the Huli and
then came to settle on land near Mt. Kare provides a powerful argument
for this clan's ritual entitlement to Mt. Kare wealth.

I include this tiny snippet of a quite lengthy and detailed document
not only to illustrate the Huli emphasis on cosmological entitlements to
Mt. Kare wealth—for example, "the people who passed their testing were
the *real* landowners of Mt. Kare"—but also to convey how landowners
anxiously and carefully select which details of their secret mythic knowledge to reveal to mining company administrators, and how they then attempt to convert this knowledge into a more "official" sounding genre
that they hope will render it compelling. Sadly, "the company" has little
use for this 20-page, single-spaced document that goes on in the same
vein, laced with cryptic symbolic references and ancestral exploits. The
failure to acknowledge the legitimacy of this genre exacerbates tensions
between landowner claimants and mining officials.

There are also gendered tensions to mining negotiations. Although
women as *tene* may own land and therefore receive money from mining
companies, they are traditionally not allowed to learn the *dindi malu* that
would establish them as rightful claimants. Indeed, traditional *mana* says
that women may not and *cannot* learn *dindi malu;* that is, as women they
are both forbidden, and thought not to have the ability, to learn complex
genealogical knowledge. Women episodically challenge this *mana,* not so
much by insisting that their fathers or brothers teach them *dindi malu,*
but by arguing that women "give birth" to *dindi malu*. In an argument
reminiscent of indigenous peoples' protests against the conversion of
their biological property (DNA) into others' intellectual property (phar-
maceutical patents), Huli women assert that they bear the persons who
comprise *dindi malu,* a labor that seems to them far more primary than
memorizing the names of those persons. As one old woman bellowed angrily into my tape recorder during an interview that was supposed to be
about her reproductive history:

• • •

You men say that women do not hold *dindi malu* and that only men
have *dindi malu*. This is not true . . . I say that when we give birth to
children, this is *dindi malu*. When you say we do not have *malu* you are
lying. You give pig intestines to women to clean out, you make women
get pregnant and give birth, you say that women have to stay in

women's houses—all this is just like saying that women do not have *dindi malu*. When you say that women do not have *dindi malu* you are lying. We name the children, so I say witness that! It is mothers who cause the *dindi malu*.

. . .

In this tirade a number of customs are represented as oppressive to women—the fact that it is women's duty to clean out the digestive tract of slaughtered pigs, the burdens of excessive childbearing now that post-partum sexual taboos are no longer stringently adhered to, the *mana* that confines women to the *anda* (the domestic, private space). Women's exclusion from important genealogical knowledge is included in this litany, particularly now that this potentially obstructs their access to mining company cash.

The Management of Desire and the Organization of Social Space

Between Tari town and the mining camps are miles and miles of rural Huli space. The Huli live in dispersed nuclear or extended family households, not in centralized villages, and each family property is encircled by moat-like trenches, sometimes eight or nine feet deep, and surrounded by high, thick stands of bushes and trees, which mark property lines and prevent easy visitation or even a glimpse of others' households. When my parents came to visit during my second year of fieldwork, my mother remarked in dismay, "these aren't villages at all; they're small fortresses." Or, as Frankel put it, "each homestead is effectively a private estate" (1986: 44). Here and there along the red dirt roads are trade stores selling rice, canned mackerel, oil, salt, flour, and occasionally, warm Coca-Cola. To get to the stores, however, you have to be able to get over the deep trenches, most of which are too wide to jump across and some of which would be difficult to get out of without a ladder should you happen to tumble in.[5] Usually the store owners have positioned a narrow plank across the ditch, and I always held my breath as I teetered across, often with someone holding my hand. The deep trenches, while marking property lines, are also paths, and the usual way of getting into the tangle of hidden residences beyond the road is by descending into these trenches and sloshing through them, often without being able to see the gardens and houses above. Eventually, as you approach people's houses, the

FIGURE 5. Trenches like this one are threaded through Huli territory and are the pathways people typically use to get from one place to another. Although muddy and slippery, they can afford a high degree of privacy if one is able to walk quietly. Sweet potato gardens flank this trench.

trenches become shallower, turn into simple trails, and suddenly open onto vast stretches of sweet potato gardens.

During my first year of fieldwork, I lived in the mountainous area north of Tari. This region is known for its especially poor land (Wood 1984; Ballard 1995), and even the earliest colonial patrol reports comment that in much of the area there is "only a few inches of subsoil over hard, grey, water-logged clay" (Jinks 1959). The households in this area are widely dispersed, and from any individual house it can seem that you have no neighbors, affording a domestic privacy highly valued by most Huli. As Huli people like to assert—contrasting themselves with urban residents, who both depend on money and must live cheek by jowl—"*mipela free*" (we are free); that is, no one can easily monitor when they get up, when or whether they labor in their gardens, when they eat, and so forth. Privacy assures them of the ability to conduct their family and economic lives as they please, and protects them from the covetous gaze. As my field assistant's sister muttered indignantly after some women had the nerve to come to her house to see me, "My cousin lives just up the hill, and I never go to her house unless she asks me, and she never asks me unless she has a specific reason. I don't even know which room she sleeps in." This cousin was part of our extended family household, and she lived with her children less than 20 yards away, but we never visited her, and she only visited us because I, as the ethnographer, had asked that I be able to socialize with lots of different women. Importantly, there is a gendered dimension to these limitations on sociality; female collectivity and sociality are particularly frowned upon and actively discouraged (also see Sturzenhofecker 1998).

The insides of many contemporary Huli houses are also organized to manage desire and its potentially malignant consequences. In the past husbands and wives ate and slept in separate houses, and men cooked for themselves and maintained their own gardens (Glasse 1968; Goldman 1983). However, the various Christian missions—citing the sanctity of the marital bond—have urged people to adopt "family houses," and according to one survey I did, two thirds of married couples now live together. "Family houses" have become a way to demonstrate one's modern sensibilities; for spouses to share a house is considered not only good Christian behavior, but also more sophisticated and worldly. Missionary attempts to replace discrete male and female domains with a shared marital space have not been entirely successful, however. The erosion of separate men's and women's houses has led to a redesign of the interior of most houses, with open sleeping platforms being replaced by a gendered demarcation of space within the home. Most "family houses" have two sides, one for husband and one for wife and children, and men's sides often have double walls, doors, and locks, while women's sides have only one wall and an open doorway separating the bedroom from the shared eating area. This spatial demarcation—intended in part to protect men from undue exposure to female substances—is also meant to prevent the theft of each other's belongings. Indeed, in two of the three rural households I lived in, the man of the household held a family meeting in which one side of the house was designated as mine. The other family members—women and children—were cautioned not to enter my space, and I was told to enforce this rule; otherwise, my belongings were sure to be stolen. Of course, there was a different dynamic in play in this situation, since I was a white foreigner who owned a range of coveted items—knee-high rubber boots, Swiss Army knife, Coleman lamp, countless pens and notebooks. Nevertheless, a number of Huli men told me that they imposed the same rules on their wives when they took the step of adopting a "family house."

Fencing in Women

This gendered demarcation of space is but one example of the way in which men attempt to control desire by controlling women. While male anxieties about menstrual or sexual "pollution" have been emphasized in much of the Melanesian ethnographic literature, among the Huli there are a range of female practices—transgressive movement, public profanity, theft, the use of love magic—that are "substantively" dangerous to men's health and well-being, and men's overarching goal is to contain and control women's potentially deleterious actions. The court case concerning my eviction from my first field site for "menstrual pollution" reflects the wide range of dangerous female substances and actions. I had been living with Tamu Mangobe, her four children, her married cousin (whose husband stayed at the nearby men's house), and her two unmarried younger sisters (Lirime and Birime Mangobe), but unbeknownst to me, her husband, who was away in the capital city, had not given her sisters permission to live in the house. Before moving into the community I had asked that, if possible, I join a household in which there were women at different stages of the life cycle, and my female host had taken advantage of this request—and her husband's absence—to invite her sisters to live with us, an atypical living arrangement. (In fact it is increasingly difficult to generalize about "typical" Huli households, largely because male out-migration forces people into what are said to be untraditional living arrangements, such as boys living with their mothers long after they should have moved into an all-male residence. Nevertheless, it is fair to say that the first household I lived in—which I found both fun and ideal for my research purposes—was, in fact, an atypical situation fabricated in part for the ethnographer.) When her husband returned to find one of his sons suffering from constipation (a symptom of menstrual pollution), he assumed that one or all of us had been preparing food for his sons while menstruating—against explicit instructions he had left with his wife—and he evicted all the extraneous women, including me.

The village court case, in which compensation was demanded from me (but not the other women) for injuring this boy, was quite instructive on a number of fronts. I learned, for example, that Huli men consider them-selves owners of "women's houses"—houses in which a man's wife and young children live. Men build them, the houses are usually on a hus-band's land, and so men refer to them as "my women's house," and they have the right to decide who will live there, who may visit, and who may not. Men rarely allow large groups of women, particularly women from a wife's constellation of kin, to live together, asserting that such an arrangement brings out women's worst qualities. (However, I also saw that men do not necessarily exert the control over these houses that they often think they do; men go back to their own houses at night, and women take this opportunity to visit each other, gamble, or cook extra food for themselves.)

The comments made by men also showed that while the case was os-tensibly about "menstrual pollution," this was not the only way that women posed threats to men's health and well-being. A number of men criticized the complainant and forthrightly stated that the whole dispute should be dismissed because "we don't believe that anymore"; in other words, they felt that he was fraudulently bringing a charge against me, perhaps because of potential monetary gain and perhaps because of lin-gering anger about the way in which his authority had been undermined in his absence. Others argued that it was, in fact, the wife's younger sis-ters who were to blame for the boy's illness since they were known to flirt with men, use vulgar language in public, go to Tari town quite frequently, attend bush discos (stigmatized rural dance parties), and then "go inside the fence" (*go insait long banis*) of morally upright men like the com-plainant. Such improper behavior intensified the dangerous quality of the young women's bodily substances, but was also polluting in its own right. The mere act of going to a disco and then crossing over onto the complainant's land was enough to have damaged the young boy's health. Ultimately it was decided that the polluting "substance" was not menstrual at all: the complainant revealed that his wife had stolen money from me, and the final consensus was that their son was sick because she had used this ill-gotten money to buy food for him. In effect, he had ingested her "sin." Thus, in this case, it was women's incessant crossing of spatio-moral boundaries, their vulgar talk, their potentially errant sexuality, their impulsive malfeasances — and the difficulties men had in circumscribing and controlling such behavior — that provoked men's unease.

One way men attempt to control women's wayward substances and movements is through the explicit gendering of objects and social space. Thus, for example, women are said to belong in the *anda,* the enclosed and private realm of the family, while men are associated with the *hama,* the public spaces of ceremonial display and oratory (Goldman 1983). In the contemporary context, women are a regular feature of public spaces such as markets, church, or the ubiquitous village court cases, but the gendering of social space is still robust and has been transposed into the new spaces of modernity (also see Sturzenhofecker 1998); women are almost never allowed to sit inside the cab of a truck, for example. Moreover, it is an unwritten rule that they should never dress or act in ways that suggest a sense of entitlement to the symbols of public prestige. Women should not — unless they are salaried employees who must do so — wear flip-flops (let alone shoes), and I heard countless stories of women who had saved up enough money to buy a radio, only to have it stolen or destroyed by jealous male kin who claimed they were punishing them for being *bighed* (self-important, impertinent).

According to most Huli I knew, both men and women, it is men who have the capacity — and the responsibility — to shape the social and material world so that women can be *wali ore* (literally "women really"; or very good or proper women). And, to some extent, it is men who have the capacity, and the responsibility, to shape women themselves so that women will act as *wali ore.* This is not to suggest that women do not themselves shape the world through their actions; however, the dominant discourse is that male agency should shape the sphere in which women can exert their own agency — or as the Huli say, women should be "fenced in by men" or "under the legs of men" (also see Biersack 1995b, 1998, 2001). Women's agency, then, is conceptualized as encompassed — it occurs within projects initiated by men and should, when properly managed, facilitate the goals of these projects. Like pigs or gardens, women must be fenced in to ensure that they are safe and that they flourish; if left unsecured, they may run amuck, be stolen by others, and fail to carry out their intended purpose. This gendered image of encompassment is seen in many social domains. For example, men and women say that while it is true that women do most of the agricultural work of tending sweet potato gardens and caring for pigs, they could not do this work unless men built the fences and drainage ditches that enclose gardens, and unless men acted as "security guards" for women, protectively encircling them while they work (although, in fact, this latter activity does not occur very often). Thus, what a researcher might diagnose as female subordination is conceptualized as a kind of encompassment, and male dominance as a kind of "fence" that is both nurturing and disciplinary.

The brother-sister relationship is said to be the ideal version of, and model for, this gendered encompassment. For example, countless Huli folktales begin: "Once there were five sisters and one brother. One day the brother decided to go on a journey. Before he left, he built deep ditches and a beautiful fence around their property and told his sisters to stay inside while he was gone." The tales proceed in a variety of ways: the one good sister may be rewarded by the brother when he returns, or the sisters may never be mentioned again as the tale goes on to recount the adventures of the brother. However, in all versions, wayward sisters who "break" *(brukim)* or "jump over" *(kalapim)* their brother's beautiful fence are severely punished; typically they are devoured by Bayaga Horo Nabaya (ogres who eat humans). A brother's fence is thus both fondly protective and disciplinary.

The brother-sister relationship is meant to be mutually nurturing, and is often spoken of as the relationship in which there are the deepest feelings of attachment, trust, and loyalty (except, perhaps, for the mother-daughter relationship). Brothers and sisters should always be able to rely on each other for requests for pigs, money, or labor, and women should be able to count on brothers to protect and support them, particularly in the context of village court cases or tribal fighting. Women who "have no brothers" (which can mean have no male siblings or, more figuratively, can refer to the small size or martial weakness of a woman's clan) are more vulnerable. For example, one woman I interviewed said that whenever she fought with her husband he would jeer at her for not having any brothers, and he boasted that he felt free to beat her because of it. Men assert that the brother-sister relationship is meant to be so emotionally intense that when a woman is severely injured or killed, her father and her brothers may come into conflict with each other: the father may be willing to settle for a compensation payment of money or pigs, but brothers—who feel a greater sense of loss—will, and should, insist on a tribal fight. For a brother to acquiesce to compensation is shameful, cowardly, and demonstrates a lack of love for his sister. On a darker note, I was often told that when women were sexually assaulted or held up by criminals they could appeal to their assailants by asking, "Don't you have a sister? I am somebody's sister too."

However, as the fence imagery suggests, the brother-sister relationship is by no means an egalitarian one. In addition to nurturing and protecting their sisters, brothers also have a moral obligation to physically discipline and control sisters; to be too nurturing and indulgent is to be negligent in one's fraternal duty (also see Dureau 1998). Almost all of the fifty women in my life history interview sample said that they were physically disciplined by their brothers when they were young. The question "did your brother(s) hit you when you were growing up?" seemed normal to women, and often brought on cackles of nostalgic laughter. The only exceptions—and women were quicker to explain to me why they had not been hit by their brothers than why they had been—were women who had been considered sickly when they were young and women who were first-born children, particularly those whose mothers had died young, and who therefore were their "mother's replacement" *(senis bilong mama)* to their younger siblings. Being chastised by a brother was, at least in retrospect, often spoken of as a sign of care, a demonstration that one's brother took an interest in one's moral development. Conversely, of a woman who is rebellious and willful, it is often said that "she had no brothers to fence her in" or, just as common, "she had no brothers to beat her." This emphasis on men's role as an external locus of control for women generates a logic in which women are almost expected to engage in willful, fractious behavior; their "innate" or "natural" volatility takes over if men aren't there to "fence them in."

The women I interviewed and lived with consistently stressed the importance of the brother-sister relationship, but they also suggested that this bond was subject to increasing stress in the contemporary context. Brothers are often away for wage labor, they said, and are not there to support and discipline sisters as they should. Moreover, many women added, with scarce cash resources, brothers choose to invest primarily in their own children, neglecting duties to sisters and sisters' children. Women, they suggested, increasingly *brukim* (break) or *kalapim* (jump over) *banis* (the fence) as a consequence of male physical and moral absence.

The labor history and migration data for the Tari area confirms women's assertions that men are increasingly absent from the community. Southern Highlands Province, home to the Huli, was one of the last areas to come under Australian colonial authority, and this occurred at a time when smallholder coffee production in other highland areas was beginning to outstrip plantation production, a predicament not anticipated by the colonial agricultural extension officers, who had envisioned smallholder production as merely supplementing plantation production (Stewart 1992). At that time the World Coffee Agreement mandated that countries could only export a certain amount, and the rapid spread of smallholder production meant that Papua New Guinea soon had far more coffee than it was allowed to put on the world market (Stewart 1992; Wardlow 1993). Thus, when coffee was introduced to the Tari area as a cash crop, it was not pushed as aggressively as it had been in other areas; moreover, since the Highlands Highway did not extend to Tari until 1981, it was difficult for Huli smallholders to competitively market their coffee. And, even now, coffee buyers who come to Tari offer relatively low prices, since they have to bear the costs of getting the beans to a more central location.

Rather than invest in agricultural development within the area, then, the colonial government cultivated Southern Highlands Province as a labor pool for plantations elsewhere in the country, with the important consequence that there have long been high levels of male out-migration for wage labor (Harris 1972; Vail 2002). Migration data for 1981, for example, shows that for the north Tari Basin area, where I conducted much of my research, approximately 45% of men between the ages of twenty and thirty-nine were absent from the community at mid-year, and throughout the 1980s and into the mid-1990s (when demographic surveillance for the area ceased), the proportion of absentees remained high (Lehman 2002; Lehman et al. 1997; see table). These numbers do not provide information about how long men actually stay away, but my interviews and more informal conversations with women suggest a wide range of behavior, with some men leaving for just a month or two and others absent for years at a time.

Given the expectation that men are meant to "fence in" and discipline women, it is not surprising that male absence has become a compelling concern for both men and women. The contemporary (and probably somewhat familiar) "myth" below illustrates current anxieties about the brother-sister bond, its failures in the modern context, and the ways in which these failures are intimately connected to wage labor and the penetration of capital relations.

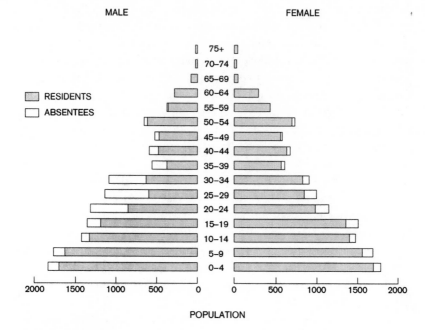

This population pyramid of the approximately 26,500 Huli people under demographic surveillance by the Tari Research Unit in 1982 shows the high proportion of male absentees between the ages of twenty and thirty-nine (from Lehman 2002).

•   •   •

Once there was a man who had two children, a boy and a girl. His first wife died, and so he took another one. This one hated the two children and convinced her husband to abandon them in the bush. But the boy overheard this plan and collected stones, which he dropped along the way so that he and his sister could find their way back home. But one morning, the second wife woke the children up when it was still dark, before the boy had a chance to collect stones, and she left them in the bush. The brother and sister walked and walked, and suddenly the boy fell down a hole in the ground. The sister waited and waited for him to crawl out of it, but he didn't come and didn't answer her calls. She concluded that he must be dead, and she wept and wept. Finally she continued on her way, and eventually she came upon a house. She went inside and it was empty, but inside there were seven beds. Later in the day the seven brothers who lived in the house came home, and the last one almost fell asleep on top of her! "Look! There's a girl asleep in my bed. Let's take care of her, and she can cook for us and wash our clothes." The seven brothers had jobs and they wanted someone to look after the house. So she lived with them for many years and worked as their maid.

Meanwhile, her brother had not died. He fell down and down the hole until he came to a beautiful, sparkling city. The paved streets were lined with white, permanent houses with corrugated metal roofing. The boy found a boss-man who gave him a good-paying job. It just so happened that the seven brothers also worked as laborers for this same boss-man. One day they mentioned to the boss that they had a young woman who took care of their house—she had lost her brother down a hole years ago, but now they took care of her. The boss-man realized that this woman must be his other laborer's sister, but he told the seven brothers, "Let's not tell them yet, let's wait a few years." So the young man worked and worked, and the boss-man's business grew very strong and the boss-man became very wealthy. Finally the boss-man told the young man that his sister was still alive. He reunited the brother and sister, and they still recognized each other after all those years, and they settled down together in one of the beautiful white fiberboard houses in town. She cooked and cleaned for him, and he continued to go to work.

• • •

The woman who told this story was mocked by the other women present. Her story, they said (and as the reader might have deduced), was an amalgamation of Huli folktales and stories that they had learned from a school workbook in the second grade. The other women had all taken turns telling "traditional" Huli myths, and in her eagerness to have a story to tell too, she had mixed them all up. In this story there are elements of Hansel and Gretel (the lost children, the stones meant to mark the path home, the wicked stepmother—although this is a theme in Huli folktales too), as well as Snow White (coming upon an empty house which turns out to be inhabited by seven men). But, there are also stock narrative elements found in Huli folktales, such as people falling down holes as they wander through the bush. And there are some elements that are actually both. This particular brother-sister duo is clearly taken from Hansel and Gretel, but protagonists in Huli myths are often brother-sister pairs. Similarly, the seven men can be seen both as Snow White's dwarves and as a group of Huli Haroli or Iba Ngiya, ritually secluded young men who are participating in a bachelor cult.

However, there are telling details in this updated version of the brother-sister myth. The seven men are bachelors, but instead of living as Iba Ngiya—the ritually purest and least secular of men—they are laborers for the "boss-man." The "boss-man," for his part, evokes the figure of Bayaga Horo Nabaya—an ogre-like figure in Huli folktales, always eating the careless and unheeding (Goldman 1998). Like Bayaga Horo Nabaya, the boss-man is a symbol of inappropriate consumption: he does not eat the brother, but he consumes the brother's labor for his own benefit. In the context of a subterranean magical capitalism, the estrangement of brother and sister only enables the "boss-man" to multiply his riches. The brother-sister link is severed, but this does not lead to the transfer of attachment to another male figure or to the formation of a new, reproductive household (as often happens in Huli myths when brother and sister are separated). Rather, both brother (through his own work) and sister (through serving the other laborers) work to enrich the boss. The only hope is that someday the boss-man will decide that he is finally rich enough—and who can predict when that will be—and will allow brother and sister to be reunited. When brother and sister are finally brought together, their transfer to respective marital relationships still does not occur. Instead, brother and sister form their own little nonreproductive refuge, laboring for the boss-man (and getting wealthy themselves), but not forming social ties with others.

Nevertheless, important to bear in mind is that the female protagonist in this story is always "fenced in"—if not by her brother, then by the seven dwarves/Iba Ngiya she lives with. Also telling is that her brother and the seven men are now themselves "fenced in" by the "boss-man," who—like the ultimate brother (if not Big Brother)—protectively but controllingly encompasses the intimate and productive lives of his laborers, using their energies for his own ends. (And, as this image suggests, men do sometimes speak of the employer/employee relationship as one that potentially feminizes the employee by making him dependent on and subordinate to his employer.) Finally, this tale is a profoundly asexual depiction of capitalist labor and its social consequences, and many Huli, I suspect, would point out that this mythic scenario does not represent what actually happens when men disappear from the community to go find work; rather, they leave their sisters and wives behind, with no one to make sure that women's potentially errant nature is properly fenced in.

CHAPTER 2

"To finish my anger"

Body and Agency among Huli Women

Long, long ago First Man approached the house of the First Woman in order to give some bespelled water to their first child. He called out to her, "Mother of Life, Mother of Life" (Habe Ainya, Habe Ainya), but the woman refused to answer. He then "turned the phrase around" *(beregeda)*, calling out, "Mother of Death, Mother of Death" (Homabe Ainya, Homabe Ainya), and this time she responded with the conventional "whoop" you use to let someone know you are at home and will see them. Perhaps in anger at the woman's behavior, the man threw the bespelled water to the ground, where a serpent consumed it and thereafter was able to shed its old skin and perpetually renew itself. The human infant, denied the water that was intended for it, drank breast milk instead and was fated to mortal embodiment. (See also Goldman 1983)[1]

In this well-known Huli myth, had First Woman responded to being called "Mother of Life," First Man would have fed their child the water that would have endowed it with an ever-renewable body. By answering instead to the name "Mother of Death," she named her child "Death," and since we are all descended from this child, she fated humanity to mortal embodiment.[2] Much like the story of Adam and Eve—which many Huli understand as a kind of structural variation of the above myth—this narrative is interpreted as a portrait of female "nature" and the tragic way in which female nature shapes the human condition. Unlike Eve, however, this woman does not succumb to temptation and the consumption of that which has been forbidden; rather, she engages in stubborn refusal: refusal of the name bestowed on her and refusal to allow her child to consume a precious gift. Eve is impulsive and acquiescent, ready and waiting for the invitation to transgress; First Woman I imagine as brooding and implacable, ready and waiting for an opportunity to be recalcitrant.

It is difficult to exaggerate the gravity of First Woman's behavior in Huli understandings of the human predicament. By endowing her child with a mortal, unrenewable body, she ushered in disease, bodily infirmity, and the fact of aging. Moreover, her actions—or, perhaps more accurately, her refusal to act—necessitated sexual reproduction as a poor substitute for the lost capacity for bodily renewal.[3] Human sexual reproduction entails a host of miseries: the potential for sexual pollution of men by women; the requirement that men exchange women in marriage, which inevitably causes conflict; the necessity of raising pigs in order to exchange women, which entails taxing physical labor and conflicts over land, and on and on and on. The whole secular realm in which pigs are bred, land cultivated, disputes mediated, and wars fought can be attributed to the actions of this woman. The closest men ever get to the way humans were intended to live—if not for this one tragic moment—is when they go off alone to the bush to hunt or, in the past, when they joined bachelor cults.[4]

I open my discussion of Huli female agency with this myth because I was repeatedly confronted by "real life" enactments of the myth's structural propositions: in every household I lived in I found myself tensely sitting by, stomach knotted, thinking "here we go again" as the male head of household approached his wife's house, repeatedly called out her name, was studiously ignored, mumbled a sarcastic insult which was rejoined with equally withering sarcasm, and then either rushed into the house in anger or, more commonly, stiffly stalked away. Familiar with the narrative of First Man and First Woman from having read Laurence Goldman's (1983) ethnography, I experienced the odd sensation that the people around me had suddenly become possessed by myth, with one huge difference: in the myth, First Woman's initial refusal to speak is dark and mysterious; she seems obstinately mute for no reason. In "real life" women have their reasons.

Like other ethnographers of the Huli, I am drawn to this myth, both because it is well known and because it encodes attributes associated with female gender (Goldman 1983; Ballard 1995; cf. Sanday 1981). However, the myth as it is usually told—both by ethnographers and by Huli narrators—is distilled to its structural components and leached of the quotidian, but highly charged, motivational elements that I believe are important for its interpretation. A simple structural interpretation leaves us

FIGURE 6. Typical rural house in the Tari Basin, surrounded by mounds of sweet potato interspersed with sugar cane and a few banana trees. The smaller house at the right edge of the picture is for pigs.

with the following symbolic antinomies (Goldman 1983: 94; cf. Ortner 1974):

Male	*Female*
Renewable embodiment	Mortal embodiment (aging, disease)
Transcendence of cyclicity	Cyclicity of life (reproduction, death)
Water (exogenous substance)	Breast milk (endogenous substance)
Ritual power (controlled)	Natural power (uncontrolled)
Transparent and benign motivation	Opaque motivation
The bush	The domestic realm
Mobility	Stasis

Other ethnographers have documented these same gendered antinomies—not only in myth and ritual, but also in daily discourse and practice—and rightly argued that such symbolic associations are deeply (if ambivalently) internalized by Huli men, as well as instrumentally deployed by them to justify male dominance (Glasse 1968; Goldman 1983; Frankel 1986; Clark 1993; cf. Biersack 2001). What is missed through a purely structural analysis, however, are the concrete social situations and gendered structures of power that drive such discursive interactions in everyday life. What sounds like an oracular incantation of doom in the myth—"Mother of Death, Mother of Death"—can be seen as sarcastic name-calling when read through everyday marital interactions. Admittedly Huli husbands do not approach their wives' houses and call them "Mother of Death," but they do call them other disparaging names, particularly when a friendlier greeting is met with frosty silence.

One way to interpret First Woman's actions, then, is as the sardonic embrace of her husband's taunting.[5] When seen through the lens of commonplace spousal situations, her behavior can be understood not as an expression of the unfathomable and ruinous nature of woman, but as an act of negative agency—a refusal to inhabit the subject position allocated to one and a refusal to cooperate with projects initiated by others. First Women's agency in this myth is figured as encompassed—she is expected to cooperate with the cosmological plans of First Man; her only other option is refusal, which is framed as opaquely willful and refractory. Thus this myth can be seen as a "charter" for Huli female negative agency. However, the structural bare bones of the myth—and a structuralist reading of the myth—mystify and efface the anger that motivates this mode of agency in women's day-to-day lives, as well as the factors that often preclude other modes of agency. It is the project of this chapter to add the affective and situational flesh to these structural bones.

Encompassed Agency: Using One's Body for Social Projects

There are, of course, myriad means by which women attempt to shape their social fields. Most visible are the culturally expected practices by which women contribute to social reproduction: a woman grows the sweet potato that feeds herself, her children, and often her husband; she raises the pigs that are used for bridewealth and compensation payments; and she raises the children who will "replace" (an idiom often used by Huli) the previous generation of persons. All these practices afford significant behavioral variability depending on any individual woman's inclination, skill, and energy. Some women pride themselves on the amount of time they spend in agricultural labor, the aesthetic arrangements of their fields, and the lengths to which they are willing to go to acquire sweet potato runners (used for planting) that promise to be particularly healthy or that will give them a harvest of many different sweet potato varieties. Some women use their personal talents to cultivate relationships with a wide range of kin in order to gain access to more land for gardening. Similarly, many women take great care in raising pigs, assiduously removing lice from their hides, assuring that they receive proper periods of sun and shade, and advocating different theories for how best to feed them. Some women become known for being such good pig caretakers that they are able to contribute pigs to various events not only through their brothers or husbands, but "in their own names," as Huli women say. Other women do not go to such great lengths in these endeavors. Thus, all of these practices provide wide scope for a more individualistic sense of agency. Moreover, on occasion women are given public recognition for their actions, as when women publicly receive the heads of the pigs they have contributed to feasts.

At the same time, most of these actions are encompassed; that is, women are expected to carry out these practices as part of larger social projects over which they have little authority or influence, and for which they receive little prestige. As other ethnographers of highland Papua New Guinea have found, it is the feast itself and what it accomplishes socially that really matters, and it is men who initiate, orchestrate, and verbally frame these events—whether for a bridewealth payment, a homicide compensation, a feast in honor of a politician, a gift of pigs to one's allies in a tribal fight, or a celebration to mark the arrival of a new mining company (Lederman 1984). Thus women are seen as importantly exerting agency within their own sphere of production and nurture, but this sphere is encompassed by the male sphere in which sociopolitical relations are shaped. Women's acts of cooperation are necessary and valued, but cooperation (or the refusal to cooperate) is the means by which women can have a social effect. It is important to emphasize that most of the time women do not see this encompassment as exploitative or disempowering. They know their work is necessary; they know that other women and their male kin recognize their skills, even if these aren't acknowledged publicly; and they often identify with whatever the larger social project may be. They too are clan members who care about clan enmities, marriages, and the potential benefits of mineral resource development. Nevertheless, the construction and enactment of female agency is largely encompassed by male agency in male-authored projects.

Moreover, implicit in Huli *mana* (customary wisdom) is the notion that women exert proper agency through using their bodies to grow and nurture others' bodies: they breast-feed babies and clean their bottoms;

FIGURE 7. *Wali ore* (good women) carrying *bilum* (string-bags) full of sweet potato runners. Visible markers of being *wali ore* include carrying heavy loads, having bare feet, and prioritizing the dress and appearance of family members over their own.

they grow and cook the food that others eat; they manage their menstrual fluids to protect the bodies of the men in their lives; they care for the pigs that enable multiple social interactions. Properly enacted, women's agency operates indirectly through others—through the pigs that facilitate social transactions, through their male children who will become effective warriors or wage earners, and through their daughters who will themselves contribute to the reproduction of the social body through their own marriages, the bridewealth they bring in, and their acts of nurture. It is through these acts of bodily agency that women age and their energies become depleted; thus, women who have had many children are said to be "older" than chronologically older women who have fewer or no children because more of their bodily substance and work has gone into the production of other persons.

I hesitate to emphasize Huli women's association with the bodily, since this risks reinscribing dominant representations, both Huli and Western, that distance women from the cultural and political by linking them with the "natural" or corporeal—with that which is both too domestic in its concern with physical needs and not domesticated enough in its sensual unruliness. Marilyn Strathern (1987) has pointed out that women are not universally aligned with "nature"; indeed, in the Huli case, both "nature" and "culture" are associated with masculinity, the former as a pure and transcendent realm untainted by feminine concerns, and the latter as the realm of *mana,* knowledge about moral and cosmological management. Huli women are, however, associated with corporeally endogenous but not easily controlled nurturant powers. Men, moreover, deliberately distance themselves from the bodily, not only by asserting their own near exclusive monopoly on *mana,* but also by embracing (at least verbally) an ascetic self-discipline in which men are not supposed to care about where the next meal is coming from or whether their wives will have sex with them. By denying the importance of bodily hungers, men delineate their difference from women, who not only do the work of fulfilling such hungers but are also said to be weakly vulnerable to them.

Avenues of Agency Foreclosed

My point here is not that female agency is "naturally" bodily; rather, other modes of agency are either not available to women or they are less socially compelling when enacted by women. For example, collective agency—having an effect through acting as one imposing social body—is associated with men. The clearest example of this is tribal fighting, from which women are excluded.[6] While a number of rationales are given for this exclusion—women are not strong enough to bend the large black palm bows, they are not nimble enough—one of the most important asserted by men is that women are innately unable to act as a unified group. The high emotion of tribal fighting would only aggravate this weakness, men assert, and the few men who were willing to entertain the possibility of women's participation laughed as they imagined women running helter-skelter in their disorganized attempts to act as a coordinated body of warriors. I sometimes argued with men that there were specific structural impediments to women's collective agency—virilocal postmarital residence, male control over female homosociality, a patrilineal ideology that emphasizes male kinship links—but most men dismissed these factors and asserted instead an innate female inability to act collectively.

Women too associate collective action with maleness, but this does not mean that they relinquish this strategy entirely. One friend of mine, in the throes of adolescent love, had a tryst and got pregnant with a young man who lived quite far from her clan territory. Her mother and older sisters were determined to coerce the young man into marrying her, but her male relatives decided that he lived too far away to threaten tribal warfare successfully, and in any case there were no witnesses to the event and he was not admitting to anything. Indeed, he felt so confident that he would get away with this sexual escapade that he publicly joked that *"em i no saiz bilong mi; em i no fit long mi"* (literally, she is not my size; she's not fit for me/doesn't fit me; i.e., she's not right for me and she doesn't "fit" me sexually). The women were so angered by the reluctance of their male kin to act that they decided to take matters into their own hands, marched to the young man's home in a group, and confronted his parents. They were jeered at, had stones thrown at them, and were sarcastically asked if they "thought they were men." They came home humiliated and were then castigated by the men of their clan for behaving in such an embarrassing manner. Their attempt at collective female agency was considered laughable.

Another potentially important mode of agency is speech. As many scholars of Melanesia have observed, speech is considered an important form of social action: it can be persuasive or uplifting or bullying—that is, it can change people's minds and hearts, convincing them to act one way when they otherwise would have acted another. My field assistant once told me of the time when he found himself on the road between two warring parties and was able to convince both sides to turn around and go home. He suddenly felt that he had it in him to be an influential community leader, perhaps even a government-appointed village court mediator; his capacity for agentive speech had been confirmed for him. However, most Huli—male and female—assert that women's capacity for effective speech is far less than men's (Goldman 1986; cf. Lederman 1984; Keesing

1985). When produced by women, words are thought of as weak, opaque, and lacking in causal force or explanatory power.[7] Few Huli people, for example, accept that a Huli woman could be an effective dispute mediator or pastor, and most doubt women's abilities to give coherent testimony during village court cases. Goldman (1986), for example, has shown that during village court cases, female speakers are asked far more "why" questions than men—why did you do such-and-such, why did you say this or that—and they are often led through testimony by heavy-handed interrogation and commentary rather than being allowed to "speak their minds" freely. Because women's minds are thought of as less knowable, they are thought unable to "speak their minds" and thus need others to build the verbal scaffolding upon which they can add their words.

The one form of speech at which women are thought to be expert is the vulgar and provocative insult—that is, the form of speech which emphasizes the uncontrolled nature of the body (also see Kulick 1993). In Huli conceptualizations, speech not only has cognitive content, it also has something like physical substance and can affect people's bodies (not just their feelings and thoughts). For example, sexual slurs or curses not only humiliate a person, they may also physically pollute him or her, and thus are actionable (although few people actually sue others just for cursing them). Relatedly, some women I interviewed expressed repugnance at even talking about menstrual beliefs and practices, asserting that speaking about such matters made their "skin feel dirty." Thus the form of speech in which women excel, perhaps not surprisingly, is the form that makes the body its object, both in terms of topic and in its aim to have a physical effect on another.

Women's insults are creative, but usually center on the inappropriate consumption of genitalia, such as "Go eat your mother's vagina" *(I ainya hamba na)*, "Go lick your own menstrual blood" *(Ini naga pugua pende bia)*, and "Go suck on your own vagina like you suck on cigarettes" *(Ini hamba mundu naga tagua bia)*. A related genre of female insult is one that relies on the opposition between outside/inside as spurious/authentic, and takes the form of asserting that a woman seems one way, but is actually something else: *"Tai yaga iegi* (on the outsides, surface) *wandari petolo peta* (she is a young girl); *kabane ha* (inside) *gonoliame karini ne peta* (gonorrhea has eaten her innards)." In other words, she looks like a young innocent girl, but really she is a slut infected by gonorrhea which is devouring her from the inside out. Or, *"Igiri mbalini mbaule ndo* (She seems like/pretends to be the sister of a man, but no). *Agalime ya* (men hold) *ariari* (line up) *piaga pasinya* (this passenger woman)." That is, she appears to be a nice, young woman properly disciplined by her brothers, but actually the number of men she's had sex with would make a long line.

Such insults are transgressive in multiple ways. First, such language often mixes consumption processes—sex and eating—that are meant to be kept separate. As is the case in many societies, sex and eating are metaphorically associated with one another; however, Huli people also say that "mouths are for eating and genitals are for sex." Thus, although the two domains inform each other symbolically, they should not over-lap in actual practice (at least according to traditional *mana*). Such insults also depict a very self-oriented sexuality, in which one is consuming one's self rather than using sexual capacities for social purposes that extend out beyond the self. Furthermore, the insults that purport to reveal their vic-tim as quite other than she appears reinforce the dominant construction of women as unreliable and capable of deception. To speak such insults in public, then, is quite transgressive. Nevertheless, just because women are said to be masterful at a particular verbal genre does not necessarily mean that this mastery is agentive. The insults in and of themselves do little to change the structures that shape gendered interaction, and if any-thing they reinforce the idea that women are volatile and incompletely so-cialized. In sum, since many avenues of agency are closed to women, it is not surprising that women's own discourses about their social efficacy tend to emphasize bodily action. Using the body—either in a nurturing way or in more resistant ways—is often the only recourse.

Negative Agency

Since women's agency is dominantly constructed as encompassed and bodily, perhaps it isn't surprising that their primary alternative is what I call "negative agency"—the refusal to use their bodily energies in the ways expected of them, and particularly the refusal to use their bodily energies for others' social projects. As discussed in the introduction, I borrow the term "negative agency" from Corinne Kratz, who uses it to describe the structurally limited courses of action available to Okiek women (2000). Analyzing the organization of Okiek marriage, Kratz shows that young women are put in the position of either cooperating with others' wishes, for which they receive no credit (it is merely what is expected of them), or refusing others' arrangements, for which they are maligned as opposi-tional and fractious. In the present ethnography I am concerned less with the aspect of prestige and more with the ways in which women's scope of action is encompassed by men, rather than the reverse, so that their av-

enues for exerting power or having a social effect are limited to supporting the sphere in which men act or attempting to undermine it through
acts of refusal.

Women's negative agency takes a variety of forms. For example, Yerime, a woman I lived with and at whose domestic violence village court
case I testified, would simply "forget" or "misunderstand" the instructions her husband gave her. He would leave his dirty clothes in a particular spot at a nearby creek, she would "forget" that this was the agreed-
upon spot, and his clothes would remain there for days on end. Not only
did her actions serve to question his authority over her, they also meant
that on more than one occasion he did not have the one set of clothes he
wore whenever he went to Tari; indirectly she thus forced him to delay
his trip. Similarly, he would ask her to bring him raw sweet potatoes that
he could go cook in the local men's house, and she would bring fewer
than he expected or would leave them behind the house instead of in front
the house, making him search for them when he simply wanted to be on
his way. Alternatively, she would "forget" that he planned to eat with us
in the evening, and would fail to cook enough sweet potato, forcing him
either to find his dinner elsewhere or to reprimand her in front of me and
whomever else was present. At one point she also told her sisters that they
could steal from her garden; they did so, with the result that there
weren't enough sweet potatoes to support the pigs that he wanted her to
care for. Not only did her actions annoy him, they effectively undermined
his ability to engage in projects he wanted to undertake and thus limited
his influence in the community. Women's options in this mode of negative agency are somewhat restricted. They rarely neglect their own pigs,
for example, or their children. They do, however, refuse to garden, cook,
and have sex, particularly if they feel a husband isn't doing enough to care
for the children he already has. In sum, refusing to use one's body for social reproduction—whether productive work or reproductive sex—is an
important form of negative agency.

Women's management of their own reproductive substances (or refusal to do so) is also an arena in which women exercise negative agency.
Most Huli women believe that the proper management of their sexual
substances is important to men's health, well-being, and success in the
world (also see Biersack 1987, 1998; Kyakas and Wiessner 1992). Just as
brothers and husbands "fence in" (protect and discipline) women, and
thereby encompass and harness women's productive and reproductive capacities, so women must "fence in" their own corporeal powers so that
the men to whom they are connected can act effectively in the world.
Husbands are particularly vulnerable to wives' bodily practices because it

is thought that men's and women's bodies become joined upon marriage. As many women put it, "An unmarried man is alone. When he marries a woman, the two become one" *(Igiri tambuni o ibini hangu. Wali tapu piria angi libu mbiyore)*. This change is described as a physical one: spouses' bodies become joined at marriage, not only during sex, but in a more enduring phenomenal way as well. For example, a number of women asserted that when a woman became pregnant, "Her husband's skin becomes bad. When his wife's body is in a bad/dangerous state, his skin stays bad. When she gives birth to their baby, his skin will become good" *(Agali dingini ko hayita. Ibu one yamu ko hayagola dingini ko ka. Ibu one kanga tapahanayagola dingini payale hole piria)*. In other words, spouses' bodies are permeable to each other's states: as long as a wife is in a weakened state, investing her bodily powers in making a child, her husband also becomes weak and his skin loses its healthy glow. Most women therefore engage in a variety of practices to "encompass" or circumscribe their bodies when they are menstruating, washing themselves more than usual, staying inside the home or at most working in a nearby garden, paring their fingernails so that blood cannot get underneath them and then get deposited in food, and refraining from handing men objects or even speaking to them. Again, the image of female encompassment is important: women follow menstrual taboos within, and as part of, a larger project of developing and cultivating male health, social success, and well-being. Since women have a stake in their husbands' social efficacy, and since married bodies are "joined," women's bodily practices have great significance.[8]

However, a woman who is angry at her husband may choose to be somewhat lackadaisical about her menstrual practices. A woman who knows her husband is unfaithful, for example, may reason that he has "stepped over her" *(anguatole* in Huli and *kalapim* in Tok Pisin; disrespected and polluted), and that she is therefore no longer obliged to ensure his bodily health and integrity. She may thus "inadvertently" step over his clothes or his bush knife. This should not be taken to mean that women deliberately use their menstrual fluids to injure a husband; indeed, the majority of women I knew or interviewed reacted to such a possibility with horror, seeing it as equivalent to attempted murder. A woman might be lax about stepping over a pile of firewood she knows her husband intends to use to cook his dinner, but she would not go so far as to take her fluids and put them in her husband's food.[9] At most, she might smear a stone with her blood and place it over the door to her house, an action thought to increase a woman's influence over her husband after he walks through the doorway by making him "under her legs," a reversal of the norm in which women are "under the legs of men." Men who fall victim to such practices are thought to lose their will; not only are they swayed by their wives' persuasive words, they also lose their own sense of purpose and intention. Thus their actions become encompassed by their wives' purposes.[10]

Negative Agency and Self-Harm

Negative agency is inherently, to some extent, an expression of a more individualized self: the actor separates herself from the desires and plans of others and refuses to commit her bodily energies to them. Ironically, however, the most extreme forms of negative agency among Huli women—suicide and finger-lopping—involve the destruction of, or damage to, the self. In his verbal autopsy study of Huli mortality, Peter Geoffrey Barss (1991) found that rates of suicide among Huli women are extremely high by international standards (27/100,000), that suicide occurs almost exclusively among married women, and that the most common methods are hanging and drowning (Barss 1991; Frankel 1986).[11] (Rates of suicide among Huli men, by contrast, are quite low.) As a few Huli husbands grumbled to me, "You say one little thing and she runs for the Tagari River" (i.e., to throw herself in).

A number of ethnographers of Melanesia have also found high female suicide rates (Counts 1993; Johnson 1981), and the Huli case can be usefully contrasted with the theories proposed to account for this phenomenon. Dorothy Counts (1993), who has extensively documented and analyzed female suicide among the Lusi, asserts that female suicide should be considered a form of agency—not an expression of despair—because it has important social consequences. Specifically, Lusi people consider suicide to be a form of homicide, and often the husband is held responsible for inducing the shame and anger that drove his wife to commit this desperate act. A wife's family can demand compensation, and the woman's ghost is thought to be aware of, and presumably able to appreciate, her husband's comeuppance. Among the Huli it is rare for men to pay homicide compensation for a wife's suicide, for suicide is not automatically considered a kind of homicide. The Huli do not say, like the Lusi, that a woman was "killed with talk" (Counts 1993: 254) by her husband. The fact that Huli women are thought to be impulsive and to lack a sense of proportion means that it is more likely that a woman herself will be blamed, and if a wife displays suicidal tendencies, a husband may publicly demand a divorce and the return of his bridewealth, arguing that the whole community "knows what she is like" and that he does not want trouble with his in-laws when she finally kills herself.

Nevertheless, many Huli women themselves consider suicide a form of agency, although not for the same reasons Counts details. Among Huli women, the most common reason for attempted suicide is being falsely accused, particularly of extramarital sex. As discussed earlier, Huli women are not fully accepted as speaking subjects in the public arena; their words are unreliable. Suicide, then, is a woman's way of authenticating her version of events and asserting herself as a legitimate, truthful speaker when other attempts to gain credibility have failed (Wardlow 1996). One friend of mine, Yamali, attempted to hang herself after her husband hit her and accused her of laughing about him with her friends. She explained that she and her friends were making jokes about a male piglet that was trying to mount a larger sow, and that the laughter that he had overheard had nothing to do with him, but her husband was sure that his masculine authority was being undermined and refused to believe her. When she ran off and he found her up in a tree with a rope around her neck, he changed his mind. Then he proceeded to hit her for attempting to "throw away his bridewealth." (In fact, Yamali's was quite a loving marriage, and both she and her husband were acting out of character during this particular incident: she had never threatened to do violence to herself before, and he had always taken a moral stance against domestic violence. They themselves attributed their anomalous behavior to the stress they were experiencing because of his family's resistance to their very intimate and affectionate companionate marriage.)

The idiom Yamali's husband used — "throwing away my bridewealth" — is a prominent one in men's commentary on female suicide, and is an important reason female suicide can be considered an act of negative agency. A man whose wife has killed herself is said to be in a pitiable condition: the bridewealth a man has given for his wife is not returned if she kills herself, and not only does he no longer have a wife to tend gardens, raise pigs, and bear children, he also still owes his own kin for the pigs and cash they contributed to his wife's bridewealth payment. Not only is he is in debt, with nothing to show for it; he's also forced to take on a woman's chores as well as his own. His wife has effectively humiliated him and reduced his socioeconomic power. Of course, men tend to use the phrase "throw away my bridewealth" to insult their wives, defining their marriages as merely instrumental and devoid of emotional meaning, even if, as was true of Yamali's husband, their conjugal love is apparent to all. Nevertheless, it is this instrumental significance that women invoke when they attempt suicide, not any emotional loss a husband might experience. As one woman said when I asked if she had ever considered *ea nogo* (hanging herself), "I thought about it, but then I thought of my brothers and asked myself, 'Is my husband's sister going to kill herself so that he knows what it is like to lose a sister? No, of course not. If I kill myself, he will just take another wife, but my brothers will be without me.' " In other words, the emotional loss caused by a woman's suicide is to her brothers, not her husband, making suicide primarily a form of economic punishment.

Moreover, according to many Huli women, suicide makes for a neat structural and semantic symmetry with false accusations of adultery. An accusation of adultery is implicitly an accusation that a wife has "thrown away" the bridewealth her husband gave for her: she has allowed her sexuality/reproductive capacity to be "used" by another man, effectively allowing this man to steal that which her husband gave bridewealth for. In a sense, then, women who commit suicide are declaring, "You think I threw away your bridewealth? OK, now I'll really throw it away!" Arguably this is the same cultural logic one finds in the Mother of Life/Mother of Death myth: just as First Woman sardonically embraces and enacts the insult, or perhaps accusation, thrown at her (Mother of Death), so women who commit suicide embrace and enact the insults and accusations thrown at them (that they have thrown away their husbands' bridewealth), even if this means the destruction of the self.

To commit suicide requires a great deal of rage, however—enough rage, women say, to overcome the fear of death. Not all women experience this degree of rage or have the courage it takes to commit suicide, so, instead, many women when falsely accused will lop off their index or pinky fingers at the first or second joint. This practice is quite common: of the fifty women with whom I conducted life history interviews, ten of them had one or two finger joints missing. Indeed this practice by Huli women is so pervasive that children say they make a point of hiding all knives and axes whenever their parents argue, not only to prevent them from injuring each other, but to prevent their mothers from lopping off their fingers. Like suicide, finger-lopping is motivated by anger and indignation, but it is highly performative as well; for example, one is supposed to maintain enough presence of mind to hurl the finger at one's accuser and yell something like, *"Keba biba haro, inaga ki bi pugu ngerogoni"* (In order to cut off/finish my anger, I'm cutting off my finger and giving it to you.) As in English, the Huli words for "cut" can refer to the physical act of severing something or to the act of bringing something to a stop.

So common is finger-lopping among women that everyone knows what to do when it happens. At my second field site, one of our neighbors continually accused his wife of adultery, and she tried to demand a court case, asserting that she was willing to accept any punishment if he could provide the name of her lover, for they both knew that she was innocent and he was only trying to provoke her. The local leaders refused to hear her case, probably because her husband was a well-liked religious and political leader. So one day, after yet another argument, she lopped off her finger and threw it at her husband. Then she quickly wrapped a string around the stump of her finger to stop the bleeding, ran to the main road and yelled for other women to summon the local dispute mediators, and then headed off to the health center, where the male nurse grumbled about having to deal with yet another finger-lopping case. Four women fainted as he injected her finger with an anesthetic and proceeded to carve out bits of bone and flesh so that he could more easily sew up her stump. Her actions had mixed results: her husband had to take on all household chores until her finger was sufficiently healed, and even after she recovered he continued to do the work that was no longer easy for her. Moreover, she had marked herself as a woman who was willing to go to extremes, and so he ceased accusing her of adultery. However, she had hoped to force the local leaders into holding a village court case: she asserted that her husband was to blame for her missing finger—if not for his false words, she never would have inflicted such damage on herself. But they were reluctant to air this kind of argument, and she was unable to convince her own brothers—both of whom worked in distant towns and were unwilling or unable to leave their jobs—to press the matter. In sum, finger-lopping is considered a lesser alternative to suicide, and similarly operates as a form of agency: it proves to others that a woman was falsely accused and it removes her body—or in this case the parts that are necessary for productive work—from encompassment by a man she feels has betrayed her.

Outraged Agency

Once there was a young man who had five sisters. One day he went possum hunting and came back with five bundles of meat, one for each sister. The oldest sister rejected her bundle and threw it at his feet. The young man wept in rage, took his bow and arrow, and left.

FIGURE 8. This woman cut off the tip of her index finger after being accused of adultery by her husband.

The last born sister followed him saying, "You are like my father—I won't leave you." Her older brother hit her again and again, but she continued to follow him. He walked on and on, and finally he stopped to rest at the top of a hill. Moved by his sister's attachment to him, he took pity on her and gave her permission to walk with him. When she got tired, he washed her, gave her some possum meat to eat, and carried her in his string-bag. The young man followed a crooked, winding path, and finally he came upon an old woman who told him that he could not stay with her because she lived with "men who eat men" (Bayaga Horo Nabaya). But the young man replied that he could go no further, and if he was killed, the old woman was to place his head inside his string-bag and hang it from a tree. When the ogres came home, they did indeed kill the man, and the old woman did as she had been instructed.

The next morning the youngest sister realized that she was hanging in a tree, and then she saw that her brother's head was lying next to her in the string bag. She wept and wept and then set off walking, taking her brother's head with her. Eventually, she came upon two pigs, which squealed at her arrival. A young man came outside to see what the commotion was. There were five young men altogether, and they were all Iba

Ngiya [members of a bachelor cult]. The first young man called out to his father, "Father, there's a girl or something—I'm not sure what it is. Come look at it." [The young man's ignorance about women is meant to indicate his isolation from them, and thus his pure, untainted masculinity].

The men decided to take her in, and eventually the young man who had discovered her married her and she gave birth to his son. All this time she had kept her brother's head: she carried it with her everywhere she went and never left it behind. One day, when she went to make gardens, she hung the string-bag carrying her baby son on one branch, and she hung the string-bag holding her brother's head underneath it. As she made gardens, she got further and further away from the tree. Her husband, who had always been curious about the string-bag his wife insisted on taking everywhere, took this opportunity to steal her brother's head.

When the woman discovered the theft, she took her baby son and hurled him to the ground, killing him. She destroyed all the drainage ditches surrounding her husband's property, cut down all his banana trees, and burnt down his and his brothers' house. She cried and cried and cut off two of her fingers. Then she looked up and saw her brother coming toward her with her husband. Her husband yelled, "What have you done?" She replied, "I had something very important in that string-bag and you took it!" The woman tried to hug her brother, but he pushed her away and sarcastically commented, "No. You think you have behaved well?" Then he and her husband vanished.

• • •

This myth encodes a number of the analytical points that have been made so far: the nurturing and yet disciplinary stance brothers are supposed to take toward sisters, as well as women's encompassment (this time in her brother's string-bag). I read this myth as a discussion of the difficulties women experience in transferring their emotional and moral attachments from brother to husband—or perhaps the impossibility of doing so—and the danger to all when women do not properly manage their loyalties. However, the aspect of this myth that I want to highlight here is the destructive agency the woman engages in when she feels her husband has wronged her. Not only does she withdraw her bodily capacities from her husband, she also destroys every symbol of masculinity and clan continuity in the vicinity—the banana trees and drainage ditches, both symbols of masculinity and patrilineality; her husband's and his brothers' house, a symbol of the clan corporate body; and the son she has born her husband. She also cuts off her own fingers, an expression of rage, but also a repudiation of her own bodily capacity for production. Her outraged agency brings social reproduction to a halt. Like the myth that opened this chapter, this narrative also encodes a kind of agency associated with women: disruption and destruction.

Of course female destructiveness is exaggerated in this myth; women rarely, if ever, burn down houses or kill their own children. They do on occasion, however, destroy crops, physically attack other people, and, as discussed above, lop off their own fingers. Nenge Tayagu's narrative below serves as an illustration. Nenge, a woman in her forties, was still bitter about the fact that although she qualified for a place at the local high school, her parents sent her brother instead. Only momentarily disheartened, she lied about her age and managed to get herself into the local nurse's aid training program when Tari Hospital needed Huli staff. After a year she was given a job, but when her family found out that a male health worker was writing her love letters, they approached her boss, got her fired, and tried to force her into an arranged marriage.

. . .

I took off my uniform in front of my boss and everyone there, and I left. I got my last paycheck and I didn't buy food with it this time, I bought beer. Why? Because they had refused to buy my school fees so I could go to high school. I was still angry about this, and even now I'm still angry about it. They just wanted to "eat bridewealth," and so I was angry. Why did they do this to me? I couldn't stop thinking about that. So I used my "finish pay" to buy beer and I just drank and drank. I got completely drunk. Then my brother found me and beat me. OK, the next day, that was it for my parents' banana trees. I cut down every banana tree and sugar cane plant. If they thought I was going to just sit quietly at home—no way! Then I started going to bush discos. If they looked for me at a Tari disco, I would go to one in Kupari, and if they looked for me at a Kupari disco, I would go to Piwa. This jump of mine went on and on [the term "jump" suggests both going outside the family "fence" and jumping over her family, a metaphor for disrespect]. When I saw relatives drinking, I would grab the beer out of their hands, gulp it down myself, and tell them, "You people refused to pay my school fees. OK—now look what you get! I'm becoming much worse than you ever expected. You yourselves did this!"

At this time my older brother wanted to marry a woman, and there was a lot of hard work to be done raising the mother pigs [the largest of the three categories of bridewealth pigs]. They wanted me to help, but

I told them to piss off. I wasn't going to help them marry a woman. If they thought I was going to help my mother and father—forget it! Your problem! You people didn't want me to have a paying job and you wouldn't help me go to high school. With my own strength I got training and got myself a job, and you got me fired. Now what are you going to do? I was really *"bighed."*

. . .

Nenge's behavior—her attempts to derail others' plans and her refusal to participate as women should in social reproduction (i.e., by refusing to raise pigs for her brother's marriage)—is a good example of women's more disruptive and destructive agency. It is also a good example of how women respond when they feel that their relatives are being "greedy for pig money"—that is, only value them for the bridewealth they will bring in. (Women's more extreme reactions to this sense of commoditization are discussed in chapters 4, 5, and 6). This form of agency is perceived, by Nenge and by those around her, as inappropriately individualistic and antisocial: her best way of punishing her family was to refuse to help in the family project of producing pigs for her brother's marriage. However, not only did she withhold her bodily energies from others' plans, she also actively damaged others' productive labor by destroying garden produce. Moreover, she refused to use her last paycheck on anything that would be helpful to her family and instead she deliberately spent it on beer, a commodity that is seen as wasteful and nonproductive. Finally, by attending bush discos, she was potentially reducing the amount of bridewealth her family could demand for her and implicitly threatening to appropriate her own sexuality, removing it from her family as a resource to be deployed by them in marriage. Nevertheless, even while acting in ways that her family saw as selfish, Nenge herself insisted that "you yourselves did this," blaming her behavior on her family. In other words, Nenge invoked a kind of relational personhood, arguing that her family's acts—their refusal to pay for her schooling, getting her fired—had "made" her in a particular way. Her antisocial individualism was socially created, according to her.

Women's acts of destruction are often quite eloquent in their way. One woman I knew, angry that her husband was gambling away all his money, took an axe to the local snooker table, yelling that if he wanted to throw away his money on snooker then she would give him the real chance to do so. As expected, the couple was ordered by the local court to compensate the owner of the snooker table for his loss. More often, however,

FIGURE 9. Man playing snooker.

women's physical aggression takes the form of attacking others. Physical fearlessness is highly valued, for women as well as men, and rather than being seen as an improper loss of control, in most instances aggression is considered an effective means of expressing and defending one's desires and one's interpretation of social reality. Little girls, like little boys, are taught the word *"ba"* (imperative form of the word for hit or kill) as soon as they can speak, and this language learning is done in the context of interactive games where little girls are encouraged to hit people who take their things or who attack their kin.[12] Moreover, both men and women view physical aggression as a marker of Huli cultural superiority, particularly when they compare themselves with cultural groups in Papua New Guinea that are said to practice magic or sorcery. Fighting is seen as a more egalitarian and less duplicitous form of aggression; as the Huli say, "Not everyone knows black magic, but everyone has two hands and can fight." And, as a number of the women I interviewed said about physical fights with their husbands, "He has strength, I too have strength. He has hands, I too have hands. I feel pain, he too is going to feel pain" *(Em igat strong, mi tu gat strong. Em gat han, mi tu gat han. Mi filim pen, em tu bai filim pen).*

The first fight I witnessed among the Huli was an all-female, stone-throwing brawl in which two people suffered concussions, one woman's arm was broken, and a few women required stitches. The incident began after church one Sunday when a middle-aged woman attempted to convene a village court case over a fight that had occurred between her daughter and two other young women. The local dispute mediators refused her request, admonishing her that dispute settlement should not take place on Sunday, the day when good Christians set aside bitter feelings and secular concerns.[13] The woman, stymied in her goal, cursed the mother of the two other young women. This woman responded by picking up a rock and throwing it at her, bloodying her face. Seven more women—kin of the two disputing parties—quickly joined in, either hurling rocks at each other or using them as clubs. Everyone else backed away, as the sphere of fighting quickly expanded, with yet more women running into the center of the fray or hurling rocks from the periphery. It was apparent that many of the women were pulling their punches; they could easily have slammed their opponents in the head, but they held back. The most frightening moment was when one of the women who started the fight grabbed an elderly man around the waist, pinning his arms to his sides, while her sister pounded him in the torso and head with a rock. He had marched into the melee in an attempt to stop it, but quickly found himself overwhelmed. Blood trickled down his face, and he looked wildly around in terror, but he couldn't break free. His youngest son, not more than seven, looked on, tears streaming down his face, arms stiffly held behind his back, a rock clenched in his hands. Finally a young man jumped into the fray to save the old man, and eventually the fight broke up as women stumbled off to the health center.

At the court case held soon after the brawl I learned that the failed marriage between Kelapi and Hiwi was at the heart of the conflict. Both in their late teens, they were forced to marry after Kelapi announced she was pregnant and Hiwi admitted to having sex with her. Hiwi's mother and sisters disapproved of Kelapi, considering her too flirtatious and worldly—she had spent some time in Port Moresby working as a babysitter for some wage-earning kin—and they spread the rumor that the baby was not Hiwi's. Hiwi himself seemed to want Kelapi, but during most of their brief marriage he was away at a CODE center (Centers of Distance Education).[14] When Kelapi moved in with Hiwi's family, his mother and sisters set out to drive her away: they shoved gum in the keyhole to her house, dumped rotten food all over her bedding, and threw her clothes down the pit latrine. Kelapi eventually gave up and moved back home. Later, when her baby contracted pneumonia and died, Hiwi's family refused to have it buried on their land or to attend the *tugu anda* (literally, mourning house; funeral ritual), effectively denying Hiwi's paternity. Kelapi's father had been away in Port Moresby during all of these events, and when he returned he furiously refused to return any of the twenty-four bridewealth pigs given for Kelapi, claiming them as *tauwa*. *Tauwa*—literally, genitals *(tau)* placed *(wa)*—is a compensation payment given to a woman's family for the "theft" of her sexuality in cases of premarital sex. It is considered an alternative to marriage; thus, when a young couple is caught engaging in premarital sex, her family will demand either *tapu* (bridewealth) or *tauwa,* depending on whether they want the young man as a son-in-law. Alternatively, a man's family may offer *tauwa* in response to demands for *tapu* if they do not want the young woman as a daughter-in-law. *Tauwa* is usually three to eight pigs, so it was scandalous for Kelapi's father to claim all twenty-four.

One day, a month or so after the baby had been buried, Kelapi and Hiwi ended up on the same volleyball team and seemed to bump up against each other a bit more than was necessary. Hiwi's sisters, their feelings still raw about the unreturned bridewealth, were furious that Kelapi was acting like a carefree young girl, flirting and playing volleyball when her baby had just died, carrying on as if her reputation had not been besmirched by past events—and, not least, daring to seduce their brother yet again! So they left the game early and waylaid Kelapi at dusk on the road home. It was this altercation that Kelapi's mother wanted adjudicated after church that Sunday.

I was shocked by this brawl for a number of reasons. For one, I was friendly with the key players in both families, and I had not been aware that tensions between them were so high. To witness them suddenly hurling rocks at each other starkly showed how little I knew about "my field site." I was also shocked because I had never before seen so many women fight with such ferocity. (Of course not all the women were equally aggressive; a few were trying only to support their female kin without inflicting or receiving too much damage.) In the West, perhaps particularly the upper and middle-class West, violence and physical force are coded as masculine. As Martha McCaughey points out, "Aggression is a primary marker of sexual difference . . . [it] is one way that we culturally tell men and women apart. The construction and regulation of a naturalized heterosexual femininity hinges on the taboo of aggression" (1997: 3). Physical aggression is rarely represented as a normal and expected part of femininity; rather, it is trivialized, as when fights between women are called "cat fights" and are thought to consist primarily of hair-pulling and scratching; it is ritually eroticized (e.g., female mud wrestling); or it is interpreted as a pathological exaggeration of a stereotypical female trait, as in Glenn Close's depiction of emotional attachment gone terrifyingly awry in the movie *Fatal Attraction* (Grindstaff and McCaughey 1996).[15] I was therefore unprepared for the intensity of Huli women's physical aggression, as well as the gravity with which it was treated by the larger community. While Huli men often belittle the reasons for women's fights, they never trivialize the fighting itself.[16] Indeed, the Huli have their own animal metaphors for representing female aggression, emphasizing both the vicious nature of women's fighting and women's supposed lack of self-control during altercations. For example, during the court case following the brawl, I learned an important piece of Huli *mana*: "When women or pigs fight, men stay out of it" *(Agali ina kamagoni agua biaga wali kungu piria ha uru nogo kungu piria ha uru ina agali nahaga)*. This aphorism was cited as a rationale for lessening the number of compensation pigs demanded from the two women for injuring the elderly man: yes, they had clubbed him in the head, but he should have known better than to get in the middle of a female fight.

Physical Aggression and Social Efficacy

It is unusual to treat female physical aggression as a form of agency (but see Burbank 1994; Behar 1993; McDowell 1992), and it could be considered irresponsible to do so without also emphasizing the fact that Huli women—like other women in Melanesia—are more often victims of male violence. In an analysis of demographic data for the Tari Basin, Peter Barss (1991) found that the female homicide rate (i.e., female victim and almost without exception male assailant) during the period 1971–1986 was 25/100,000, an extremely high rate by international standards (6/100,000 for Thailand in 1981 and 4/100,000 for the United States in 1987), and appeared to be on the increase. As Barss puts it, "The endemic severe violence to adult females appears to be unprecedented for a country not under active attack during time of war" (chapter 7, p. 29). The combined female suicide and homicide rates suggest that Huli women may have one of the highest documented rates of death due to intentionally inflicted injury. Moreover, regional and national surveys have repeatedly found that domestic violence occurs in 70%–85% of rural marriages in Papua New Guinea (Toft 1985; Bradley 1988).[17] Thus, my shift in perspective is in no way meant to diminish the fact of violence against women. However, that women are often victims of violence does not mean that their own physical aggression should be made invisible or thought of as merely defensive. Huli women tend to be quite proud of their fighting skills, and in my interviews with them they were usually more eager to tell me about fights they had been in than to answer my questions about marriage, reproduction, or pig raising.

Before examining the social consequences of women's fights, I must point out that their aggression is effective in the limited physical sense of causing injury. In an analysis of all adult inpatient injury cases at the Tari Hospital over a two-year period (roughly 240 cases, which excluded tribal fight injuries, unintentional injuries, and anyone under the age of eighteen), I found that women were responsible for inflicting almost one third of all the injuries.[18]

	Female Assailant	Male Assailant
Female Victim	50 (26)	82 (50)
Male Victim	23 (16)	85 (40)

The numbers in parentheses narrow the inpatient cases down to those people who were in the intensive care unit of the hospital. While most of the hospital injury inpatient records provided information about the gender of the victim and the assailant, they did not always specify the kinship relationship between the two, making it impossible to make any generalizations about the relationships that tend to be the most violent. Where the relationship was specified, it ran the gamut from spouses, to mothers beating daughters, to sons beating mothers, and so forth. Indeed, Tari Hospital staff were unsure how to code various injuries in the reports they sent to the national health department each month: one of the coding categories was "domestic violence," and most staff had been taught that this category should only be used in cases of fights between spouses, which to them seemed an arbitrary criteria since fights just as injurious occurred between people related in other ways.

One reason that women's aggression is so harmful is that women rarely use their bare hands; rather, when fights break out, women immediately grab weapons—rocks, sticks, knives, and pieces of scrap metal being the most common. Of the 73 cases in which women caused the injury of the patient, 25 involved knives, 21 involved a stone or a stick, and 6 involved other dangerous implements such as axes, scrap metal, and metal spades. Some of the descriptions of the cases in which women were the aggressors included "deep head wound from being beaten with spade," "fracture of forearm; bashed up by lady opponent," "chopped by a lady with a bush-knife on left thigh; required internal sutures and stitches," "attacked by other woman in town with knife and stone, and burnt on body," "stoned in leg by daughter; leg broken," "bitten by another female on thumb; required amputation," "brought in unconscious;

FIGURE 10. Waiting for a village court case to begin after having participated in an all-female brawl. Ultimately this woman had to give compensation pigs and money to the women she had injured, but she also received compensation for having been injured by them.

beaten by two ladies with stones," "beaten by five ladies with sticks," "son lashed with bush-knife by mother on forehead," "woman beaten by daughter-in-law; broken jaw," "hit with stone by wife in abdomen; vomiting blood," and "stabbed by wife in the upper chest and left forearm; unconscious; required stitches and blood." Thus, from a purely physiological standpoint, women's aggression can clearly be quite "effective."

Female fights are also dangerous because they often become group melees. The rate and degree of female aggression is exacerbated by the expectation that one's female friends and kin will jump in whenever an altercation arises—perhaps the one situation in which women do act quite collectively. Women rigorously keep track of which women help them in a physical fight—referred to as *sapot sapot* (support support)—and this is important in determining one's real friends. It is assumed that one's sisters and mother will *sapot sapot*, but one's *nenege* or *besty* (respectively, Huli and Tok Pisin for best friends) should come to one's aid as well. Indeed, one question many women posed to me when I was a few months into my fieldwork was whether I *sapot sapot*-ed Yerime when she and her husband or her mother-in-law fought. I had to confess uneasily that I did not, and my friends were disappointed, but not surprised: I only confirmed what they had suspected about white women—that they were weak and fearful.[19]

Not all women fight, of course, for as a nurse at Tari Hospital told me, "Some women are too weak, some women are cowardly, and some women don't have good mothers who teach them to fight." Nevertheless, most women do express a readiness to engage others in physical conflict. In my set of fifty life history interviews, all but five of the women had physically fought with other women, and of their 73 marriages, 56 entailed physical fighting with husbands, 15 were free of any physical conflict, and 2 women said they were hit by their husbands but they did not fight back or ever initiate physical fights.

A Pause to Reflect on Methodological Issues

Women's aggression is also socially (not just physically) effective; that is, it can be considered a powerful mode of agency because it does often have consequential effects. First, however, I will take a moment to examine some methodological and interpretive issues. Many theorists have noted that an examination of agency often requires privileging the actor's point of view; it is only through documenting the way in which actors interpret and act upon the social structures around them that the researcher can ascertain how actors reproduce or change the structures that animate and constrain them. And while it is possible to do "prospective" case studies in which the ethnographer follows the life of a person over the course of one or many fieldwork periods, tacking back and forth between the ethnographer's and the person's own versions of his or her life, the most feasible and common actor-oriented method is the life history. However, life histories cannot be read as transparent statements of autobiographical fact. Myriad factors shape interviewees' narratives of their lives: their perception of the interlocutor, their understanding of what the narrative will be used for, the identity they are trying to craft at that particular moment, the local conventions for orating such narratives, and so forth (Stewart and Strathern 2000a; Keesing 1985). An analysis of agency is particularly vulnerable to the effect of such factors since narrators may represent themselves as highly agentive or as passive role players in accord with such factors. In other words, the life history method itself necessarily has implications for an analysis of agency because retrospective narratives force actors to decide just how they will present their own past and present abilities to have a social effect.

Huli women's accounts of themselves often seemed contradictory: they either asserted what seemed to me an exaggerated agency in which, for example, they boasted with bravado of physical fights in which they vanquished both a husband and his illicit lover, or a complete lack of agency, when, for example, they claimed that they went to a "bush disco" only because a husband or brother was not there to stop them. Such statements can and should be read simultaneously through a number of different lenses. They are at once statements about specific events, expressions of a more general Huli tendency to present the self in a triumphalist manner, and commentaries on the moral disappointments and failures of contemporary relationality: one's brother or husband should care enough to stop one from *"brukim banis"* (breaking the fence, transgressing expected female behavior), one's husband should be punished for taking a lover and deterred from doing it again. In other words, one can read life history interviews not only as factual statements (once the facts asserted are cross-checked with others) about an actor's social efficacy, but also as social critiques and as examples of a particular narrative genre.

Another portion of my interview with Nenge Tayagu illustrates these points. In this portion Nenge discusses a fight she had with her husband's second wife. Confirming some of the factual details with other people showed that Nenge's fighting abilities did have social consequences and were, in fact, an important mode of agency. At the same time, the reader will see that Nenge's narrative encodes critiques of contemporary marital relationships and serves as a portrait of a bold and righteous conquering hero. After being fired from her job as a nurse's aid, Nenge gave in to her parents' desires for her to marry a neighbor who was a soldier in the Papua New Guinea defense force. However, Nenge soon deserted this marriage, ran away to live with some relatives in Enga Province, and later returned to marry a man who worked as a headmaster in an elementary school. As a salaried employee he could afford to marry more than one wife, and so he did, leaving Nenge and their children in a bush house while he lived with his second wife in permanent housing on a school compound outside of Mendi, the capital of Southern Highlands Province and a five-hour ride from Tari.

In the narrative below, Nenge has made the trip to Mendi on a Friday because she wanted some money from her husband, and she knew he would be paid that day. There she happened to see her husband and his second wife doing their Friday shopping—carrying bags of rice and canned corned beef to the school truck. As she was rarely able to afford such foods, had no access to a private vehicle, and had born her husband two children, she was furious that the second wife was the beneficiary of all this largesse. Nenge claimed that later in the day this second wife snuck up on her and attacked her; others, in contrast, asserted that Nenge deliberately chose to go to a store where she thought she would find the second wife. (My comments to the reader and responses to Nenge are in brackets.)

. . .

I heard the whoosh of air from her stick, and quickly I grabbed it so it didn't hit my head. And I said to this woman, "Why have you come to hit me?" "Mmm?" she said. She couldn't speak Tok Pisin well. So I said, "You want to steal my husband? You can't find a man as young as yourself? He's an old man. Why are you so eager to steal married men?" That's what I said. I had suffered this problem for long enough, and my body was sick and weak because of it. I said to her, "Do you usually carry your husband's cock around in your mouth? Or do you usually carry it around in your hand?" [You said that?] Yes. I said that to her. "You don't even count to your husband. He is going to carry his thing, his cock, around to any woman he wants. It's not just you who is going to sit down all nice and comfortable in that house. I am going to go live there too."

Then she spoke to her two companions as if I wasn't there, "He was looking for someone brand new and he found me. Now his old whore has come back." Please. Now I thought I would be able to keep my cool, but this old worry kicked me, and I was so tired of getting sick for no reason. This woman kept saying hard things like that, and so I grabbed her stick and I clubbed her in the head. That was round one. Then round two went to me too. OK, the third round I hit her again. Her mouth was bleeding and I kept hitting her. Her two friends came at me and I jabbed them with a knife. There were three of them and one of me. I kept hitting that woman and I ripped off her skirt and threw her down naked on the highway. I said, "Now your husband is going to come here carrying his cock and he is going to see you naked like that, just what you were waiting for."

I was so angry that after that I went and I drank some beer like it was Coca-Cola. So angry! I kept thinking to myself, "What can I do, what can I "finish"? I can finish the beer! [In Tok Pisin the verb "pinisim" can refer to the act of finishing the consumption of something or to destroying or killing something, so Nenge is playing on words here. She would like to "finish" the second wife, or she would like to "finish" her anger over the situation, but instead she will "finish" the beer.] Man, I drank twelve and there were twelve left in the carton, and while I was drinking my husband arrived. "Oh, Mother of Daisy [Daisy is the name of their child], what are you doing here?! You think this is your land so you can sit there and drink beer?" [Her husband is both shocked to find her in Mendi and shocked to find her publicly drinking beer]. "I don't think you should be talking to me right now. You should probably go fix your wife's problems. I'm not sure where she is, she could be in the hospital. You might want to look for her and take her there—she collapsed," I said. And my husband said, "Why were you hitting my wife?"

The two Mendi women reported me to the village court, and they said that I had to show up for the case on Tuesday. This is what they said in their report: this *"pasinja meri"* stabbed us with a knife. In the space where they were supposed to write my name, they just wrote *"pasinja meri."* [They said your name was *"pasinja meri"*?] Mmm. So we went to court. We sat down, and everyone from the school was there. And they asked me, "Where did you come from, and what is the real reason that you came here to Mendi?" And I said, "I came to find that man over there" [i.e., her husband]. "Who is this man to you that you came looking for him?" And I said, "He's my lover." And he got up and yelled, "Hey, she's lying! That woman is my first wife." And then the court magistrate said, "Those women said she was a promiscuous *pasinja meri,* a gonorrhea woman who brings sickness wherever she goes." And my husband yelled, "No she's not! She's my first wife. They are lying. Which women said that my wife is a *pasinja meri?*" "Those two Mendi women sitting over there, and it was your wife who told them to say it," I said. "OK. You women have damaged the name of the school and our reputations as well. So you have to pay compensation." That's what they told the three women. Then one of my friends stood up and said about me, "She—she didn't use this kind of language, and she didn't do anything to start the fight. It was all of you women—you were the ones who were so eager to fight with her. Her husband has said that she's his wife, but you damaged her name and started the fight. You should pay her compensation." So the women had to pay K50 each, but my husband's other wife didn't have any money. The court gave me the K100 they collected, saying that I should take it because those women had said those things about me.

Then the two Mendi women said, "That old woman cut us with a knife. Aren't you going to do anything about that?" "Who is she to you? You don't even know her. You didn't even know where she came from. You can't just go around jumping into other women's fights for no reason. The wives of one husband, a family of sisters, or a family of brothers—they have a right to fight with each other and jump into each other's fights. But you put yourselves in the middle of something that doesn't concern you. So it's your fault and your problem!" [That's what the court said?] Mmm. So then, my husband's wife didn't have any money on her, so she couldn't pay me. She saw my husband getting some money out of his pocket and she thought he was going to help her. "No! I'm looking for the bus fare for you!" Then I said, "You don't have any rights here. Only I have a name here. You, get out!" "He's my husband," she said. "You go. You damaged the school and you're not fit to live here." So they kicked her out. They gave her the K40 bus fare, and I told her, "Go back home. You're not fit to live here. You could damage the name of the school again." So I thought she was gone for good, and I was here to stay. I went and fetched my children, and we all went and lived at the school.

· · ·

In this narration Nenge emphasizes her fighting skills—for example, she was able to beat up three other women. She also frames her violence as a morally justified course of action: she only traveled to Mendi because her children required money, and moreover, the second wife started the fight. Indeed, the second wife is represented as thoroughly ignominious: she can't speak Tok Pisin, can't fight, is guilty of slander (describing Nenge as a passenger woman), foolishly thinks she is special enough to have a monopoly on her husband's affections, is selfishly consuming resources that should go to Nenge's children, is incapable of behaving with the decorum appropriate to the representative of a modern institution like a school (she picks fights in public), and doesn't have the money to pay for her own transgressions. In contrast, everyone is on Nenge's side: her aggression is acceptable because she did not start the fight and she was performing as a mother, defending her children's interests. Moreover, she presents herself as verbally quick and clever: when asked by the court magistrate who she is, she brings the other women's slander to public attention by asserting that she is her husband's lover; she suggests the second wife's uncertain control over their husband by asserting that the only way to be sure of his fidelity is to "carry his cock around in her mouth." Thus, a number of structural oppositions are at play in this narrative: first wife/"other" wife, righteous anger/greed, maternal identity/sexual identity, good fighter/poor fighter. Such oppositions work to suggest that Nenge is victorious physically *because* she has moral right on her side; her effective fighting skills are a result of her moral integrity.

Nevertheless, although this narrative is clearly shaped by Nenge's desire to paint herself as highly agentive and morally triumphant, it is also true that the outcome of this fight and subsequent court case did, in fact, result in the second wife being sent back to Tari. Nenge successfully ensconced herself and her children in her husband's *haus kapa* (literally, house copper; a fiberboard house with a corrugated metal roof) where they had store-bought food, money, access to the school truck, and the prestige of being affiliated with a modern institution. And while I selected Nenge's narrative because she is a lively and articulate storyteller, it is the case that most Huli women tend to claim that their physical fighting is highly effective. That such accounts are clearly part of a particular genre or style of narrative does not necessarily undermine the potential efficacy of women's physical aggression; they can be used by the researcher both as evidence of agency and as examples of a particular female discourse about agency.

Making Conflict Public

In the above narrative, Nenge puts as much emphasis on the village court case as she does on her actual fighting, and the same was true of other interviewees' narratives. The fact that physical injuries make conflict public and visible ultimately renders women's physical aggression socially consequential and agentive. Village court decisions usually have material consequences—that is, one party must give compensation to the other—but they can also mandate changes in structural arrangements, as in Nenge's case when one wife is sent home and the other is allowed to take her place (which also has material consequences). However, women's access to the village court arena is not automatic. Among the Huli, all the government-appointed village mediators are men, and it is they who decide which matters should be public and which private, which are worthy of village court cases and which are not. Recall that both Kelapi's mother and our neighbor whose husband accused her of adultery were unsuccessful at persuading the local leaders to hear their complaints until they inflicted injury—one by instigating a big, public fight and the other by injuring herself. In the face of men's trivialization of women's conflicts, women see fighting as the one reliable means of forcing public intercession in matters that men have deemed *"praivet samting"* (a private matter) or *"liklik samting"* (literally, small thing; an insignificant matter). Women often provoke fights in order to bring their conflicts into the public sphere, where local mediators will have to review their contentious history and where women will have to articulate their version of events for others to hear. It is often only after repudiating words in favor of weapons that women's words are taken seriously.

For example, another all-female fight I witnessed was triggered by a dispute between the women of two different clans. In this case, Kiya, a man who had made money working as a gold buyer during the Mt. Kare gold rush, convinced some men who belonged to another clan to lease him some of their land so he could invest his profits in a large trade store. The trouble started when he allowed his cross-cousin (father's sister's daughter), Liname, to cook food and sell it on the land where his trade store was located. Liname had almost had her arm chopped off by her husband, and Kiya felt sorry for her.[20] However, women who belonged to the clan that actually owned the land on which the store was located did not. They asserted that if any women were going to be allowed to sell cooked food out of Kiya's trade store, it should be them. They confronted Kiya numerous times about this perceived injustice and reminded him that he himself was only leasing the land from a clan to which they themselves belonged, but he refused to make any changes. So one day the women attacked Liname and broke her arm, the same arm that was still healing from her husband's attack. In this particular case the women got their way: they had to pay compensation to Liname for breaking her arm, but she was no longer allowed to sell food out of Kiya's trade store and they succeeded in taking her place.

That physical fights make visible conflicts that might otherwise remain obscure or be dismissed is particularly important in marital relations. The nuclear family home, in which husband and wife eat and sleep in one house, has become an important marker of being Christian and modern. One consequence of this is the construction of marital disputes as "family problems" (Huli use the English words) or *"praivet samting"* (literally, private things) that should be resolved domestically, rather than interclan problems that should be resolved publicly. Indeed, when a marital dispute occurs in a public place, particularly in Tari town, someone is sure to snicker that the couple must be backward, *"bush kanaka"* people who still live in separate residences, for if they shared a house, as many Huli couples now do, they would have fought at home instead of running into each other in a public space. Public fighting between married couples thus suggests that a man is both failing to control his wife and living a backward, un-modern life. Not surprisingly, then, men feel that marital disputes should take place in the *anda* (the domestic realm) and should be kept private.

Women are well aware that this so-called modern and Christian ideology works to their disadvantage. I had one friend, Lucy, whose husband often hit her, though never severely, and on one occasion she stabbed him, accidentally, she claimed: in the middle of a dispute he ran into a knife she was using to peel potatoes. He was taken to the hospital, and his family wanted to demand compensation from her; that is, because *she* had injured *him* they were quite ready to bring this dispute into the public sphere, which had not been the case when she was the injured party. She jeeringly threw back at him the phrase he had so often said to her, *"Em family problem, yia."* In other words, just as her own injuries at his hands had been defined by him as a "private" matter for which she should not seek support, so she was defining his injury at her hands. She was quite proud of her clever appropriation of the phrase men typically use to avoid public exposure of marital problems.

For the most part, however, women dislike this "privatization" of conjugal arguments, and they usually seek ways of making spousal tensions more public by confiding in siblings, pastors, catechists, nurses, and government-appointed village court mediators. And, if all else fails, they resort to what is increasingly defined as shameful *"bush kanaka"* behavior (i.e., public fighting) in order to make their problems public. Public fighting always results in a court case, and court cases always entail articulating in minute detail the whole marital history which led up to the fight. Thus, fighting ultimately enables a woman to do what she wanted to do all along; that is, testify publicly about what has taken place in her marriage and have others collectively decide what is to be done.

Attention to women's negative agency—when they refuse to lend their bodily energies to others' plans or use these energies to disrupt others' plans—shows that women's actions both reproduce and change the structures that generate them (MacLeod 1992). Women's negative agency is generated by a range of social and ideological structures: women are discursively constructed as ineffective social speakers, and spatial arrangements and kinship organization limit the possibility for collective action. Moreover, women's productive and reproductive work is conceptualized as encompassed by larger, more important processes of social reproduction over which men have jurisdiction. Thus, women's agency is channeled through the body and into acts of refusal and disruption. Women see these acts as both momentarily resisting encompassment by others and as potentially instigating more enduring structural changes. However, these same acts are framed by men as impulsive and chaotic, and thus they work to reinforce ideologies that women are volatile and lack a sense of proportion, that they are unpersuasive speakers, and that they need to be disciplined and controlled by men. Thus, women's negative agency can be seen as both changing some of the immediate structures that shape women's lives but reproducing others.

The causes of Huli women's anger have likely been gleaned by the reader, but it is important to conclude by addressing some of these causes more directly.[21] These causes fall into three overlapping categories: domestic economy, money, and sex. In part because of male absence for wage labor, agricultural work is increasingly defined as "female" activity. Male abandonment of gardening activities has contributed to strained marital relations, a situation that I often thought of as "kaukau politics" — that is, the gendered struggles over sweet potato. On the one hand, the construction of Huli masculinity says that men are not supposed to worry about where their next meal is coming from, or other such creature comforts; it is women who are so physically weak and self-indulgent. However, where the next meal is coming from can be a real issue for men who do not maintain their own gardens. Thus, on the other hand, many men invoke a commoditized discourse about bridewealth, arguing that their wives must feed them — and perform other chores — because they "have paid for them."

And, as is discussed in more detail in the next chapter, women for their part often complain that husbands do not give them enough money. Husbands argue that a woman has no need of money until she has children to care for, and moreover that wives, as outsiders who have "married in," do not necessarily have the interests of husband and children in mind. Some husbands, suspicious of wives, try to give money or food directly to their older children in order to avoid giving it to their wives, whom they claim will selfishly "throw it away" on cigarettes and clothing for themselves. A vicious cycle can develop between husband and wife: when a husband does give his wife some money, she may already be so disgruntled about not receiving money in the past that she will defiantly and publicly spend some on cigarettes and food for her own consumption, thereby confirming a husband's accusations that she is selfish and wasteful. However, it is not only suspicion of wives that discourages men from giving them money, but also the competing demands on men for rural wages that are small. Men have children, sisters, mothers — as well as their own images of themselves as modern men — to maintain. A man who has a wage is likely to feel that at the very least he shouldn't have to do garden work, he has a right to gamble with his friends, he should be able to eat store-bought rice in the local men's house, and that he should wear jeans, Australian work boots, a watch, sunglasses, and some sort of hat. Maintaining the image of the modern man can be more expensive than men expect and than women realize.

Women, however, often assert that men do not contribute enough to "making" children, by which they mean that a husband does not give them enough money to buy food for the household or to pay for children's clothes and school fees.[22] Arguments over money can lead directly to marital fights or can lead to a woman's refusal to have sex, which can also result in conflict. Women invariably phrased their refusal to have sex as the refusal to have more children when a husband was not adequately providing for the ones he already had. Indeed, a number of women told me that they had *beregeda* (turned around; reversed the meaning of) a traditional saying about cassowaries to reflect their anger at men about this issue. As is true in many areas of Papua New Guinea, cassowaries are believed to be female and to reproduce through parthenogenesis (Tuzin 1997; Gardner 1984). Thus, traditionally when a young woman was reluctant to marry, her family or even her intended would taunt her by saying, "Do you think you are a cassowary and you can have children by yourself?" Women told me they had appropriated and "turned around" this witticism to berate their husbands by asking, "Do you think I'm a cassowary and I had these children all by myself?"

Even worse is when a woman knows her husband is using money to *gris* (entice, persuade) *pasinja meri*. Indeed, twenty-one of the fifty women I interviewed physically fought with husbands about their liaisons with *pasinja meri*. Five of these women knew they had contracted an STD from their husbands. Traditional *mana* teaches that a man's sexual infidelity can make his wife and children weak and vulnerable to disease because he is *anguatole* (literally, stepping over them; disrespecting and violating them; see Frankel 1986).[23] Moreover, as wives see it, men who have sex with *pasinja meri* are removing sex from its proper reproductive purpose: they are *"guap guap nating"* (literally, go up, go up nothing; having sex for no reason and with no purpose), and are wasting scarce cash resources to do so. What men experience as the heady capacity of money to transcend the bridewealth system—that is, to facilitate access to sex without the encumbrances of marriage and affinal relations (LiPuma 1999; Nihill 1994)—as well as a source of modern prestige, women see as an inexcusable waste of cash.

CHAPTER 3

"I am not the daughter of a pig!"

The Changing Dynamics of Bridewealth

One December late afternoon, as I rounded the Tari airstrip on my way to the hospital compound, some young men, who must have been home for the holidays and who probably thought I was a tourist, yelled out to me, *"Misses, kam likim mipela"* (White lady, come lick us). It had been a long day, and my first impulse was just to ignore them and walk on. There were many people sitting in groups talking and playing cards by the side of the road, and I was embarrassed by this sudden, very public eroticization of my racial identity. I wanted to flee in the most dignified way possible, and so I walked on as if nothing had happened. But then I caught myself. I had been there long enough to know that ignoring the young men would likely be construed as cowardly passivity on my part and was most definitely not the way most Huli women would respond. So I forced myself to turn around, march up to the fence behind which they were drinking and playing darts, and yell that they had *rabis pasin* (despicable behavior) and that I was going to *"kotim"* (take to court, sue) them for *"diskraibim"* me. (The Huli have adopted the English word "describe" to mean verbally sexualizing a person or talking about a person's body in public.)

Taking them to court was, in fact, an option. A woman has the right to file a complaint against men or women who publicly speak to her in this fashion and to demand compensation for what is conceptualized as a verbal assault on her personhood. Clearly taken aback by my unexpected (and delayed) reaction, the young men were unable to muster a unified response: one yelled that I had misunderstood what they were saying, another weakly retorted that they had not been talking to me but to somebody else, while another ran off mumbling something like, "It was them, not me." To my relief, they quickly backed down. There were witnesses, after all—people who knew me and who had started yelling at the young men, gleefully assisting my performance as a *"Huli wali"* (a Huli woman). The young men disappeared into the bush behind the fence and I continued on my way, accompanied by a young boy who puzzled over why I hadn't reacted assertively in the first place. "Are you hard of hearing?" he asked.

Arriving home, I reported the incident to my friend Yamali, who peremptorily summoned her husband to discuss whether we should gather all the nearby men, with their bows and arrows, to demand compensation. Hers was a somewhat exaggerated response, but she explained that the young men's behavior was not only a form of sexual intimidation, but also a racial one. They believed, rightly according to Yamali, that white women were too scared and weak to defend themselves. Yamali dissected the event word for word and gesture for gesture. She praised my confrontational reaction, but sternly added that I should have picked up some big rocks, hurled them at the speakers, and yelled, "Where are your pigs?! I don't see my bridewealth pigs! Where is your mother? I am going to go sit down in your mother's house, and she can go line up all her pigs for me!" *(Pig bilong yu we? Tapu bilong mi, mi no lukim! Mama bilong yu we? Mi, bai mi go sindaun insait long haus bilong mama bilong yu, na em inap lainap olgeta pig bilong em na givim mi!)* I was somewhat disconcerted, for the last thing I wanted was to suggest that marriage would be a good outcome to this incident. However, Yamali's script for me was, of course, a rhetorical strategy. Referencing the young men's mothers and their bridewealth pigs would have immediately resignified my sexuality as something properly reproductive and embedded in kinship, rather than an individually possessed, erotic behavior. The point behind such a retort was to let the young men know that I knew that the sexuality of *wali ore* (real women, good women) is about bridewealth, reproduction, and relationality. By angrily invoking pigs and mothers, I would have signaled my identity as a moral woman. (Such a retort was also meant to intimidate the young men and remind them that men's sexuality too is properly about kinship and reproduction; demanding bridewealth would have been a good way to undermine their performance of modern, publicly libidinous masculinity). Although Yamali relished the idea of my distributing compensation money to her and her kin, ultimately we decided that my response had been adequate and that we didn't need to pursue the matter further.

Such trivial incidents—perhaps particularly the ones that put the anthropologist on the spot—can be ethnographically useful, for they can be employed to make people's tacit cultural logics and values more explicit. In this case, because I was only able to come up with a partially "correct" response to the young men, Yamali and I were able to discuss why it was strategic to invoke bridewealth in such situations and how bridewealth confers value and dignity on female gender. In this chapter I discuss the way in which bridewealth is both a totalizing discourse—in that it profoundly structures women's sense of self-worth and constrains the imagined possibilities for action—and, increasingly, a source of conflict. The cultural meanings and subjective experience of female gender are shaped by the fact of bridewealth, but, at the same time, the proper practices and outcomes of bridewealth are hotly contested as they are encompassed by capitalist social relations. Conflicts arise over whether bridewealth should be given in pigs or in cash; what proportion of bridewealth a woman's father or mother should receive to distribute to their respective kin; what obligations husband and wife have to each other once married; what obligations affines have to each other; and whether bride*wealth* is becoming bride-*price*—that is, becoming a commoditized transaction. Are sisters "inalienable possessions" (Weiner 1992) that brothers should strive to keep and protect, or are they "trade stores" (Jorgensen 1993) through which one secures cash resources? How bridewealth articulates with the economic and discursive processes of the nation-state, and how this articulation shapes the subjectivity and agency of women are the issues of this chapter.

The following summary of Turume's early marital experience provides a preliminary sense of just how important bridewealth is, as well as the conflicts it can generate. I met Turume—who at that point was not married—during my first few days in Tari. She was exuberant and flirtatious, and she was proud of the fact that her father had been an important local leader with many wives, each of whom had given birth to at least six children. As she put it, "I can walk around and everyone is related to me. My kin fill up this place" *(Mi inap wokabaut igo na olgeta manmeri, em lain bilong mi tasol. Lain bilong mi pulap long hia).* When I saw her again, more than a year later, I noticed that the tip of her index finger was missing. When I first met her she struck me as a young woman on a mission to be hip and modern: she occasionally wore trousers, something Huli women never do, and she was familiar with the songs of many Papua New Guinea bands. I was thus surprised that she had apparently resorted to fingerlopping—a behavior I had come to associate with older, more rural, and less educated women. When asked to explain, she launched into the following story of her tumultuous marital history, all of which had taken place in the year or so since I had first met her.

•   •   •

She had been set to marry Moxi, an educated Huli man who had a salaried job in Port Moresby. In fact, she had already been taken to his father's land, where she was staying with his grandmother, while he and his kin assembled the thirty *tapu* (bridewealth) pigs that their two families had agreed upon. Unexpectedly, her previous *lawini* (beloved), Togobe, appeared and told Turume in Tok Pisin (which the grandmother didn't understand), "I have known you since you were a child who didn't know how to talk. I was like a brother to you and taught you how to speak. I have been your *lawini* since before you had breasts. How could you not tell me you were marrying someone else? He is not your true *lawini*, I am." She could not resist his sweet words, and she agreed to run away with him. When Moxi returned, Turume was gone. Since his thirty pigs were assembled and it was too difficult to take them all back to the numerous relatives who had donated them, an alternative wife quickly had to be found.

Knowing that her relatives would be furious with her, Turume hid out with Togobe's kin for two weeks, working in his mother's gardens, assuming that Togobe was assembling her bridewealth. Instead, he asked her to run away with him to Kimbe, capital of West New Britain, an island province of Papua New Guinea. His younger brother worked there, Togobe explained, so they could walk to Mt. Kare, take a plane to Porgera, take a bus to Lae, and then a ship to Kimbe. Offended, Turume replied, "Good man, this kind of behavior is no good. I am the daughter of a man. I am not the daughter of a pig that you can just take me away like that. You must take me back home, straighten all this out, explain everything to my mother, and pay my pig-money [bridewealth] properly. I won't stand for this kind of thieving behavior. If you want to take me, bring bridewealth and then come take me" (*Gutpela man, dispela kain pasin ino gutpela. Mi pikinini bilong man. Mi no pikinini bilong pig na yu inap kisim mi igo olsem. Yu mas kisim mi igo back long haus, na bai yu stretim gut na klirim mama bilong mi, na pigmuni tu bai yu givim stret. Dispela kain stil pasin, mi les. Yu laik kam kisim mi, karim pigmuni ikam na kisim mi*).

Turume's relatives, for their part, were furious at the loss of Moxi, an educated man with a salary, and irate about her insubordination, and so they increased the bridewealth payment to forty-five pigs, a very high number. Togobe's relatives were able to muster up only half that amount and proposed that the rest be given later, but Turume's relatives refused and filed a suit at the Tari courthouse demanding that To-

gobe pay *tauwa* (a compensation payment for the "theft" of a girl's sexuality from her family). On the day of the court case, Turume ran into
Ibabe, yet another *lawini*. At that moment, she claims, he performed
some kind of "black power" on her which made it inevitable that she
would marry him. At the court case she could have been adamant about
marrying Togobe, but she found herself confused and tongue-tied. Ultimately Togobe paid twelve pigs and K500 (approximately US$300 at
that time) as *tauwa* for Turume and ended up with no wife at all.

After the court case Turume went back home to live with her own
family, and found herself thinking and dreaming about Ibabe. One
night he appeared to her in a dream, led her out of her family's house,
and brought her to his own house. When she woke up in the morning,
there she was in his mother's house. And there she stayed. He told her
that she had arrived the day before, and in the risky tradition of Huli
women in the throes of love, had sat down in his mother's house, insisted on helping her in the garden, and thereby made it known that she
wanted to marry him, which he wholeheartedly supported. She claimed
to have no recollection of this. His kin were in the process of paying
compensation to clans who had been allies in a recent tribal fight, and
thus they did not have the resources to pay her bridewealth in full.[1] It
was therefore agreed by the two families that Ibabe and Turume would
live on her clan's land until the payment was complete.[2]

One day, Turume saw Moxi (her first fiancé) back in town. He told
her that he still wanted her as his wife, offered to buy her a plane ticket
to Port Moresby, and said that he would square accounts with Ibabe by
reimbursing him for the *tapu* (bridewealth) pigs he had given her family so far. Turume agreed, reasoning that since Ibabe had not yet completed paying her bridewealth she was still a free woman. On the day of
departure, in order to allay any suspicion, she didn't pack anything, she
didn't wash, and she wore old dirty clothes. Everyone would think she
was on her way to her gardens. She went to the airstrip and took her
seat on the plane, but one of the employees at the airstrip was related to
her husband and alerted him. Ibabe suddenly appeared and dragged her
off the plane. After this incident Ibabe was watchful and wouldn't allow
her to go into town for a number of months.

She and Ibabe lived peaceably together for a while. However, it grated
on her that he did not give her a larger portion of the paycheck he received
as a store clerk. She argued that if he wasn't going to pay her bridewealth
quickly, then he ought to give her more of his pay as some kind of compensation. He responded that he had to save for her bridewealth, contribute to
a homicide compensation payment, and had a mother and sister to think

about as well. Moreover, they didn't have any children yet, so what did she want more money for? Increasingly resentful of this situation, Turume toyed with the idea of going to the Tari welfare office and arranging for Ibabe's wages to be garnished each fortnight, but she worried that Ibabe and his relatives would be furious with her. So instead she went to his boss and complained—falsely—that he was spending all his money on black market liquor, gambling, and *pasinja meri*. His boss fired him. Turume missed having the cash, but at least it wasn't an object of contention any more. And she had shown Ibabe that she could get the better of him.

Some time later her kin invited them to a *nogo tagandia* (a private party in which one family kills a few pigs and invites kin, and sometimes friends, to eat the cooked pork and take some fresh meat home with them). Turume was irate. How dare they invite her husband to sit down and eat pork with them when he hadn't completed paying her bridewealth? She refused to go and wouldn't eat any of the pork he brought home for her. To further display her anger, she went to town the next day and refused to work in her gardens. A few days later Ibabe's mother and sister arrived and proceeded to admonish her about not attending the *nogo tagandia*. Turume lost her temper and yelled that they had not yet paid her bridewealth and had no right to complain about her behavior. Ibabe's mother responded by jeering that they had not paid her bridewealth because they knew that she was so pathetically in love—"tears and snot were dripping down her face"—that they could get away with it. After all, she had suddenly appeared in their house and insisted on the marriage. Humiliated, Turume cut off her index finger with an axe and threw it at her mother-in-law.

Ibabe then arrived on the scene, yelled at his mother and sister for interfering in his marriage, and, according to Turume, punched both of them. At the ensuing village court case it was decided that Ibabe would have to pay compensation to his mother and sister for hitting them, but that they would have to pay compensation to Turume for her finger because it was their provocative talk that drove her to it. Turume gloated that the local leaders had decided that Ibabe's kin were the *tene* (the ultimate cause) of her lost finger. She also reasoned that her lopped-off finger could be counted toward *"pinisim pig bilong em"* (literally, finishing his pigs); that is, reducing the amount of bridewealth that would have to be returned if she decided to divorce Ibabe.

· · ·

Important to this narrative is that despite the soap opera quality of her experience, the choices Turume made, her appraisal of her possibilities, and her interpretation of her social relations were all structured within the logic of bridewealth. This is not to say that she was motivated by bridewealth in quantitative terms; she rejected her first suitor despite his proven ability to make a bridewealth payment and despite the whole-hearted support of her kin for the match. Rather, at every step Turume knew there would be consequences for her that would be framed in terms of bridewealth. Thus, after fleeing the first match, she hid from her relatives and urged her second suitor to raise the bridewealth necessary to appease them. His suggestion that they flee the bridewealth system altogether and run away to Kimbe pushed her beyond the limits she was willing to go and violated her sense of herself as a virtuous woman. Although willing to buck the system somewhat, she wasn't willing to repudiate bridewealth entirely. Flight from the bridewealth system would only serve to define her all the more in its terms. Her kin might even call her a *pasinja meri*—a woman who gave sex away or selfishly kept a man's resources for herself. Moreover, there were subjective, internal consequences to this possibility: she herself experienced Togobe's desire to avoid this transaction as an affront to her personhood. As she angrily put it, "I am not the daughter of a pig . . . If you want to take me, bring bridewealth and then come take me." In other words, her sexuality was not the unregulated behavior of animals; it was embedded in the bridewealth system.

Similarly, when she decided to run away to Port Moresby to marry Moxi, she attempted to make sure that he would "reimburse" Ibabe for the number of pigs he had already given her family as bridewealth. This might prevent Ibabe from retaliating against her, and would go some way toward alleviating the anger and shame of her kin. When living with Ibabe, she felt that because he had not paid her bridewealth in full, she was "less married" and could therefore act more autonomously. Until he made the payment in full she did not consider herself fully under his authority, let alone his mother's, and she was angry when her own kin treated them as if they were fully married. In this case, her definition of her marital status did not accord with others' interpretations, but her idiosyncratic and expedient logic was still informed by the calculus of bridewealth. Finally, despite losing part of a finger, she immediately figured that its loss would make it easier for her to obtain a divorce: because blame for the damage had been attributed to her husband's female kin, it would count against any bridewealth that would have to be returned to them. Clearly bridewealth structured Turume's understanding of her options, her subjective experience of herself as a moral person, and even her own injured body.

At the same time, encompassment by the nation-state and a monetized economy introduces new tensions, confusions, and possibilities into the bridewealth calculus. How much of her husband's salary does Turume have a right to, for example? Since bridewealth has already been given for her, some Huli (primarily men) would argue that her husband owes her very little—none if she does not yet have children to care for. The nation-state, on the other hand, says that working men have an obligation to maintain their wives and children, and a woman can go to the local welfare office and petition to have her husband's salary garnished if he doesn't provide her with adequate support. Turume's solution to this contradiction was less unusual than one might think—she was not the only woman I interviewed who had attempted to get a husband fired after failing to convince him to hand over more of his wages.

Bridewealth and Social Reproduction

A number of ethnographers of Melanesia have suggested that as bridewealth transactions become encompassed by capitalist social relations, women—as wives—are increasingly treated as commodities. And certainly some Huli women I knew told of husbands who resorted to commodity idioms in order to justify claims on a woman's labor, saying, for example, "I paid bride-price for you and so you must do my laundry" (a task that women describe with disgust as nontraditional and polluting). In other words, bride-price was the idiom through which husbands attempted to legitimate their authority over wives and their entitlement to wives' services. The husband of one friend—who at a crucial moment during a marital spat couldn't quite bring herself to lop off the tip of her own finger—flattened the finger with a stone, angrily asserting that "since he had paid bride-price for her, her fingers belonged to him, and if anyone was going to damage them, he would be the one to do it." Since Huli women themselves express concern—and sometimes rage—about the possible commoditization of bridewealth, one might wonder why they don't resist the system altogether. Thus, in the next few pages I discuss the centrality of bridewealth in Huli social reproduction and elucidate the many ways that women themselves have a huge stake in maintaining the practice, whether from the subject position of bride, mother, or clan member.

Huli bridewealth practices, to borrow from Foster's description of Tongan mortuary rites, are "the practical locus for social reproduction, the privileged site for producing and fixing, again and again, social identities and relations imagined as preconditions for future action" (1995: 8). Arguably processes and institutions other than bridewealth also contribute to Huli social reproduction; for example, in the past, complex multicultural rituals were crucial for periodically renewing the fertility of the land and the health of the social body (Glasse 1995; Ballard 1994; Sturzenhofecker 1998). But, if any one social institution can be designated as that which works to ensure the continuous reproduction of Huli clans, gender relations, means of managing land tenure, and a sense of socio-historical continuity, it is bridewealth marriage. Bridewealth secures the reproductive substances and the gestational labor necessary for creating the next generation, and the processes of giving, waiting, and recuperating wealth link people vertically and horizontally over time.

Huli bridewealth practices have particularly significant material consequences for the father of the bride. As with the neighboring Duna, "A daughter's marriage is the prime occasion for a man to emancipate himself from the role of indebted husband and move into that of the distributing father. Thus in this role the man is beleaguered by a crowd of creditors anxious to ensure that they will receive an appropriate return for the investment they made a generation earlier" (Sturzenhofecker 1998: 102). Thus, in order to amass the bridewealth, a groom must draw on the resources of his kin, and while he may have opportunities over time to repay these kin, the Huli (unlike many other highlands groups) do not engage in elaborate networks of ongoing competitive exchange in which the payment of personal debts may be enfolded. Moreover, there are no return payments from affines that might be used to offset debt to a groom's kin. In sum, a man enters marriage owing people in the previous generation and expecting to be able to repay them, or their descendents, through the marriages of his daughters in the next generation. Further, a woman's brothers also have a stake in her marriage, for it is her father's ability to repay his debts—using the bridewealth brought in by her marriage—that will convince kin to assist in her brothers' bridewealth payments for their own wives.[3] Stéphane Breton, writing of bridewealth among the Wodani of West Irian, stresses the material aspect of this practice, asserting that clan solidarity "is actually nothing but an accumulation of debts . . . the clan is essentially a community of shareholders bound up together in matrimonial investment projects" (1999: 555–66). In other words, what holds the clan together, and what enables social reproduction from one generation to the next, is the collective payment and receipt of bridewealth for women.[4] Breton's narrowly economic definition of "clan" certainly departs from standard anthropological understandings in which a "clan" is usually conceptualized as a political unit in relation to other similarly organized units. However, his provocative description captures something fundamental about the role of bridewealth and the way in which it binds one generation to the next.

But bridewealth among the Huli concerns more than a materialist notion of debt; it is also about creating and sustaining relational identities. For example, Huli people would often take me aside, point to a child, and say in a proud and wonderstruck tone, "We paid (or received) pigs for that child's mother, and look what *we've* created!" The act of participating in bridewealth exchange makes one an agent of biological reproduction, and even wealth objects, when properly channeled, are indirectly "reproductive substances": pigs and money properly distributed improve the likelihood of successful reproduction; improperly distributed, or given only in installments, reproduction may be more chancy. Bridewealth thus ensures the continuity of the clan and family, effects the proper physiological transformation of single bodies into marital bodies, and safely encompasses potentially dangerous reproductive substances. As the Huli conceptualize it, the giving and receiving of bridewealth is at once social, bodily, and historical work (Biersack 1995b). The village court case described below illustrates the importance of bridewealth—and the specifics of its distribution—to notions of relationality.

Wangale, the elderly woman who brought the case, was demanding compensation because she had been beaten by the adult son of her half-brother, Igibe. Unbeknownst to Igibe, Wangale had been given permission to harvest sweet potato from their half-sister's garden (Igibe, Wangale, and this half-sister all had the same father, but different mothers). So, when Igibe and his son found Wangale there, an argument ensued, and Igibe's son beat Wangale with a stick, damaging her arm and shoulder. In fact, Wangale claimed, she had caught *them* stealing from their half-sister's garden, and Igibe's son had hit her because he was embarrassed at being caught. Whether Wangale deserved compensation for her injuries, and how much compensation, hinged on whether Igibe and she were considered brother and sister. If they were, then Igibe deserved her forbearance for this misunderstanding and had less of an obligation to publicly compensate her. If they were not, then he had no right to hit her at all, and every obligation to compensate her. Wangale repeatedly asserted that the "truth" of their relationship could be read from the fact that Igibe had not given her any of the bridewealth he had received upon his daughter's marriage a number of years before. That he had not signified that he did not really regard her as a sister.

Wangale: Did you give me any of the compensation you received? I don't know you. Who are you? *(Inaga abini I latale binibe? I manda napito ko. I ai?)*

Igibe: Bring an X-ray and summon the local leaders, and then we will discuss your bones. The government is in charge now, so do as they tell us to do. That's what we do. (*Agali manali ibu lowa piksa moyalu ibalimu. Amugoni kuni naga laminia ndobe. Government power muwa. Ai agua biyatago. Agua bia laragola piaga ndobe.*)

Wangale: You mentioned your compensation and your daughter's bridewealth. Is this lies or is it the truth? You yourself ate your compensation and the bridewealth. I never saw any of it. I am like a stranger to you. I am a foreign woman to you. I don't know you and you don't know me. (*I abini la I wane tapu la larigo hawabe henene? Abini narego na handaga tabuni narego na handaga. I wali tara ndotabe? Wali tara petogo. I bi I manda napi. I bi I manda napi petogo.*)

Igibe: There is a law about this now that says you should get a medical report and bring it back. (*Mana mbira agua nga. Paper ogo mulene. Muwa yalu taipuwa.*)

Wangale: Oh! When my real brothers are here you won't be able to get away with this! I didn't come here to listen to your bad talk. I don't talk with Igibe. You hit me for no reason. You don't share your karuka nuts with my son. You hit me for no reason. You and your son stole from that garden and then hit me for no reason. If you want an X-ray, your wife's son must give me the money to pay for it. I am not paying for it. I do not have a single garden on my mother's and father's land. Now give me! Give me! Give me! (Sarcastically) Somebody said you were a man. You have mentioned your compensation and your daughter's bridewealth. I didn't receive any of it. (*O! I mbalini kale ho porona wiere. I bi ko ogoni hale ho ibini ndo. I Igibe la bi yu nahaga haruni. I page bete. Anga mbira igini Aiopa la nangua laruguni. I page bete. I igini libu page baribi. I mabuli ndo page barebigoni. Piksa ogoni Igibe one igini tigua muni ibi loa bira. Ina ndo. I apa ainya dindini mabu mbira nawi larugoni. O ayutago ngi! Ayutago ngi! Ayutago ngi! Igibe agali layago mbirame. I inaga nogo agi larigo inaga nogo wariabu larigo—I ndo.*)

Igibe: I said to go get an X-ray if you want to have a dispute about your bones. (*Inaga kuni naga piksa mia larugoni.*)

Wangale: Why?! Ah! Go eat your own cock! [To her son's wife, who accompanied her] Here, take my string-bag. [Handing off one's string-bag to another woman is usually a sign that a woman intends to engage in physical aggression, and so Igibe began backing away from Wangale]. Where will you run to? You are living underneath your mother! Where are you going? You aren't a real man. I will hit you, I say! All this verbiage about sharing your daughter's bridewealth with me—as if you were in the habit of sharing with me. I don't think you are my father's son. Now give me the money! *(Aginaga?! Ah! Ininaga wi na! [To her son's wife] Inaga nu ya. [To Igibe] I hariga ago pole bere? I ainya ke wara ha anda pu kego. I ani pole bere? I agali ndo. Ina pole bero laro. I wane tapule I habini hai bibiya larigo ina I ngiakabe. I i apa anda honowinitalo manda napi I kogoni. Ayu ngitaba!)*

Wangale, demonstrating behavior that only old women engage in during court cases, refused to sit quietly and listen to others' testimony and constantly interrupted Igibe with hand-claps, screeches, muttered oaths, and jeering laughter. When it was her turn to speak, she argued that Igibe was not really her brother. Rather, she was a *wali tara* (literally, woman stranger) to him: he had not given her any pigs from his daughter's bridewealth, he had not given her any land, and he had not shared food with her son. The men participating in the dispute, though disgusted by Wangale's improper verbal and bodily conduct, told Igibe that she was correct in her reasoning; they really didn't seem to have a brother-sister relationship.

Igibe, having failed to define Wangale as sister, attempted to reframe the issue and shifted from a bridewealth-oriented idiom to a legalistic one: as a citizen, he asserted, he had the right to demand official evidence of Wangale's injury—an X-ray of her shoulder—in order to determine whether the case had any merit. The village court mediators—all men of Igibe's age—showed signs of being convinced by this latter logic, and so Wangale, frustrated by this turn of events and by what she perceived as sophistry on Igibe's part, handed her string-bag to her companion and attacked Igibe with her walking stick. While other men gingerly fended off her blows, Igibe ran away and hid in a trade store. Ultimately, Wangale and her companions left in anger because it was decided that she did, in fact, need to provide an X-ray and that she would have to pay for this herself.[5]

Bridewealth and Female Subjectivity

In addition to being fundamental to social reproduction and relational identity, bridewealth is also a pervasive discourse through which female subjectivity is constituted. It may seem somewhat odd to think of bridewealth as a "discourse," for anthropologists usually conceptualize discourses as symbolic productions—myths, rituals, conversations, speeches, textual representations—that are analytically distinct from the more sociological and economic practices of marriage or exchange. Recent critical theorists, however, have attempted to blur the distinctions between social action and cultural production, or at least to point out how these distinctions are the analyst's own heuristic tools. As Sherry Ortner has said in her explication of practice theory (herself using marriage as an example), "An institution — say, a marriage system — is at once a system of social relations, economic arrangements, political processes, cultural categories, norms, values, ideals, emotional patterns, and so on" (1984: 148). Thus, bridewealth and other exchanges of wealth are not only social and material practices, but also structures of knowledge or "truth regimes" (Dirks et al. 1994: 20) about how persons and societies are reproduced. In this sense they systematically discipline individuals, constrain the choices they can imagine for themselves, and shape the ways that they experience themselves as persons.

Indeed, it has already been argued (although not in the language of critical theory), that bridewealth and other exchanges do structure Melanesians' experience of themselves. As Marilyn Strathern and others have pointed out, Melanesian persons are not autonomous individuals who author themselves, but rather "dividuals" (Strathern 1988) who are, as Aletta Biersack has said, "always already social" (1995b: 232) and who have been created from a whole web-like history of marriages, gifts given and received, and substances exchanged and mixed. One arrives in the world already the product of multiple strands of exchanges, and upon marriage one is expected to create more such persons who are themselves the products of gifts given, women circulated, and substances mixed. At birth one is positioned as an outcome of this relational economy, and through marriage and reproduction, one is positioned as a potential contributor to, or actor in, this economy. I prefer to think of this relational economy as a kind of discourse rather than, in its more rigid versions, as a kind of essentialized Melanesian mode of personhood. Thinking of bridewealth as a kind of discourse enables one to see that there exist other competing discourses and embodied practices, such as wage labor and commodity consumption; that different discourses can be invoked by actors at different moments for different agendas; and that actors are differently positioned by these various discourses.

For example, while both men and women are inextricably woven into the bridewealth system, social expectations of them differ. While many Huli men do not marry until they are in their thirties, and in the past some never married at all, marriage for women is universal, and marriage is defined by the fact that the parents of a girl receive and distribute *nogo*

FIGURE 11. Pigs acquired from various relatives of the groom and gathered in one place, ready for presentation to, and distribution by, the bride's family. In this case the bridewealth pigs remained in limbo for three days while the groom's family waited for the bride's brother to give permission for the marriage. Pigs must be led in and out of the sun at regular intervals, and care must be taken to ensure that they are usually in the shade. They also, of course, require food and water. "Liminal pigs" such as these are highly problematic since it is unclear just who should be performing these tasks.

tapu (marriage pigs) for her. It is difficult to exaggerate the extent to which female identity is enmeshed in the notion of bridewealth. As the well-known Huli aphorism goes, *"Igiri yagua danda danda; wandari yagua damba damba"* (If it's a boy, then bows and arrows; if it's a girl, then bridewealth bridewealth) (Goldman 1983: 69). At marriage a woman is a lost resource to her own clan, the instrument through which another clan will reproduce itself, and the "road" between the two clans, which have been brought into permanent relation through the woman's ability to embody all these meanings and capacities (Strathern 1972). Not surprisingly, married women know exactly how many pigs were given for them in each category (there are three categories, discussed later in the chapter), how many pigs were actually given as pigs and how many as cash, how many their father distributed and how many their mother distributed, and to which relatives the pigs were given. Bridewealth also has a strong moral valance to it. Almost invariably, when Huli women were getting to know me, they would ask whether it was true that white people did not pay bridewealth, and when I confirmed this shocking rumor, they were embarrassed for me (though also fascinated) that I belonged to a society in which every woman is *"stil marit"* (theft-married)—in other words, not really married at all. It is bridewealth that makes adult women *wali ore* (real woman): "real women" are those who are "defined in terms of enduring relations to others, men especially" (Nihill 1994; cf. Rubin 1975, 1997), and it is bridewealth which establishes these enduring relations.

Bridewealth and Female "Sexuality"

Sexuality—men's as well as women's, but women's more so because of their gestational, lactational, and nurturing role—is embedded in the bridewealth system and is thought of as a family and clan reproductive resource. As discussed in the introduction, female sexuality is embodied in an individual woman, but is in the custody of her family. Perhaps the easiest way to illustrate this particular construction of sexuality is through an examination of the meanings of pre- and extramarital sexuality. When a young, never-married woman's sexuality is compromised—either through rape or through consensual sex with a boyfriend—her family typically demands that the couple marry or that the man's family pay *nogo tauwa*. Illicit sexual activity—whether "consensual" or "nonconsensual"—is understood as the theft of a woman's reproductive capacity from her natal kin, or from her husband if she is married (see A. Strathern 1985 for a similar discussion). Thus when Togobe suggested to Turume that they run away to Kimbe and forget bridewealth altogether, Turume described this as disgraceful *"stil pasin"* (theft).

   To put it otherwise, the dominant concern in cases of illicit sexual activity is not whether a woman consented, but that her family did not. Since a woman's sexuality "belongs to," or is a partible aspect of, her family, the locus of consent resides with them. While the issue of forced sex may be important to a woman herself and probably her nuclear family, it is not the most salient aspect of an illicit sex case to most of her kin. All that matters for the purpose of demanding marriage or compensation is that the sex happened. Indeed, when I asked about past court cases concerning premarital sex, people quite often did not remember whether or not the sex in such cases had been consensual. If pressed they would sometimes recall whether the woman had been pregnant or not, and this was often considered an indicator of consent. Since pregnancy is believed to require more than one sexual episode, and since, they said, it is unlikely that the same woman would be forced by the same man more than once, young pregnant women were probably not raped.

Of the women in my interview sample, sixteen were made to marry because of premarital sexual activity. Six of these women said they had been "consensually" intimate with a *lawini* (beloved, boyfriend), and three of them said definitely that they were forced to have sex against their will by men they vaguely knew but did not consider *lawini* and did not want to marry. The narratives of the remaining seven women, however, suggested that they were, for lack of a better term, "sort-of-raped." That is, in each case the woman knew the young man, and she usually considered him a *lawini*, but he surprised her when she was alone in her garden or on a path and forced sex on her, usually at knifepoint.[6] It is difficult to categorize these incidents as rape, since the Western construction of the concept depends on a highly individualized, self-determining notion of "possessive sexuality" in which one knows decisively whether one wants to have sex or not (also see Dasgupta and Dasgupta 1996). Huli women do not "own" their sexuality in this way, and these women found it impossible to say whether they had "consented" to sex at that particular moment.

Disconcertingly, the English word "rape" has been adopted by Huli Tok Pisin speakers as *"repim,"* and is used to describe both consensual and nonconsensual illicit sex. One Peace Corps volunteer I knew was so distressed by this usage that she made it her mission to "correct" people whenever they "misused" the word *"repim."* It was a difficult task: what is most important about an illicit sex case for persons outside of a woman's immediate family is whether compensation is paid for the girl's "theft," whether a marriage ensues, whether warfare is threatened by the girl's brothers, and the resulting shifts in the sociopolitical field. Most women tend to accept and internalize this construction since they themselves identify strongly with their clans. If compensation is given to their families, then they themselves feel vindicated.

Other Female Identifications in Bridewealth

Women's stake in bridewealth does not rest solely in their role of transacted valuable, however. They too are clan members, persons who have contributed to the work of "making" other nubile women, and thus potential recipients of bridewealth. For example, Lirime Mangobe—of the Mangobe sisters, discussed in the introduction—once held a machete to

the throat of her sister's four-year-old son and threatened to kill him because of a conflict over her sister's bridewealth. Her sister was pregnant
yet again by a man who had not yet completed her bridewealth payment,
and Lirime was irate that her sister was bearing more children for a man
who had no real rights to her reproductive resources. Lirime refused to
treat this man as an in-law, often, for example, addressing him in public
by his given name, taboo behavior between affines. So what if this man
regularly gave her sister money for his son, she said; what about her own
family's work at making her sister? If a man didn't give bridewealth, he
shouldn't get the benefits of a wife, such as children. If her sister got pregnant again, she coldly stated, she would slit Philip's throat and throw him
down the pit latrine.[7] Thus bridewealth is a discourse which structures
Huli women's desires and values, whether they are in the role of potential wife or watchful sister.

And, if anything, women have an even greater stake than in the past as
potential recipients of bridewealth. In the past it was common for a
mother to receive one third or less of the bridewealth pigs, and the father
two thirds (Glasse 1968). Since the bride's father had given bridewealth
for the bride's mother, it only made sense that he would receive a greater
proportion when his daughter married and would thereby be able to pay
back those kin who had helped him marry his own wife. This is still primarily the case. However, in the context of male absence for wage labor,
mothers are increasingly successful at arguing that they have put more
work into raising a girl and therefore deserve more of her bridewealth.
Moreover, if a father is absent, it is expected that his contribution to the
work of "making" a girl will take the form of remittances sent home to
pay for school fees, clothing, soap, and food. If a man does not, or cannot, send cash home, then his wife and her relatives will claim that he has
contributed little to the upbringing of the girl and therefore deserves little
bridewealth.

Nine of the fifty women I interviewed stated that their mothers had received at least half of their bridewealth pigs to distribute, a significant increase from the norm of the past, and in all cases this was attributed to a
father's absence, either because of an attempt to obtain wage labor or because he had apparently abandoned the marriage. Significantly, these nine
cases were almost all among young women whose marriages had been in
the last ten years. Most of them claimed that at the bridewealth distribution they themselves had publicly insisted that their mothers receive a certain number of pigs because they felt that their fathers had not put
enough work into "making" them. One assertive young woman tried to
keep her absconded father from finding out when her bridewealth distri-

bution was to take place, and then distributed the pigs and cash herself, giving her mother's relatives the bulk of it. Our neighbor, a cousin of the bride's mother, gleefully came home that day with three pigs in tow, one of which was a pregnant sow, a very valuable gift. However, a week later the bride's father threatened to make "trouble" (Huli use the phrase *mekim trabel* [make trouble] to refer euphemistically to threats of violence), and she was pressured into returning the sow so that he could have it. Thus, bridewealth distribution is increasingly a kind of argument with pigs (instead of words) in which women can express indignation at a husband's or father's failings, and mothers can assert their own greater reproductive work.

Women also have a singular stake in bridewealth as mothers through *imane aka*. *Imane aka* (literally, in-laws' cloth or clothing) is a relatively new category of bridewealth payment meant specifically for mothers. It is said to compensate mothers for the pollution they endure by cleaning up a baby's excreta; the "mother's cloth," then, may refer to the towels and diapers that women use to clean babies' bottoms, although none of the men and women I asked knew the origin of the term or of the practice itself. In any case, *imane aka* is typically at least K100 (US$75 in the mid-1990s), usually paid in cash, and belongs solely to the mother: she is under no obligation to distribute it, and the payment does not affect the number of pigs she receives from the other bridewealth categories (also see Strathern and Stewart 1999; Guyer 1995). Indeed, my friend Yamali wanted me to help her write and submit a proposal to obtain WID (Women in Development) money from AusAID or the New Zealand High Commission for the purpose of forming a women's group that would petition village court mediators and local politicians to increase *imane aka*. She had a six-month-old daughter at the time and asserted vehemently that if she had her way, she would receive at least K1,000 when little Kwarima was old enough to marry. Notice, then, the attempt by specifically positioned actors to draw on relatively new resources—international development aid in this case—in order to reproduce and intensify the existing means of social reproduction. Thus bridewealth distribution and *imane aka* have become spheres in which women can assert their own hard work and dedication as mothers and can complain about male physical and economic absence from the work of raising children. Far from attempting to emancipate daughters from bridewealth, mothers depend on it as an arena for claiming what they feel is due to them. Given women's multiple positions within the bridewealth system it is not surprising that female agency works primarily to reproduce it.

Bridewealth in the Context of the Nation-State

Having shown the myriad ways in which Huli women are invested in the continuity of the bridewealth system, I can move on to the ways in which bridewealth discourses and practices variously articulate with the discourses and practices of the nation-state and its economy. The actions of various male and female actors are influenced not only by whatever subject position they occupy in relation to any particular bridewealth transaction, but, in the contemporary context, also by policies, laws, and social agendas pursued by church and state (Jolly 1994). While the intentions of church and state often seem to be to "emancipate" women or put them on more equal footing with men, social policies do not always have the effect intended and can actually be encompassed or pressed into service by the logic of bridewealth. For example, the law of "maintenance" under the Deserted Wives and Children Act is intended to ensure the financial support of mothers and children should an employed man refuse his familial economic obligations. This act states:

> A wife and children who have been deserted may claim maintenance in the District Court or the Local Court under the Deserted Wives and Children Act . . . Only a married woman may claim maintenance for herself and for the children by her husband . . . A wife cannot claim maintenance after dissolution of their customary marriage . . . A woman must show that she and/or the children have been left without means of support . . . the words "has left his wife or children without means of support" has been defined to mean . . . actual desertion, going away from them and leaving them, or it may be, without committing any act of desertion in the ordinary sense, by leaving his wife and children in his house and making no provision for their maintenance. A wife can therefore obtain maintenance from a husband for herself and/or the children if the husband gives her no money or makes no provision for their maintenance even though they live under the same roof. (Law Reform Commission of Papua New Guinea 1989)

According to this law, a woman married to an employed man can sue for maintenance if she receives no economic support from him. He need not even be physically absent for her to qualify for this maintenance; even if they are under the same roof—and in the Huli case, under different roofs if they live according to *"kastom bilong tumbuna"* (traditional custom)—she is eligible, as long as she can prove her employed husband's failure to provide economic support. Half of all the marriages by women in my interview sample—meaning first marriages and any subsequent marriages—were to men who had been or were currently employed, usually

as store clerks, security guards, or as laborers for mining companies outside of the Tari area. And, women's complaints about husbands often included a husband's long absence from Tari and his failure to send remittances home. Nevertheless, of eight women who had children and who
were currently separated from a husband who worked but did not send
any money home, only one had tried to make use of this "maintenance"
law to garnish her husband's wages.

Most women are not aware that the law exists, and of the women who
are, many assert that it is a lesson in frustration since men—having the
money to begin with—can bribe the magistrates who administer this law
(an assertion that was confirmed for me by a man who had once held this
position). Women who knew of the law also asserted that they were afraid
of how working husbands would react if they tried to garnish their wages.
And, indeed, most men I spoke with who knew of the law were incensed
by it. When my field assistant had a job at the Porgera mine for two years
and sent no money home for his two children, his wife's sisters encouraged her to apply for maintenance and have his wages garnished. In response, he quickly came home and threatened to kill her. (In general he,
and just about everyone else in the community, made a point of im-
pressing on me his equanimity and gentle nature. However, in this case,
he felt that his cause was so well justified that he had no qualms about candidly discussing with me his murderous rage toward his wife.) She was
intimidated enough to give up the idea despite support for the idea from
her natal family.

Importantly, the idea of "maintenance" contravenes the logic of bride
wealth: if a man has *"putim pig-muni pinis"* (already given bridewealth),
it is improper for a wife to feel so entitled to his pay that she would coerce him into giving her money. Men also claim that women do not understand the many competing demands for men's small wages. Men have
sisters and mothers—as well as their own images of themselves as modern men—to "maintain." Indeed, some men and women (in their role as
sisters) seem perplexed by the state's privileging of wives (as opposed to
sisters or mothers, for example) as deserving special access to a man's resources. What will a wife do with the money if you give it to her, men
would ask me—just give it to her own relatives, they would answer themselves, which isn't fair since a man has already given them bridewealth for
her. Just as infuriating to men is the possibility that a woman would be
"bighed" (impertinent, willful) enough to *"go autsait"* (literally, go outside; make the matter public) and solicit state intervention in a man's domestic affairs. As an alternative, then, women do as Turume did—that is,
intervene directly with a husband's employer, either to obtain some of his

wages or to get him fired. One woman in my interview sample, whose husband worked as a government driver, went directly to the government paymaster in Mendi, the provincial capital, and asked him for her husband's paycheck. When he initially refused, she told him about her children and about her husband's escapades with his *pasinja meri* girlfriend, and asked, "Don't your wife and children have to eat?" The paymaster capitulated after she agreed to give him some of the money (not as a bribe, mind you, but to thank him). She boasted to me that she then stuck a few toiea in a bar of soap and sent it to her husband as a form of *tok box* (literally, boxing talk; insulting, provocative language): the soap to remind him that previously he'd only given her enough money to buy the occasional small item, such as soap, and the penny coins to pay for the sexual services of his *pasinja meri*. In sum, the Deserted Wives and Children Act, intended to benefit women, has been interpreted within the framework of bridewealth and has been rejected as unreasonable by most men and unfeasible by most women.[8]

Another law that that has been "encompassed" by the logic of bridewealth is intended as the complement of the one just discussed. If women have a means of redress for husbands who desert them or fail in their domestic duties, so do men have an analogous recourse. Thus, when a wife absconds, a husband has the legal right to take out a court order compelling her to return and pay a fine of approximately $US150, or, if she refuses, be thrown in the local prison for up to three months. The logic of this law again pivots on bridewealth. A man may abscond from a marriage or unilaterally decide to go live with a second wife or girl-friend, and there is little a woman can do except try to have his salary garnished (if he has one and if she dares). If a wife absconds, however, the logic of bridewealth dictates that her husband may sue her and set in motion a chain of legal procedures. He and his family have given bridewealth for her, and thus he has certain rights over her and where she may go.

Most husbands in this situation do not actually want to send their wives to jail and only resort to this law as a form of intimidation: once word spreads that the police are on the lookout for a particular woman, her kin will usually persuade her to return home. However, some men do pursue the law to its ultimate end. Indeed, when I went to Hawa prison to interview women who had been incarcerated for violent crimes, the prison records showed that many of the female inmates for the past two years had been jailed for violation of court orders. Many of these court orders concerned the subject's failure to pay compensation for injuring another woman, but many concerned flight from a marriage and refusal to return.[9] Women who had spent time in jail for such violations had a range of reactions: some missed their children and regretted running away; some were angry that their own kin refused to pay their fines and thus release them from jail; some had explicitly told their kin not to pay the fines, arguing that they preferred jail and would not give their husbands the satisfaction of getting paid for behavior that had driven them off in the first place. (In point of fact, these fines were paid to the courthouse, not the husband). Further, the system was quite flexible, in that a husband could drop the charges if his wife returned home and compensation was paid to him directly.

Bridewealth Payments and the Gender of Money

If national laws can be said to have been encompassed by and subordinated to the logic of bridewealth, the same cannot be said about the articulation of bridewealth with the national cash economy. Increasingly bridewealth is becoming a means for unemployed rural Huli to access money. Bridewealth pigs are still divided into three categories: huge sows (*nogo angibuni* in Huli; *mama pig* in Tok Pisin), medium-sized gelts (*nogo haguene* in Huli; *head pig* in Tok Pisin), and smaller pigs of either sex (*nogo daga* in Huli; *ol liklik pig* in Tok Pisin) (Goldman 1983). A payment usually consists of the same number of pigs in each category; thus, for example, when I asked women how much their bridewealth payments had been, they would usually say 7,7,7 rather than 21, to specify how many pigs had been given in each category. In the 1950s, when Robert Glasse conducted his research, bridewealth was generally a standard 15 pigs, 5 in each category (1968: 54), whereas from the 1970s to 1990s—when most of the women in my sample married—bridewealth ranged from 18 (6,6,6) to 30 (10,10,10) pigs, with a norm in 1996 of 24 or 27. Thus, inflation has been between 2 and 4 pigs in each category (or between 6 and 12 pigs altogether) over the past forty years.

These days some of the "pigs" take the form of cash. The cash portion of a bridewealth payment is not given in one lump sum, but rather in discrete packets, each representing an individual pig from one of the three categories. Thus, during the bridewealth presentation ceremony the groom's father will hold up a wad of money—K100 for a pig in the second category, *nogo haguene*, for example—and declare, "here is one pig." Women are proficient at switching back and forth between these two currencies when talking about their bridewealth payments: when asked how much her bridewealth payment was, a woman may say that her *tapu* was 8,8,8, or she may say it was 8,5,5 plus K450 (each *nogo haguene* being worth approximately K100, and each *nogo daga* being worth K50, meaning that three pigs in each of the two latter categories were actually given in the form of cash).

For the purposes of the marriage ritual, then, money "is" a pig; nevertheless, everyone knows that bridewealth transactions are increasingly used as a direct and efficient means of access to the more fungible medium of cash. Men, in particular, often seem to be on a mission to increase the proportion of bridewealth given in cash. Money, they argue, can be distributed more widely than pigs, and is a fluid currency, easily used to buy trade store goods, PMV (public motor vehicle) fares, school fees, and so on. Of course, in the contemporary context pigs are no longer confined to the arena of ritualized exchange; they can be, and often are, sold for cash. Indeed, in Tari town there is a particular fence along which people line up their pigs for sale every Friday. Since pigs can be sold as commodities anyway, one might wonder why Huli men would urge each other to acquire bridewealth payments in the form of cash; after all, a man could presumably receive a bridewealth pig and sell it. If it was a female pig he could breed it and then sell it and its offspring, potentially making yet more money.

However, it is important to bear in mind that in order to sell a pig a man must have a woman (a wife, mother, or sister) who is willing to care for the pig until a buyer is found. If a buyer cannot be found, and one's female relatives are reluctant to look after the pig, then it can be killed and the cooked pork sold in pieces at market, but this will bring in far less money. The same pig that would have sold for K100 alive will only bring in K60 after being killed, "operated" (as many people now refer to the process of cutting a pig into pieces), cooked, and sold for its meat at market.[10] Thus, if one ultimately hopes to use a bridewealth payment for plans that require cash, it is more efficient to get the cash up-front than to try to sell the pig later. Indeed my field assistant told me that he and three kinsmen once unexpectedly received a pig as part of a compensation payment, and they were at a loss as to what to do. The "traditional" expectation was that they would kill it and eat it together in the men's house (Goldman 1981: 67), but none of them wanted to do that, and none of the younger men in the group wanted to care for the pig or ask their wives or sisters to care for it. Finally the oldest man in the group, more of a traditionalist, offered to pay the other three men K20 each and to take the pig himself and have one of his wives look after it. The pig was worth about twice that amount, but the younger men in the group were happy to be spared the burden of finding a woman to care for it and then feeling indebted not only to the other men in the group, but also to whichever women had invested work into the pig's care. This one small incident demonstrates the decline in significance of male commensality, as well as the increasing value placed on individual consumption and autonomy. Also important is that, at least in this case, the value of cash is not only its easy divisibility or fungibility, but also the way it fosters men's autonomy by allowing them to bypass the productive sphere of women.

Not surprisingly, then, women generally prefer to have bridewealth given in pigs, not cash. Women are more likely to subscribe to the common saying that "money is like a passenger woman—in the pocket of one man one day, in another man's pocket the next." Like passenger women, money is transient, mobile, and nonreproductive (Simmel 1990)—at least in terms of socially sanctioned reproduction. Pigs reproduce when embodied work is put into them; money does not. And cash, women say, is simply too easy to part with. There is always something that cash can be used for, whether it is a can of Coke, a stick of sugar cane, or cigarettes—what does one do when the cash is gone? It is better to keep one's wealth in the form of pigs, which will always be on hand when a compensation payment or a school fee must be paid, and which grow and reproduce. Moreover, while some men do look after one or two pigs of their own, it is more often women who care for their own pigs, one or two of their husband's pigs, one or two that they have decided to own jointly, and occasionally one or two that a brother or cousin has asked them to care for. Regardless of how these pigs are eventually disposed of, the female caretaker can be sure that she will get something out of it: she will publicly receive the head of the pig if it is killed at a *nogo tagandia* (a small party between kin and friends); she will receive some acknowledgment if it is used for a bridewealth or compensation payment; and if she or someone else sells it, she will receive at least some of the cash. Thus, while men try to monetize the bridewealth system, many women express doubts and hesitations about this trend.

Bridewealth or Bride-price?

One of the first village court cases I attended concerned an elderly couple who had been living together off in the bush. The man was thin, sinewy, white-haired, and stood impassively, listening quietly to the case against him. The woman was also white-haired, but unlike the man, was fractious and derisive, intermittently clapping her hands, swearing, barking out strident laughter, refusing to answer questions, interrupting the dispute mediators, and occasionally rocketing toward other speakers as if to attack them. Both old people had been married before to other spouses now dead, their children were adults with children of their own, and they were clearly past their reproductive lives. However, the woman's former husband's clan members were demanding that the old man pay bridewealth for her. Her own son and daughter were supporting this claim, perhaps hoping to receive some of the payment, perhaps only trying to shame their mother into assuming the proper nonsexual role of an old woman. The woman's interlocutors asked intimate questions about what exactly the two did together in the bush—who slept where, did they have separate houses, did she work in his garden—trying to assess whether the man was benefiting from her as a husband would. She responded with taunts and jeers: she had long ago brought in bridewealth for her kin; she had produced children for her husband's clan; what more did they want from her, an old woman? Clearly she had *"pinisim pig"* (finished, paid off her bridewealth pigs). Did they really believe that she was going to be producing children for that skinny, white-haired man over there? So what if she worked in his garden; he helped her with her gardens too. They were two old people living out in the bush bothering no one; why should they be anyone's concern but their own? Her own children were trying to "sell" her, she yelled.

Everyone around me indignantly whispered that everything about the case was outrageous: that those old people could be having sex was inappropriate, but even more disgraceful was that the opposing party would bring the case in the first place. The old woman was right; she had done her social duty to all parties involved. And her children! Hoping to "eat" (profit from) their own mother's vagina! Her former husband's kin shouldn't win, but they just might because they were "strong" (belonged to a large clan known for its military might) and the old man was weak and alone. The woman's children and her former husband's clan members, my friends declared, were the epitome of what was wrong with Huli people today: they were "just jealous and greedy for money."

This court case goes to the heart of a central debate in Melanesian ethnography: does the increasing monetization of bridewealth automatically entail its commoditization? Are women becoming more like commodities to be bought and sold, or are they still the valuable gifts that cement ties between families and clans? Are marriage transactions in the contemporary context more accurately called "bridewealth" or "brideprice"? Bride*wealth* suggests that marriage-related exchanges are embedded in a larger system of reciprocity, and that the valuables given for a woman are conceptualized as an intrinsic, almost bodily part of the

bride-receiving clan. Bride*wealth* serves to join two families and their respective clans, not alienate them from each other; it implies enduring relations of obligation between two families. The term bride-*price,* on the
other hand, suggests contractual—and even venal—motivations and outcomes in which women are alienated from their families, affinal relations
are not prioritized, and men (and their families) invoke the idiom of
bride-*price* to assert dominance over women as wives. In the recent past
ethnographers of Melanesia have been quite careful to use the term
bride*wealth* in order to steer clear of imposing Western commodity logics on rituals clearly replete with other, culturally specific meanings and
consequences. However, the inflation of bridewealth, the increased use
of cash instead of pigs or other valuables, and the apparent attenuation
of extended family and affinal obligations can make the exchange look
somewhat like a commodity transaction.

The question of whether bridewealth has become commoditized is a
vexing issue, both for ethnographers and for Melanesians themselves
(Filer 1985; Valeri 1994; Marksbury 1993). Jolly asserts that bride-*price* is
"an increasingly legitimate idiom" (1994: 132) to describe the marital
payments of South Pentecost people, and she criticizes the failure of
ethnographers to "acknowledge the importance of the colonial experience
and of an encroaching capitalist system in importing a new language of
persons and things" (117). Similarly, Jorgensen carefully asserts that while

> much of what we know of the behavior of cash in systems of exchange in
> the highlands of Papua New Guinea suggests that cash has, if anything, en-
> hanced indigenous systems of transaction . . . this argument cannot easily
> be applied to contemporary Telefol bridewealth, because transactions seem
> to aim less at the establishment or maintenance of debts and claims than at
> their liquidation, which has resulted in shrinkage rather than expansion of
> the exchange networks . . . The tendency is toward commercial investment
> or consumption rather than distribution, with a general disengagement of
> each marriage from other exchanges. (1993: 74–75)

More bluntly, Zimmer-Tamakoshi discusses the "process that has resulted in Gende women being sold or offering themselves for sale to the
highest bidder" (1993a: 87).

Just how to determine whether bride*wealth* is becoming bride-*price* has
been the subject of debate. Valerio Valeri, in an article called "Buying
Women but Not Selling Them," suggests that current formulations of
bridewealth cannot be considered commercial transactions because (1) a
woman, unlike other forms of property, cannot be further alienated by
her husband—that is, he cannot give her away to a third party, and (2) as

he puts it, "in a purchase, the equivalent given for a thing of one kind may be exchanged for a thing of another kind . . . But the equivalent given for a woman may only be converted into another woman" (1994: 3). Among the Huli, the first criteria is certainly true—husbands cannot sell their wives to a third party—but the second is not. What is given for a woman now—cash—can, of course, be converted into all sorts of things, which is exactly why people want to use it.

Perhaps more important than the nature of the actual transaction is the nature of the relationships established through and after the transaction. As Marilyn Strathern has pointed out, "It is not buying and selling as such, of course, that are at the heart of anthropological understandings of commoditization, but the quality of relationships" (1996: 518). This ad-monitory reminder, although important, makes the diagnosis of bridewealth/-price difficult, for "the quality of relationships" can only be analyzed through time, and any shift toward commoditization will likely occur in a piecemeal fashion through the practices of individual actors. I suggest, however, that there are at least four questions one can ask in an attempt to assess whether or to what extent bridewealth is undergoing commoditization: Do people recognize the exchange of money for per-sons as a process of alienation? Are women forced into marriages for the express purpose of obtaining bridewealth for them? What is the nature of the affinal relations established by marriage? Do husbands say that the use of cash gives them certain rights over wives?

Some of these questions are more easily answered than others. Ad-dressing the first question, among the Huli there are other kinds of ex-changes involving persons and money that are, in contrast to bridewealth, recognized as a kind of alienation. For example, the nurses in the mater-nity ward at Tari Hospital were roundly criticized for their "sale" of babies born to mothers who didn't want them. The nurses facilitated adoption by finding other, often infertile, couples to take these babies, and they would usually charge for this facilitation, giving most, but not all, of the money to the biological mother. Although this practice was infrequent, there were unmarried teenagers and passenger women who took advantage of this service, and there were rare stories of married women who had attempted to do so as well, particularly if their husbands were absent and had not sent remittances home for existing children, or if they knew the pregnancy was due to an adulterous liaison. Most Huli people spoke of this practice as an egregious development, for, unlike bridewealth, it was flatly interpreted as "selling" human beings—that is, completely alienating them from their makers in order to gain cash. The nurses at Tari Hospital tried to resignify the payment as "compensation" for the women's embodied labor of gestation and birth, but most people interpreted this rhetorical move as a facile attempt to mask a blatantly commercial transaction. Thus, a distinction was drawn between this practice and bridewealth, with the argument that married women remain related to their kin and, particularly through childbearing, bring two families and their respective clans together. A woman's husband and brothers have obligations to each other, newly married couples sometimes live on the woman's clan territory with her family, and after a period of restriction when a newly married woman may not be allowed to spend time with her family, she accrues increasing liberty to do so and potentially greater power to facilitate ties between her husband and her natal family. Thus, bridewealth was ultimately about increasing relationality, not severing it.

And yet some women asserted that the above description of affinal ties is no longer accurate—that families have become more nuclearized and that relations of obligation between a woman's brothers and her husband are no longer as strong, with the consequences that (1) a woman's role "in between" them (Strathern 1972) is no longer as important, and (2) women do, in fact, feel more "alienated" from their kin. Women cited examples of husbands refusing to attend the funerals of women's natal kin or refusing to participate in basic cooperative activities such as house or fence building. Similarly, women complained of not being allowed by husbands to attend the funerals of natal kin and not being allowed to participate in productive activities with natal kin, such as gardening with sisters. It is difficult to assess whether such reports actually indicate a trend toward decreasing affinal obligation, whether they reflect momentary strains in particular affinal relations, or whether this is an idiom through which women express complaints about marriages. Most men I knew did have close—if occasionally strained—relations with their wives' brothers and other natal kin. Those few who did not usually cited labor migration as the reason why they had neglected ties with their affines. Labor away from home was said to structure their time so that they were unable to fulfill affinal obligations or, more rarely, was said to make affinal obligations less necessary, less compelling, and more burdensome.

Similarly difficult to assess is whether women are coerced into marriage by natal kin expressly for the purpose of acquiring bridewealth, a possible indicator of its commoditization. Out of my interview sample of fifty women and their seventy-three marriages, there were only two women who described something like this occurring. One said that her father owed another man money and forced her to marry him in order to pay off the debt, despite the fact that he was much older and that she objected to the marriage. Another woman said that her husband had been chosen by her brother, and although she herself was amenable to the match, she resented that her parents had pressured her to agree to the match because her husband had bribed them with money and store-bought gifts. (A few other women said that they had been coerced into arranged marriages; however, these were often to solidify political ties, and bridewealth was not the immediate motive.) Nevertheless, many women complain that families are "too greedy for bridewealth" (*jelas tumas long pig-muni*), and they sometimes assert that they are being treated "like market goods" (*olsem maket*). Similarly, women assert that in the past women were the "objects" of value for which people gave wealth items, but now money is the coveted object of value for which people give women. Most often this feeling seemed to stem not from being forced into venally motivated marriages but from feelings of abandonment by natal kin after marriage, a subject that is taken up in the next chapter.

The question of whether the payment of bridewealth is used by husbands to assert rights over wives has been addressed earlier. Men do invoke the idiom of bride-price to demand certain services, and often these are services that were not included in traditional obligations of wives to husbands; thus, for example, many men expect their wives to cook for them, a task that men performed for themselves in the past. Most women, however, speak happily of this change as a sign of greater intimacy and companionship. However, some tasks—doing a man's laundry and fetching things for him, in particular—are conceptualized by many women as duties forced on them because bride-price was given for them.

Moreover, men invoke a commoditized discourse about bridewealth in their attempts to control women's reproductive lives. The best example of this is Huli men's attitude toward modern contraceptives or "family planning," which, during the period of my research, was primarily hostile. In Papua New Guinea, it used to be law that only married women could receive contraception from government clinics and that both husband and wife had to sign the consent form. Although the law has changed so that a woman no longer needs her husband's permission, it was standard practice to require this in the mid-1990s when I conducted my fieldwork. Nurses working in the Tari Hospital MCH (maternal/child health) mobile clinic said that in the past they had attempted to give informational talks about contraception to the mothers and fathers gathered for baby weighing and immunization. However, they were threatened multiple times by men who yelled that the nurses could give depo-provera shots to their wives only when the nurses had refunded their bridewealth. Eventually the nurses abandoned these educational talks. They added that the clinic nurses were supposed to inform every pregnant woman about the possibility of contraception so that they could "space" their families. However, their actual policy was to delay any mention of contraception until a woman had four children because too many husbands had threatened to sue or burn down the clinic when wives who had used depo-provera in the past had difficulties getting pregnant. In my own casual conversations with men about family planning, many were contemptuous of arguments about women's and children's health—for example, a woman should space her children in order to minimize their risk of malnutrition. If a woman behaved properly and abided by traditional *mana*—working hard in her gardens, never going to town, and so on—then she would remain healthy, they claimed. It was only women's rebellious insistence on going to Tari market, talking to their friends on the road, and other inappropriate behaviors that made them sick.

Women's resentment about male authority in the productive and re-productive realms may be aggravated by a sense that "modern" marriages should be more companionate. On a few occasions, women I was interviewing abruptly stopped talking, looked around, and said, "marriage should be like this—sitting at a table, smoking together, talking and laughing like this together." As one friend of mine put it, husbands and wives should *"wok wok, helpim helpim, story story, bung wantaim na lotu"* (work together, help each other, have nice conversations together, and go to church and worship together), implying that a marriage characterized not only by respect and cooperation but also by psychological intimacy is both desirable and an essential part of being a good Christian (Wardlow in press). Many couples do, of course, achieve a marriage where they work side by side in their jointly owned gardens and cooperate to raise money for various endeavors such as providing bridewealth payments, opening a trade store, and managing to put all their children through school. Nevertheless, it may also be the case that women are coming to expect more companionate marriages as the proper conjugal form for modern persons, and that failure to achieve such expectations contributes to their perceptions of being *"olsem maket"* (like market goods). For example, Jakili, a married mother of two children, physically fought with her husband and eventually ran away from him. In response, her husband humiliated her by publicly announcing that since she had absconded from the marriage and her family had not yet returned his bridewealth payment, any man from his clan had a right to her. (Everyone knew that this declaration was rhetorical, and no man would have acted on it.) She asserted to me that by announcing that she was available for the taking her husband was treating her *olsem maket* (like a commodity); arguably, however, he was not using a market idiom at all and was actually invoking a highly relational, noncommodified notion of bridewealth in which his bond with her was eclipsed by his membership in the male corporate group that had helped him marry her. In other words, it was his deliberately insouciant, and very public, trivialization of their marriage—in the face of her expectation that modern spouses should value each other over other relationships—that wounded and infuriated her.

Pinisim Pig and Divorce

If it is, in fact, the case that bridewealth is becoming commoditized, then women themselves would probably say that the transaction is more like a long-term rental agreement than a sale. Many women desire to return to the land of their natal clan once their childbearing and child-rearing duties are over, and upon leaving many feel that they have no further obligations to their husbands or their husbands' clans. Moreover, most of the women in my life history sample and many of my friends seemed continually poised for flight from their marriages. To continue with the language I have invoked, they seemed always to have an eye out for reasons the "rental agreement" could be terminated, and particularly the ways to terminate the agreement that would limit a husband's claim to have his bridewealth returned. Thus, women often engaged in what I came to think of as the *"pinisim pig"* (finishing bridewealth pigs) discourse, routinely calculating and revising estimates of how many pigs would have to be returned if they tried to obtain a divorce.

Divorce is quite difficult for Huli women to achieve. If a woman demands a divorce or is found to be at fault for the divorce, then her family must return most if not all of the bridewealth given for her. Conversely, there are a number of socially recognized reasons for a man to demand a divorce and still have his bridewealth returned in full (menstrual pollution, adultery, running away to one's natal home, showing suicidal tendencies), and men sometimes take advantage of this greater leverage, particularly early on in a marriage, before any children have been born (Glasse 1968). If, however, a man demands divorce, has no "reasonable cause," as it were, and is found to be at fault for the dissolution of the marriage, then the bridewealth to be returned to him may be quite small or forfeited altogether. However, the latter scenario almost never occurs, for if a man is dissatisfied with a marriage he can simply choose to live elsewhere and have little to do with his wife. The complex multiresidence system of the Huli (Glasse 1968; Goldman 1983; Allen 1995) affords men great flexibility in terms of where they can build and maintain households. Many men, particularly in the older generation, regularly move between a number of residences on their father's father's land, their mother's father's land, the local clan's men's house, and so on. Women, on the other hand, are expected to live in the house a husband has built for them on a husband's land surrounded by a husband's kin; thus, a woman's only real "exit strategy" from a marriage is divorce. And, as Sturzenhofecker (1998) found for the Duna, divorce has become more difficult for women in the contemporary context because of bridewealth inflation. The increasing amount of bridewealth means that prospective grooms must call on more relatives to help them make the payment, and women seeking a divorce must convince more of their relatives to help them return the payment. Consequently, women wanting to exit a marriage are always on the lookout for ways to *"pinisim pig"*—that is, for reasons why this return payment should be reduced.

Reproduction is the most straightforward way of "finishing" a man's "pig-money." When a woman told me she wanted to leave her husband, I would usually ask what was to be done about the bridewealth, and often she would respond something like, "I've given birth to three children! I've finished his pigs!" *(Mi karim tripela pikinini pinis, yia! Mi pinisim pig bilong em!)* The other way that women "finish" bridewealth is through tolls taken on the body. Women who were beaten severely or frequently by their husbands would assert that their injuries had "finished" their husbands' pigs. More recently, acquiring a sexually transmitted disease from one's husband has also been used by a woman's kin in court cases to argue for a divorce with a reduction in the number of bridewealth pigs returned. Women therefore scrupulously make sure that any and all injuries or sicknesses that can be attributed to a husband's behavior are recorded in the clinic books that most Papua New Guinea people receive either at birth or when they get their first immunizations. Women spoke of these books—tattered, soot-stained, and smelling of smoke—as moral/bodily histories detailing all diseases and injuries suffered since they were born. As such, they can be used as evidence for court cases. In sum, women sometimes speak of bridewealth as a debt that need only be paid off through the bodily expenditures of reproduction, injury, and disease before they can return home.

Because it can be very difficult to convince relatives to support one in a divorce, an alternative exit strategy for a very few women was to keep boyfriends waiting in the wings with the hopes that the second husband would simply give his bridewealth to the first husband, enabling them to escape. This is a tricky game to play, however. One has to be sure that the second man has serious intentions, and one has to be sure not to get caught. Since a woman's sexuality is supposed to belong to her husband, and since sexual propriety is so central to the definition of being a *wali ore,* playing this game automatically puts one's reputation and safety in jeopardy.

The principle reasons given by women I interviewed for seeking divorce were excessive beating—with the use of a weapon, for example—or a husband's promiscuity. The case below illustrates these reasons.

. . .

Norin married an older man whose clan territory was contiguous with her father's. She vaguely knew of him because his first wife was an agnate of her father's clan and because he had a job at the local health center. Norin's bridewealth, thirty pigs plus K400 *imane aka,* was relatively high because she had a grade 6 education, was premenarcheal, was known as a diligent and responsible garden worker, and was the daughter of quite religious parents who disapproved of her marrying a man who already had a wife. Indeed, her mother refused to distribute her portion of the bridewealth because of her religious objections to the marriage. After the bridewealth distribution ceremony, Norin and the first wife lived in the same house, an unusual arrangement, and, atypically, got along quite well, perhaps because Norin was young, they had known each other before Norin became the second wife, and because their husband had followed the more traditional steps of informing his first wife and gaining her approval for the marriage.

Neither wife got along very well with this husband, however. After excessive beating, the first wife ran away, although she was forced by her own family to return. Norin got pregnant too quickly for her husband's liking, and they often fought about his insistence on sex during her pregnancy and subsequent breast-feeding, violation of taboos that Norin, like most Huli women, took very seriously. He then took a third "wife," a woman who was rumored to be a *pasinja meri* because she had been seen at *dawe anda* (traditional courtship parties which are now somewhat like brothels; discussed in chapter 6). Norin refused to recognize the marriage, primarily because of the woman's reputation, but her husband insisted that all three wives live together. Norin became sick with a sexually transmitted disease, probably syphilis, and in anger, she attacked her husband and his *gonolia meri* (gonorrhea woman), as Norin referred to her. During this fight her husband slashed her hand with an axe.

At that point Norin decided she wanted a divorce. Her brothers and the local leaders from her father's clan suggested that she go into Tari town and seek a divorce through the district court system there. They warned her that because her husband was a strong local leader from a strong clan she might lose the case if she tried the local village court mechanism. She knew they were right: on those occasions when she had fought with her husband about his promiscuity he had often jeered at her that "your beardless little brothers—what are they going to do about it?" *(Ol liklik brata bilong yu nogat grass—ol bai mekim wanem?* that is, your clan is a lot weaker than mine). So Norin secretly went to Tari carrying explanatory supportive letters from the local leaders, as well as her clinic book, which documented her pregnancy, STD, and the axe injury to her hand. According to her, the Tari district court granted her divorce and ordered that only seven of her thirty bride-wealth pigs had to be returned to her husband.

•   •   •

Unlike Norin, most women do not have the knowledge or the gumption to go directly to the higher district court system. When wives instigate divorce locally, their families usually have to return a much larger portion of the bridewealth, primarily because local court officials, while genuinely seeking a just settlement, primarily want to keep the peace and send both parties home relatively satisfied. Thus a woman's family will often have to return much of the bridewealth given for her, even if she feels she has *pinisim pig*.

What often happens then, instead of a definitive divorce (defined as the return of at least some of the bridewealth), is that a wife will move back home with her parents or into a brother's household for an extended pe-riod of time and the future of the marriage is left ambiguous. Indeed, of my sample of 50 women, all but one of whom were or had been married, 14 were currently living with their husbands; 6 were old women whose husbands were dead or who had moved back to their own territory with their husbands' permission; 7 were officially divorced (meaning some bridewealth pigs had been returned); 4 were separated from their hus-bands solely because of his work, not because of any conflict; and 18 were contentiously separated from their husbands with no agreement about what would be done about bridewealth.[11]

This is not a comfortable state of affairs. Indeed, just as I was finishing my fieldwork a woman and her brother were murdered by her husband be-cause of a bridewealth dispute (mentioned briefly in the introduction). As the story went, she had left him because he beat her excessively and be-cause he ran a *dawe anda*. No bridewealth was returned, and they had lived tensely, but uneventfully, apart for a number of years until he learned that she had been boasting that a cousin had bought her a plane ticket to Tabubil, a town in another province, and that she was planning to leave Tari permanently. He was said to be consumed by *"madane"*— he was furious that she seemed to think she could get away with never returning his bridewealth, and resentful that she had become so *"bighed"* that she was publicly boasting about her wealthy kin and her own freedom to do as she pleased. I did not know or interview any of the key players, but all the narratives about this incident implied that the initial murder stemmed from profoundly gendered conflicts about marital relations in the contemporary context: Is a husband entitled to extramarital relationships, or are such relationships reason enough for a wife to leave? Is it an unacceptable assault on a husband's masculinity for a wife to boast about her wealthy relatives or to flaunt her ability to escape an unwanted marriage? The conversations about these incidents always came back to the issue of the unreturned bridewealth. Thus, if nothing else, one can conclude that anxieties and anger about contemporary gender relations get channeled into, or framed as, conflicts about bridewealth, since this is the idiom for gender relations in which everyone is fluent.

The bridewealth system, for all its current permutations and ambiguities, is central to the construction of female identity and the reproduction of society. Bridewealth is what makes women *wali ore,* and it is the pervasive calculus through which women interpret the social world and act on their interpretations. Women often see their worth as the amount of bridewealth they can bring in to their families, and bridewealth is the idiom through which they argue that they have invested more labor in raising daughters, claiming more bridewealth pigs and larger payments of *imane aka.* And, women strategize to leave their marriages by constantly calculating how many of the bridewealth pigs they have worked off. At the same time, there is increasing tension about the perceived trend toward the commoditization of bridewealth transactions. In the past, women, pigs, and other valuables, such as shells or cassowaries, all moved within an enclosed circuit, but with monetization the circuit has split open, and bridewealth has become an important site through which the "grassroots" can obtain the cash that will pay for PMV (public bus) fares, school fees, clothes, guns, and so on. The actions some women take in response to the commoditization of social relations is the subject of the next chapters.

CHAPTER 4

"You, I don't even count you"

Becoming a Pasinja Meri

Megeme said that she made up her mind after she was raped for the second time. Her kin condemned the assailant's behavior and belligerently demanded *nogo tauwa* (literally, pigs for genitals; compensation for "stealing" the sexuality of a woman), but later seemed to forget about her. She recalled the heady atmosphere of righteous indignation as dozens of relatives gathered for the village court case—the women vehement and quarrelsome; the men somber, letting their loosely held bows and home-made guns speak their intentions. At the time, Megeme was proud that her kin had threatened tribal war if the assailant's family did not give them fifteen pigs, but what she then perceived as support and solidarity later seemed to her to be more like greed. After the court case, she often ran into kin who had received these *tauwa* pigs, and they never bought her soap or cigarettes or food, and when she asked them to pay her school fees, they refused. As she bitterly pronounced, "The first time a man raped me I supplied fifteen pigs for my father's family, and the second time a man raped me I supplied fifteen pigs for my mother's family, but my relatives never give me anything."[1]

It was at this point, she said, that she started to *"pamuk raun"* (have sex with many partners) and to act like a *"pasinya wali"* (or *pasinja meri* in Tok Pisin). She would sneak off to the local "bush discos" (rural, late-night dance parties) and later have sex in the underbrush for a few kina. She was the firstborn child in her family, so there were no older brothers to physically stop her, and her father was not a typical Huli man: gentle and quiet, he was known in the community for his eccentric belief that it

FIGURE 12. Armed men display their willingness to go to war. In the mid-1990s automatic weapons had not yet made it into Huli territory; battles were fought with bows and arrows and homemade guns.

was wrong to hit dogs. So he wasn't about to beat his daughter, even if she was going around wearing tank tops, being a *"show-off meri"* in her "Bruce Lee" shoes, hopping on PMVs (public buses) to Mendi, and having sex with men in the bushes.[2] In any case, everyone has always been a little nervous around Megeme. She exudes a kind of minatory magnetism, drawing people to her while intimidating them at the same time. Notorious for her hair-trigger temper, she claims she almost killed one of her husbands by slashing his arm with a bush knife. Everyone knows she's a *pasinja meri*—even I guessed as much the first time I saw her—but no one says so to her face.

• • •

Ogai had two children and had suffered through a difficult marriage for a number of years before she began to *"raun long laik"* (literally, go around as I please, which implies promiscuity when applied to women). Her husband worked in the mess hall of a mine site in another province, but he rarely gave her money and rarely came home. He once promised to take her to Mt. Hagen during a leave from work, but he took his girlfriend instead, and she later found naked photos of this woman in his pockets when she did his laundry. Nevertheless, it was only after she was raped and her brothers and husband refused to do anything about it that she decided to leave him. It was after this incident, she said, that she abandoned him and their children and began exchanging sex for money.

When she explained to me the series of events that led up to her decision to become a *pasinja meri* she was clearly preoccupied with the rape itself, turning it over and over in her mind and reiterating that the sex had not been consensual. Having spent a long day collecting thatch for the roof on a relative's new house, she had hurried to her garden alone at dusk to get some food for dinner. Her sister's daughter had recently been raped and killed, and so Ogai was wearing her funeral finery of Job's Tears necklaces, red T-shirt, red face paint, and a grass skirt—attire that the aggrieved female kin of a murder victim often wear until vengeance is exacted and attire that should invite respect from others. As she bent over to dig up some sweet potato, she noticed a man watching her. Luckily, or so she thought, the husband of one of her cousins happened to come by, scaring the man off. Made bold by her in-law's presence, she insulted the man as he fled, telling him to go look at his own wife's *"pindu"* (literally, possessions or belongings; a common euphemism for genitals) if he was so "hot."

She went back to working in her garden, assuming that her in-law had continued on his way. However, as she left her garden, the in-law snuck up behind her, held a bush knife to her throat, and whispered that he, like the other man, had become aroused seeing her bend over in her grass skirt, watching the other man stare at her, and hearing her *"tok bilas"* (provocative or insulting language). He demanded that she have sex with him, threatening that if she struggled, he would kill her and throw her body in a ditch. No one would find the corpse until it started stinking, he taunted, and when it was found, who would know that he had done it? No murder compensation would ever be demanded for her; no one would take up arms to avenge her death. And anyway, he sneered, "You think your 'thing' [i.e., vagina] is a good thing? I've had sex with/raped white women, so you, I don't even count you" *(Yu ting samting bilong yu em gutpela samting? Mi save repim wait meri, olsem na yu, mi no save kauntim yu).*[3] Conventional wisdom among Huli women is that physically resisting rape infuriates assailants and can get one killed. As Ogai put it, fighting back sends that the message that "you think you are strong" *(yu ting olsem yu strong)* and have the right to reject sexual advances (see NSRRT and Jenkins 1994: 104 for similar stories). And there Ogai was, in mourning for a niece who had suffered exactly what this man was threatening to do to her. She summed up the situation: "And he wasn't my brother after all [i.e., it wasn't an act of incest], so forget it [i.e., forget trying to resist], we just did it right then and there" *(Na em no brata bilong mi. Maski, mipela wokim long hap).*

When she later told her brothers about the assault, they responded that she was a married woman—her husband had given bridewealth for her—and so it was her husband's responsibility to take this man to court. According to her, however, her husband refused to leave his job and come home, and when he finally did, he said that since there were no witnesses anyway, it wasn't worth bringing the case to court. Voice shaking, she said that she was so angry at the apparent indifference of her brothers and husband that she considered committing suicide, but instead deposited her two children with her sisters and ran away from home. She began by sneaking off to the local bush discos, where she would dance with a number of men and then have sex with one of them in the underbrush for a few dollars. Later she joined a group of women who also self-identified as passenger women, and they cooperated in organizing liaisons with groups of men, often sneaking into clan men's houses—residences that are strictly off-limits to all women—in the dead of night. As Ogai said:

> We would go sleep in the men's house. The house in the middle is the men's house. All the houses around it belong to a man's relatives and his wives. So they would go talk with their wives and relatives while we snuck into the men's house. He would sit there and talk with his wife, so she would think that he was going alone back to the men's house, and then he would come back and we would have sex. When it was time to leave, we would leave, before it was light, before anyone was awake. So we would hide and do it. In the men's house they would divvy us up—like if there were two men living there, then I would go and bring a girlfriend of mine for the other man. . . . and if there were seven or eight men, six, five, like that, I would bring lots of women.

Eventually Ogai hopped on a public bus and decided to take her chances on the roads and in the towns of Papua New Guinea. She lived this way for approximately five years and claimed to have had sex with hundreds of different men.

• • •

Tarali's family thought she had married well: her husband owned trade stores in Port Moresby and a few other cities, and he took her with him whenever he traveled, instead of leaving her at home to make gardens and raise pigs. But then he infected her with gonorrhea, the doctors she went to in Port Moresby declared her infertile, she and her husband began to fight all the time, and eventually he sent her back to Tari. When she later heard that he had taken a second wife and was returning home, she and her sisters waited at the airstrip and attacked the couple as they got off the plane. In the melee her husband punched out her front tooth. The gonorrhea and subsequent infertility, her lost tooth, and the strength of her father's clan were all persuasive arguments during the subsequent divorce case, and none of her bridewealth was returned to her husband, a remarkable outcome in Huli divorces.

But afterward Tarali became depressed. Even her younger sisters were married and had children, and there she was, back at home with her father, who blamed her for the failure of her marriage and the consequent lost connection with her wealthy ex-husband. Moreover, when her mother died soon after Tarali's divorce, her father refused to let her go to the funeral, an unconscionable act according to most Huli women. Her mother had run away to become a passenger woman when Tarali was young, and her father, angry and ashamed, had done his best to sever contact between them. Tarali asserted that all these incidents culminated in her decision to become a passenger woman. Her husband's promiscuity, her consequent infertility, and her father's refusal to let her attend her mother's funeral all resulted in a consuming rage. So Tarali started going to bush discos, and when men asked to have sex with her, she would. She said that she didn't ask for money at this time; she just felt angry, and, as she put it, she had sex with them simply because she could. Her older brothers tried to restrain her from being a *pasinja meri,* but she argued that she had provided bridewealth for them already, and so she should be free to do as she pleased. *"Laik bilong mi"* (My choice), she said.

• • •

Megeme, Ogai, and Tarali, despite their quite varied life histories, typify Huli *pasinja meri* in a number of ways.[4] Like Ogai, most of the passenger women I interviewed had been married (fifteen out of eighteen), and they often had children (thirteen out of eighteen) before they decided to run away. In other words, for the most part, it is not young, never-married women who become passenger women. Like Ogai and Megeme, many passenger women leave Huli territory, and most of them are quite proud of the journeys they have taken and their skills at adapting to new places and to people from other cultural groups. And like all three women, most passenger women I interviewed had grown up in rural areas, but usually had at least a few years of education and knew how to speak Tok Pisin, the lingua franca of Papua New Guinea. Also, like all three women, many passenger women do not initially expect to receive money in exchange for sex. Instead, they begin by running away and having a number of extra-marital sexual partners and only later come to insist on receiving cash in exchange for sex. Often they have an encounter in which a man offers them money, or they meet other passenger women who teach them that they can and should demand money from men if they offer sex. And, per-haps most important, like all three women, many passenger women de-scribe their entry into this social category as triggered by incidents of vi-olence and motivated by feelings of betrayal and anger (thirteen out of eighteen). In other words, to the extent that these factors can be disen-tangled, it was emotion, not economics, that first impelled them to en-gage in extramarital, monetized sexual exchanges.

Megeme, Ogai, and Tarali also demonstrate the wide range of factors that can play a part in pushing Huli women onto the path of exchanging sex for money. Like Tarali, some passenger women, but by no means all, suffer from infertility, and a husband's rejection or a sense of irremediable social failure influences their decisions to abandon the seemingly unattain-able role of *wali ore* (real or good woman). Also like Tarali, some passenger women's mothers had themselves run off to become passenger women, an eventuality that may increase the likelihood that a woman will also do so. Indeed, women who are angry with their husbands sometimes deliberately recruit their own daughters to become passenger women, arguing that such behavior is a sure way to punish the husband/father for his negligence or violence (although this was not the case with Tarali). Finally, like Ogai and Megeme, some passenger women experience rape before they become pas-senger women, an issue taken up in more detail later in the chapter.

In this chapter I do not attempt some kind of regression analysis to de-termine which of the above factors is most common or potentially causal in shaping women's decisions to become *pasinja meri*. Rather, I discuss the range of women's experiences prior to becoming passenger women, the tendency of women to rhetorically frame their decisions to become *pasinja meri* as voluntaristic and effective acts of female negative agency, and the potential tensions and disjunctures between passenger women's narratives and their life histories.

Defining "Passenger Women"

"Passenger woman," a term used widely in Papua New Guinea, may de-rive from the fact that women who sell sex can be found at roadside mar-ketplaces where public buses stop as they traverse the Highlands Highway

(Hughes 1997). In other words, passenger women are the women who provide sexual services to passengers on public buses. Among the Huli, however, the term has somewhat different meanings: people say that passenger women are called by that name because they jump on buses and run away from their families; that is, a *pasinja meri* is literally a female passenger—a woman who will not stay put, either physically or sexually.[5] Most self-identified Huli passenger women exchange sex for money, making it tempting to gloss their practices as prostitution or sex work; however, the nonsexual and non-monetary dimensions of *pasinja meri* identity are equally important to passenger women themselves. Moreover, as is discussed in the next chapter, local discourses about the significance of passenger women do not correspond to received theorizations or descriptions of sex work in other world areas, what Kamala Kempadoo has called "the 'canon' in prostitution studies" (1998: 13). As she says, "Little research or theorizing to date is, for example, grounded in the lives, experiences, definitions and perspectives of Third World people in sex work, allowing western categories and subjects to be privileged in the international discourse on sex work" (13). Throughout this chapter and the following, then, I attempt to do this grounding, showing how cultural and economic structures shape Huli *pasinja meri*'s motivations and experiences.

To begin with, both self-identified *pasinja meri* and other Huli emphasize mobility as an important component of *pasinja meri* identity—mobility both in terms of their daily freedom of movement and in terms of their autonomy. *Pasinja meri* usually frame this mobility as both a consequence and a manifestation of agency: their life history narratives are often structured around their travels outside Huli territory, and they proudly emphasize all the places that they've been and their contacts with men from other cultural groups. They often use phrases such as *"mi brukim banis pinis," "mi raun long laik," "laik bilong mi,"* and *"mi fri"* (I've already broken out of the fence, I go where I please, it's up to me, I'm free) when asked how they are different from other Huli women. This "freedom" does not come easily, as Tarali explained to me:

· · ·

This is what I was thinking: I already provided pigs and money [i.e., bridewealth] for my relatives, so why should I stop myself and stay at home? I am going to go. I would go to party houses [*dawe anda* and bush discos], and my brothers would beat me up, punch me in the mouth, that sort of thing. Then they would drag me back home and leave me there. And I would think, "That's OK—now they can beat me; tomorrow I'll just go again." So that was the pattern: they would beat me and beat me, and finally they just got tired and left me alone. They said, "She provided bridewealth for us already, so why should we boss her? If she wants to stay here [at the bush disco], it's her choice, let her stay." They said this, and so now I go where I please. All this happened, and now I'm free.

. . .

Here Tarali represents her "freedom" as something actively fought for; however, this is not always the case. Although Megeme liked to boast about all the places she had been, she once glumly stated that she believed someone had put a spell on her that made her incapable of settling down and being happy in one place: "I always feel restless to just go, go, go, wander, wander, wander" *(Mi save sikarap long go, go, go, raun, raun, raun).*[6] Such contradictory constructions of mobility point to a more general ambivalence women experience about identifying as *pasinja meri;* sometimes women claim the label as a sign of bravery, autonomy, and defiance; but often they are acutely sensitive to the stigma that attaches to that label, and they attempt to repudiate it.

While *pasinja meri* themselves are often proud of their mobility and describe it as something actively fought for, it is always constructed by others as purposeless and passive: *"pasinja meri* are merely passengers, not the driver," people say. To those of us who have grown up being passengers in buses, planes, or cars, the concept of "the passenger" may not seem terribly fraught with meaning; however, to be a passenger is a relatively new concept and experience in Papua New Guinea. "Passenger" connotes unwonted mobility combined with a frightening passivity and loss of self-determination. Ultimately, wherever the driver goes is where the passenger ends up. A common saying among the Huli—"money is like a passenger woman"—similarly conveys the sense that *pasinja meri* are rootless and subject to others' whims and desires. Why? Because neither is permanently attached to other people: they belong to one man one day, but are in the pocket of another man the next. Unlike pigs, land, and proper women, they do not stay put and generate more wealth for their custodians. The pivotal notion in this construction of *pasinja meri* mobility is that they are socially unconnected—not protected, nurtured, or "fenced in" by any particular man or clan—and thus without larger purpose. *Pasinja meri* mobility contravenes everything that defines *wali ore:* they do not "sit under the legs of men," and their sexual/reproductive powers are not dedicated to the project of social reproduction.

Passenger women are also sexually peripatetic, but their liaisons can take a variety of forms. Megeme claimed to have had sex with hundreds of men, but the nature of these interactions varied considerably—from brief commercialized transactions, to serial romantic affairs, to bouts of marriage, to liaisons that had little to do with the partner at hand and more to do with another partner against whom she was retaliating for some perceived slight. Ogai's and Tarali's sexual histories can be similarly characterized as amalgams of commercialized sex and opportunistic affairs, punctuated by periods of marriage. At one point after Ogai left her husband, for example, she lived with a truck driver from Mt. Hagen and planned to marry him; indeed, he gave her the bus fare home so that she could inform her family. Upon arrival, however, she ran into kin who had struck it rich panning for gold at Mt. Kare and who wanted her to join them. So she gave up the Mt. Hagen man—and all the belongings she had left behind with him—and went by helicopter to Mt. Kare, where she helped to manage a "video house" and occasionally exchanged sex for money. Tarali also had a relationship with a man who worked as a truck driver. When he and some friends held up a luxury hotel and did not give her a portion of the money, she turned them all in to the police and secured a job for herself as a maid at the hotel, where she occasionally slept with some of the expatriate guests for money, but also did their laundry, earning about the same amount for each service.

What it means to be a *pasinja meri,* then, cannot be clearly defined because it is an emergent category that encompasses a range of practices, motivations, and personal meanings. Nevertheless, what binds and unifies these diverse trajectories is that women who are designated or who self-identify as passenger women are thought to have "gone outside," as people say. That is, by engaging in sex outside of the institution of bridewealth, they have evaded the physico-moral "fences" meant to enclose, discipline, and sustain women. As will be seen, it is the problematic of bridewealth that is central to the local significance of *pasinja meri,* and it is the threat that passenger women pose to the bridewealth system that makes them such a powerful and emotionally charged symbol of people's desires and anxieties about modernity.

If you ask Huli people why some women become *pasinja wali,* they usually give one of three reasons: they are *"jelas"* (excessively desirous) for money, they have lived outside of Huli territory, or they had "no brothers to beat them" (i.e., both to physically prevent them and to physically socialize them into more proper female behavior). Blame for female sexual impropriety is located in individuals rather than attributed to the way women are positioned by changing cultural and economic structures. It is widely acknowledged that people in general—not just *pasinja meri*—are *"jelas"* for money these days; indeed, *"jelas,"* as discussed in chapter 1, is a new emotion term that can be seen as an implicit critique of increasing disparities in wealth and what is perceived as an attenuation of broad transactional networks and an ethos of reciprocity. Nevertheless, women are said to be more *"jelas"* than men in that they are "naturally" myopic about goals that transcend the individual (Goldman 1983; cf. Lederman 1984). *Pasinja meri* are perceived to be the most *"jelas"* of all since they are willing to trade their sexuality—something that "belongs to" the clan—for personal gain. Thus, the assertion that passenger women are *"jelas* for money" takes a collective anxiety about the present moment and locates it within individual women, who are then stigmatized for the behaviors that give them greater access to cash.

Similarly, any Huli person who lives outside of Huli territory is thought to be vulnerable to the corrupting influences of the less disciplined and immoral people of the *"nambis"* (in Tok Pisin, *nambis* means the coast, but Huli use this word to refer to anywhere outside of the highlands). Women, however, are thought to be especially vulnerable, and indeed some women are gossiped about as passenger women simply for having lived outside of Huli territory for long stretches of time. Again, passenger women—because of their autonomous mobility—epitomize this potential corruption. Likewise, all women are thought to require the physical discipline and protection of men, but *pasinja meri* are those women who did not when young, or do not as adults, have brothers to beat them. (This logic implies, of course, that all women are potential *pasinja meri*, but for the guiding minds and hands of brothers and husbands.)

If you ask self-identified *pasinja meri* why they deserted their marriages or began exchanging sex for money, they often say *"keba"* (rage)—not desire for money, but rage—and three themes are prominent in these narratives of rage: sexual and other forms of violence, the perceived absence or indifference of male kin, and bridewealth. Below I discuss each of these in turn.

Sexual Violence

The threat of rape looms large in the everyday consciousness of Huli women: until women are married and have a few children, they rarely stray from familiar territory alone, and most would never walk to town or a distant garden without a husband or brother to accompany them. I, for one, was never allowed to go anywhere alone when I lived in rural areas, and when living in Tari I was warned not to wander off the road circling the airstrip, and even to avoid walking on this quite central road after about 3:00 P.M., when Tari emptied out and only small groups of young men loitered about playing darts. The high prevalence of sexual violence was often discussed, though its proposed causes varied. Some people attributed rape to the *jelas* (excessive sexual desire) of the modern generation of men who had not been properly schooled in traditional *mana* about the importance of sexual-avoidance taboos. Others asserted that violent sexual behavior stemmed from *madane* (rancor, resentment) about women's increased autonomy and *bighed*-ness (willfulness, autonomy, impertinence), and was motivated by a desire to control and punish women. Others said that the loosening restrictions on women were to blame: women no longer stayed in the *anda* (domestic realm), as they were supposed to, and some men simply took advantage of the opportunities that this situation presented. Whatever people's thoughts about the causes of sexual violence, there was agreement that the nature of rape had changed: no longer only directed at the men to whom a female victim was connected, it often seemed to have more to do with the individual woman herself.

This uncertainty about what rape means in the contemporary context can be seen in women's own meditations about such incidents. As Ogai explained in response to my question of when and why she had started being sexually promiscuous:

· · ·

I thought to myself, "You [i.e., her rapist] didn't want to do anything [i.e., hurt her]—you just wanted to do it [i.e., have sex], and so you threatened me and so we did it" . . . I said to my cousin, "Your husband 'pulled' me and he threatened to knife me with a huge bush knife, and so I had sex with your husband" . . . "You [i.e., her husband] left me alone for a long time when I was still your wife, and this man accosted me and did all sorts of things to me, so I want to testify. You should take this man to court and get compensation from him. He attacked me and did it to me.

"Look, I'm married. You [i.e., her rapist] should give compensation to my husband. It wasn't like I wanted you and accosted you. It was your lust, your desire, you wanted to do it to me, and so you did—so now we should marry. Hey, cousin, you go marry my husband, and your husband can marry me" [this was said very sardonically] . . . This is what I was thinking: "I spoke out about what happened; it wasn't I who did it; I had no intention of doing it. He threatened me and terrified me into doing it, and I wanted to testify against him." But that man was strong. He hid. He went from place to place and hid and never killed a pig for me. That was when I started messing around. It was this event that started my befriending [i.e., having sex with] lots of men.

· · ·

While feminists in the West have argued forcefully that rape should be conceptualized as a crime of violence, among the Huli it is in many cases understood as a crime of desire (also see Gregor 1990). This is what Ogai means in the beginning of her quote when she says, "You didn't want to do anything—you just wanted to do it"; in other words, she is saying her rapist didn't really want to hurt her; rather, he was overcome by the desire for sex, and so he threatened her in order to get it. However, later in her narrative, Ogai expresses confusion about her rapist's motives, unsure whether the motive was simple sexual desire or something more vindictive. Zimmer-Tamakoshi has asserted that men use violence against women (and, I would add, the threat of violence implicit in labels such as *bighed*) "to assert or regain a sense of dominance" (1997: 539), and she emphasizes that such violence needs to be interpreted in a context of emerging class differences in which elite women in particular are scapegoated by men of all classes "as symbols of all that is wrong with contemporary Papua New Guinean society" (539). In Ogai's case, however, the rape seemingly has very little to do with class and perhaps more to do with race: she was discursively stripped of value by the assailant's invocation of a racially based hierarchy of female sexual worth. By implying that because she was black she didn't even figure in his implied tally of victims, her assailant essentially forced her into the subject position of being "un-rapeable" through the very act of rape (Sharpe 1991).[7] Then, from her perspective, her male kin tacitly accepted this devaluation by allowing her violation to stand unavenged.

Ogai became very upset talking about this incident and its aftermath, and it is therefore very difficult to keep track of who "you" refers to in the above passage. She was angry at all the people involved in this incident: the rapist; her cousin (the rapist's wife, who refused to support Ogai, knowing that she would be responsible for providing the compensation pigs); and her husband for not vigorously pursuing a court case. In this passage Ogai is struggling to articulate a concept of consent and the fact that she did not give it: "It wasn't like I wanted you and accosted you. It was your lust, your desire, you wanted to do it to me and so you did . . . it wasn't I who did it, I had no intention of doing it." Dominant constructions of Huli female sexuality emphasize its reproductive and relational dimensions, as well as its proper custody by a woman's family or husband. Indeed there are strands of this relational logic in Ogai's own narrative. For example, one of Ogai's thoughts before she capitulated to her rapist was "After all, he's not my brother" (i.e., not from her clan), evidence of a concern with incest and kinship violations rather than the violation of herself as an individual. Similarly, she imagines herself saying to her rapist, "It was your lust, your desire, you wanted to do it to me, and so you did—so *now we should marry,*" thus framing the rape in terms of relationality and kinship, rather than as a personal violation, while at the same time subverting this frame through sarcasm. In the same vein, she sneers facetiously to her cousin, "Hey, cousin, you go marry my husband, and your husband can marry me." Her tacit assumption that her husband is the one who is owed compensation for her rape also suggests a sexuality embedded in relationality and properly safeguarded by male kin.

The more possessive or individualistic aspects of female sexuality are not culturally reinforced or elaborated, often making "lack of consent" difficult for women to convey in their narratives about such events. In point of fact, Ogai makes her lack of consent quite clear; however, she was not able to invest this representation with a moral and cultural weight that had significance for others. Since women are normatively "fenced in" by others, rape is primarily about the theft of a woman from these others. All that matters for the purpose of demanding compensation is that the sex happened. It does not matter whether the woman agreed or was forced; it does not matter what her assailant's motivations were; and it does not matter whether or how he humiliated her during the attack. But all these factors clearly mattered to Ogai: she was outraged that she was not given the opportunity to assert in a public forum that she had not initiated or consented to the illicit sex with her cousin's husband. She was also angry that her consent, or lack of it—as well as the verbal humiliation she endured—was of no structural or political consequence.

While rape was prominent in many women's accounts of what had led up to their acting as *pasinja meri,* other forms of violence—sometimes to themselves and sometimes to female kin—also figured in their narratives (twelve out of eighteen). Such incidents, like the rape described by Ogai, were often characterized as "trigger events"—moments of dark epiphany—and included the rape or murder of female kin, public humiliation by one's husband, and excessive marital violence.

Absent Men, Angry Women, and Economic Structures

While incidents of violence are quite striking in passenger women's narratives, and are asserted by many women (although not all) to be causal in their decisions to become passenger women, ultimately, it is the response by kin—or, more often, lack of response—to these violations, humiliations, and injustices that are of more import to passenger women themselves. Indeed, when women talked about the *keba* (rage) that motivated them to become passenger women, they were invariably talking about rage directed at their natal kin or husbands—not rage toward rapists or others who had transgressed against them. For example, it was Ogai's husband's and brothers' failure to demand compensation for her rape that prompted her to run away; it was Megeme's feeling of abandonment and exploitation by her kin after the court case concerning her rape that provoked her pattern of revenge promiscuity. Earlier in this chapter I asserted that it was emotion, not economics, that motivated passenger women. By this I meant to suggest that it is not rural poverty that initially drives Huli passenger women to sell sex (at least at this point in time), but anger at male kin. However, emotion and economy are not so easily disentangled: it is largely changing economic regimes, and the consequent conflicts and contradictions within social relations, that motivate women's wrath. In other words, it is useful to separate analytically motives that are directly economic (i.e., just trying to make money) from motives that are fostered by changes in economic structure. While passenger women's discourse of voluntarism and self-determination is quite striking (an issue discussed in more depth later in the chapter), their acts occur within and can be seen as a response to a changing economic context over which they have little control—in particular, the commoditization of social relations through wage labor and monetization of the local economy.

What women complain about most in their narratives of rage is the absence or apparent indifference of kin, particularly male kin, to women's experiences of violation or to their expectations of male support and reciprocity. As discussed in chapter 2, women tend to accept and internalize the notion that they need to be protected, disciplined, and "fenced in" by men. However, this internalization is not an unquestioning acceptance of male dominance or clan encompassment; rather, women perceive this organization of gender relations in some ways like a contract (also see Gregg 2003). Specifically, women—and men—say that it is men's responsibility to create an economic and social world in which women can act as *wali ore,* and women accept their encompassment by this world as long as men live up to their masculine obligations. One explicit expectation is that brothers and husbands uphold the value of female sexuality by demanding compensation, threatening tribal warfare, or exacting revenge when a woman is transgressed and appropriated by others. Additionally, those who benefit from the wealth a woman brings to her family and clan—whether through marriage or through compensation given for rape—should feel some sort of indebtedness to her (as long as she doesn't make a shameful habit of getting herself into situations where *nogo tauwa* must be demanded for sexual transgressions). What many women felt acutely after trigger events of violence—whether to themselves or to those they loved—was a failure of kin to fulfill obligations of reciprocity. Incidents of violence made them feel estranged from their kin—appropriated and transgressed by others—and then their kin failed to reestablish their relationality by failing to redress these injustices or, as in Megeme's case, by treating the incident as a venue for obtaining cash (or at least this is how Megeme perceived it in retrospect). Women's anger tends to be directed toward men because men are understood to be a synecdoche for the clan or family: it is men who publicly represent families and clans, who formally demand compensation pigs, and who take action by using, or at least threatening, collective violence.

However, as discussed in chapter 1, because of migration for wage labor, men are not always present to fulfill these obligations. The various mining companies that employ Huli men, for example, generally do not provide family housing, and many Huli women believe that men prefer it this way. Huli women often commented to me: "Tari men don't bring their wives with them to their places of work. The companies forbid it, and the men think this way also" *(Ol man Tari, ol no save kisim meri raun raun long ples bilong wok. Kampani save tambuim ol, na tingting bilong ol man tu olsem).* Moreover, a number of contemporary myths suggest that male places of work, mine sites in particular, are construed as analogous to the sacred sites of the past—places where men perform important cosmological work that requires the exclusion of women (Wardlow 2001). That men rarely come home and rarely bring their wives to their places of work is thus seen by women as conscious and deliberate decisions on the part of men. Ogai, for example, asserted that after she was raped, her husband *refused* to come home. She may have been right in her interpretation; however, what women often understand as men's refusal can feel to men like constraints beyond their control. Men employed in wage labor often say that while they enjoy the benefits that money brings, they also find employment unreasonably disciplinary, with employers deciding when they must get up, when and what they eat, how they use their bodies, when they can stop to rest, and when they are eligible for leave. Thus, men are not always able to come home and risk losing their jobs if they do. Moreover, as men increasingly sell their labor to mines and other distant companies, their identities become less embedded in the web of clan interests and obligations. Clan disputes often seem less compelling to them, and their moral attention and emotional investments shift to other arenas (also see LiPuma 1999). Modern constructions of masculinity—with their emphasis on commodity consumption, travel, and access to cash—reinforce this shift in identification. Women experience men's incipient individualism as a lack of clan support and solidarity, and some women—in response to trigger events such as those discussed above—respond with an act of negative agency: removing their bodily capacities from the custody of clan or husband by exchanging sex for money and keeping the cash for themselves.

Bridewealth and Negative Agency

The third theme prominent in passenger women's narratives—in addition to those of violence and men's moral and physical absence—is bridewealth. While the specific details may differ, the bridewealth system is implicated in each of the narratives that opened this chapter: Megeme felt her relatives were profiting financially from the forcible appropriation of her sexuality; Ogai felt her husband should have shown that he valued her sexuality by demanding *nogo tauwa* or threatening war after she was raped; and Tarali felt she had bought her own "freedom"—including sexual freedom—by supplying bridewealth to her father and brothers, and, moreover, wanted to deny her father any future bridewealth in order to punish him for his violent treatment of her mother and his refusal to let her attend her mother's funeral. These stories employ the same cultural logic: all of the women felt, in one way or another, disappointed, betrayed, or exploited by the bridewealth system—or perhaps more accurately, the contradictions and failures of the bridewealth system as it is currently practiced—and all of them saw promiscuous sexuality as a logical, if emotionally driven, response.

In women's narratives, bridewealth is both the social structure through which encompassing economic structures make their effects felt by Huli women and the instrument through which women enact their anger by exchanging sex for money. While one result of the incursion of capitalism into the Papua New Guinea economy is the physical absence of men due to wage labor—and the consequent social and moral vacuum in which women sometimes seem to find themselves—another result is people's need and *jelas* (desire) for money. And, as discussed in the previous chapter, one of the important means by which jobless men gain access to cash is through bridewealth: increasingly, men ask that a greater portion of bridewealth consist of cash instead of pigs. This increasing reliance on cash, combined with the anxiety that men are no longer upholding their end of the gendered social contract, leads many women to assert that women are now treated *"olsem maket"* (like market goods). By this they mean that they sometimes feel that women are valued primarily for the bridewealth they bring to their kin at marriage, and that once bridewealth has been received, kin are all too willing to abandon their obligations to women. For example, Ogai and Megeme both angrily complained that as clan members they had a right to economic assistance from their kin, but that kin often refused them this support. As Ogai put it:

• • •

Now when women are young their relatives look after them, give them money and soap and all sorts of things . . . but once you're married, our husbands are supposed to take care of us. Once we've given pay [i.e., bridewealth]—. It's all to do with bridewealth; "we gave it already" [your relatives will say]. "You're already married." They [your kin] won't see you [i.e., take care of you].

• • •

While many women may feel disgruntled by this loss of value, it is incidents like rape and the failure of kin to pursue traditional justice that expose the current contradictions of the bridewealth system and the ways in which its meanings—and the meaning of women in it—have changed. These incidents serve as triggers for some women to repudiate the system altogether and withdraw their sexual resources from sociality by exchanging sex for money. In order to understand the perhaps counterintuitive assertion that choosing paid, multiple-partner sexuality is a form of negative agency, one must remember just how central the bridewealth system is to the construction of female identity and subjectivity. Bridewealth is what "women are for," as the Huli say, and the bridewealth given for their sexuality (conceptualized as reproductive capacity) is what makes women *wali ore* (real women). Women are taught to be proud of the bridewealth they bring in to their families, and while women may not know and should not say clan genealogies, they proudly assert that they "create them" through the reproductive sexuality which the payment of bridewealth makes possible. Thus, while women may not be beautiful and pure in the way that men are, and although their physical sexuality is often denigrated as *"ngubi"* (smelly), they know that it is through them, and the reproductive energies and wealth that they embody, that Huli sociality and history endure.

Since women are "for bridewealth," the most disruptive thing any individual woman can do if she feels the bridewealth system has failed her is to thwart this system, and the most effective way of thwarting it is to remove her body from it. For example, Agili, one of the younger passenger women I knew, and one of the few who had embarked on this path before marriage, started to "passenger around" (that is, have sex for money) after her father killed her mother. She decided that she was going to "ruin herself," as she put it, so that her father would not be able to receive any bridewealth for her. She vowed never to let the man who had murdered her mother profit from her marriage, and if this meant never getting married and becoming a *pasinja meri,* then so be it. Eventually she met a man at a *dawe anda* who wanted her as his third wife, and she agreed, but only on condition that he not pay bridewealth to her father.[8] Thus, women who become *pasinja meri* enact negative agency by taking aim at their kin—particularly their male kin—precisely where women can hurt them most: through disrupting social reproduction by abandoning or refusing marriage, appropriating their own sexuality, selling it, and keeping the resources acquired for themselves. Indeed, *pasinja meri's* sexuality threatens human history as the Huli conceptualize it, which is primarily in genealogical terms: it suggests the possibility of a world in which women are no longer exchanged, valuables are no longer distributed, affines are no longer created, and the identities of children become indefinite.

Ambiguities of Agency: Problematizing Women's Narratives

One consistent dimension of passenger women's narratives is the degree of voluntaristic, self-determining agency they ascribe to themselves, both in their decisions to become passenger women and in their lives afterward. To provide an extended example, below is Megeme's description of a two-week period during her fourth marriage when she and her husband lived in Port Moresby. Before this marriage, Megeme had alternated stints of more commercialized sex work with stints of living for periods of time with men, some of whom gave bridewealth to her family in order to formalize the relationship as marriage. This fourth marriage dissolved soon after the events described below.[9]

• • •

He fought all the time and he never gave me money. I was tired of fighting. I would beat him bad enough to put him in the hospital, but he didn't feel it. He would just say, "That's OK. Cut me. Here's an axe," or "Here's a bush knife. Let's play." [He would say that?!] Yes, that's what he said. Please! We fought and fought. Not a day went by when we didn't fight. This was in Moresby . . . His ways—he drank and slept around. [And when you were with him in Moresby, did you sleep around too, or you were married and so you didn't sleep around?] Oh, when I was with him, it was hard to, very hard to—. I just stayed at home. It was too difficult [i.e., she was too closely monitored by her husband].

There was just one time when I [giggles], he told me, he told me it was his payday, and he told me to come, and I didn't know my way around town very well. So I took this woman from Kagua and another woman from Hagen. We went together to meet him, and then my husband wouldn't even talk to me. He didn't say the normal things like, "How did you get here?" or "Did you come to get some money?" He didn't say anything to me. He just took off in a bus and left us standing there like pieces of wood [i.e., her husband had specifically told her to meet him at work so he could give her money, but when she arrived, he ignored her. Megeme did not offer an explanation of his behavior, but it is likely that he objected to the women she brought with her, either because they had bad reputations or simply because he didn't want other people witnessing their private economic transactions]. I had something to say about that but my throat was blocked. I was so angry! I wanted to say something, but please! Tears were rolling down my face. [Huli people, women in particular, often describe extreme anger in this way—as a force that rises up from the stomach and so overwhelms one that one cannot speak. Only retaliatory physical action of some kind—fighting, suicide, finger-lopping, and more recently, revenge promiscuity—can alleviate this situation.]

I sat there for one hour until my throat was open again. Then I quietly asked the two other women, "Do you two know about the Boroko Hotel?" [The Boroko Hotel is known as a place frequented by prostitutes and their customers.] "Yeah, we know." "Let's go." So we went, and when we were outside the hotel a car pulled up to us. "Hey, you women!" "We're not doing anything." "Do you want to drive around with us?" "Let's go." So we got in and we drove all the way out to Sogeri, where the men bought some beer. They asked us, "Do you women want to drink?" The two other women looked at me. "I want to drink," I said. I was angry, so I wanted to drink . . . When we were finished drinking we went to Bomana, where the war cemetery is. We had sex, and then the men went to their house to get money and they said, "Let's go back to Boroko." They left us in the Dark Room [a bar where people drink and dance, known as a location where men can buy sex].

There were lots of people from Tari there. People from all over. And there was lots of dancing! Lots of beer! We sat at a table and some men came and gave us beer. So I got really drunk and I started dancing. They had to stop me from dancing—I was doing a sexy dance! And the security guard said, "If you dance like that all the men are going to come 'choose' you. You should take it easy." That's what he said. "Oh, did you pay my entrance fee? Did I come here because you told me to? I came because I wanted!" [Megeme, invoking a cultural logic of reciprocity and opposing it to one of autonomous action, is sarcastically asserting that because the security guard did not pay her entrance fee, he has no right to tell her what to do.] That's what I replied to the security guard, and then I punched him. Then he took me outside.

Outside I saw this warden-policeman that I knew from before. "How did you get here?" he asked. He was from the Sepik, and he previously had taken me to court here in Tari. I was married to a Sepik man before, and this man was his brother. I beat up my Sepik husband, and so this policeman took me to court. He had moved to Moresby and he was surprised to see me there too, and he told me he was working and asked me what I was doing there. "Oh, I'm working here too," I said. I was angry, so I said that. [Megeme feels the Sepik man is boasting about the fact that he has a job, so she is trying to mock and embarrass him by suggesting that she sells sex and that sex work is a job just like his.] . . . Then he told me to come with him. But me, I don't give anyone space. When I'm drunk no one else can say a thing to me. "Who are you talking to? Am I drunk because of the beer you bought for me? Did you buy me beer and so you think you can talk to me?"

[Again invoking a logic in which a "gift" confers the giver authority over the receiver's actions, Megeme is belligerently asserting that because this man did not buy her beer he has no right to assume that he can tell her what to do.] I said that, and then I hit him in the face with a Coke bottle. He fell down, and then he knocked me down and kicked me in the eye. Before all this happened a Tari man had come and seduced the two women I was with. He wanted to have sex with them, and so they had already left. I was all alone. I was bleeding and my eye was swollen shut.

Then a police car came up to us and they took the men to prison, but they took me to the hospital. They dressed my eye, and then the policeman took me to his house. [The policeman took you to his house?!] He said, "Your eye is messed up, but 'down there' you are just fine. Let's fuck." [He said that?] He said that. And I thought, "Small things. He saved my life and took me to the hospital, so why not?" So I stayed with him for one week. It was hard for me to see. My eye was swollen shut, and when I tried to look at something it felt like someone had forked me in the eye, and it was really red.

So we stayed together for one week, and one day he asked me if my eye was alright. It was better, and so we went to a movie theater. [The Starlight Drive-In or Wards?] Yeah—Wards. He took me there, and it was a James Bond movie. He was fighting with some black men. It was a magic one. [Oh, I know. There was a snake.] Yeah—the snake went inside the bathroom and wrapped itself around James Bond's neck. [Yeah—I remember.] It was a good movie, but it was hard for me to watch. When it was over I ran into one of my sisters [i.e., a woman with some sort of kinship relationship to Megeme]. She was living at the university and she came to see the movie. I went and stayed with her for one week, and she told me that my husband had been looking for me. He'd left his job at the airport, and he was searching for me, wondering if some people had killed me. He was checking in drainage ditches wondering if he would find me there alive, or if my body was already rotting.

So I went back home, and I found out that the women from Kagua and Hagen were in jail. My husband had said to them, "You two took my wife with you, and then you just left her somewhere, so you can go sleep in the jail cell!" So I went there and got them out. I told the jailers, "I'm still alive and I'm not a baby. They didn't put me in a string-bag and carry me around with them. I have legs, I have a brain. It was my decision to go." [The two women were released when Megeme demonstrated that in fact she wasn't dead and argued that in any case they were not responsible for anything that had happened to her.]

Then we went back to my house, and oh man, my husband saw me and said, "Please. Shake my hand!" I responded, "My hands are clean. You can touch my feet." I said that because, you know, feet are dirty. [Megeme's husband is making a friendly overture to her, but she is trying to provoke a fight. She suggests that he should not touch her hands because they are too clean for him.] He was in a state of shock and just stood there. Then he said, "Let's go inside. You can tell me your story inside the house. You can tell me what you've been doing for the past two weeks." So we went inside, and he told me to start talking. And I said, "You first. You're the man, you go first. Let's hear your story." "OK. That Friday when I got my pay I got really drunk, and I went to the house of this old woman from Simbu Province." "So how was the sex? Was it good with an old woman?" He didn't say anything. "Speak up! How was it? Don't worry. I've got a story to tell too." So we talked like that—real honest and crude and down to the bones. The Bible, you know? The road to heaven is there. [Passenger women often emphasize how important it is to be candid about one's sins, and Megeme, for one, often claimed that because of her candor she was more virtuous and Christian than the churchgoers who stigmatized her.] So he talked about how he had sex with this old Simbu woman. Then he said, "OK, your turn."

And I said, "OK. That day, after you left, we went to the Boroko Hotel. We were there in the doorway when a car pulled up and picked us up. We went all the way to Sogeri, and on the way the men bought two cartons of beer, and they asked which of us women wanted to drink, and I insisted on being the first one." That's what I told him. "Then we went to Bomana, to the cemetery, and then we had sex—one at a time in the car." Oh, he was upset. His throat was completely dry. He had no saliva, and he just stood there. "Is that all?" he said. "No—there's more," I replied. "When we finished, the men dropped us at the Dark Room and we went dancing and drank some more, and when we came outside I got in a fight and smashed the face of this man who was the brother of my previous husband. Then a police car came and took me to the hospital. They dressed my eye, and I told my story to the policeman, and he felt sorry for me, and he didn't care about you, about the fact that I had a husband." That's what I said to him. "So then we went to his house and did our 'business' for a week. We had sex for a whole week." That's what I said to him. "Aiya! Lies or the truth? Is she telling the truth or lying to me?" He said that.

Then he came at me and bit off my earlobe. [Megeme's earlobe was, in fact, tattered.] When he let me go, I grabbed a board that had nails in it and plenty of splinters, and I hit him here and here, and a nail went through his leg. So now it was equal: we were both bloody. I hit him and hit him and hit him. Later they had to stitch him up; I had slashed his veins, and his blood was flowing. It looked like he wouldn't have any blood left. I beat him up, and later he had to go to the hospital. But we were still fighting. We were fighting in the ocean. We were living in one of those houses on stilts over the ocean, and we were standing on the veranda, and then I jumped into the water. But the ocean has tides, and it goes and comes, and it was out when I jumped, and I cut my foot on an old tin can. Then he went and got an axe, and he wanted to cut me. I tried to hide behind some old scrap metal from World War II and cut myself again on my head. My head was cut and my foot was cut and there wasn't a person around who knew what was going on. We were in the sea, and no one saw us. He threw the axe at me. If I wasn't strong, my life would have ended in that water. We kept fighting, trying to find out who was strong and who wasn't strong. "I don't want to die from your fucking hands!" I yelled, and I won.

· · ·

This snippet from Megeme's quite tumultuous life history is dense with many of the issues discussed earlier: women's pride at their lack of physical fear and their fighting skills; the tensions between husbands and wives over men's wages; the way that *strong* (Tok Pisin) or *hongo* (Huli)—physical strength—is invoked as a metaphor for moral legitimacy; and the way that women respond to marital conflict by *"brukim banis"* (breaking the fence; flagrantly transgressing expectations that a wife will stay in the home). Moreover, it is important to note that Megeme's adventures do not conform to conventional or received notions of sex work; rather, they seem more like a combination of commercial transaction (the men in the Bomana cemetery), opportunistic affair (the policeman), and revenge promiscuity (the incident as a whole).

Here, however, I want to highlight the way that Megeme emphasizes her own agency—continually asserting her self-determination, her conscious (if not always "strategic") decision making, and her success in various social encounters because of her own individual skills and determination. Throughout this segment, Megeme emphasizes that her actions were deliberate and self-initiated: she dragged the two women with her to meet her husband and to the Boroko Hotel, she insisted on drinking the beer first, she determinedly performed her "sexy dance" to provoke the crowd, she resisted the guard's attempts to calm her, she started the fight with her Sepik former in-law outside the Dark Room, she got her two friends out of jail by arguing that only she was responsible for her actions, she provoked her husband into a physical fight, and she won both the game of sexual one-upmanship and the fight itself. Much like Nenge's narrative in chapter 2, Megeme's account is saturated with a seemingly self-authoring, autonomous "I"—the kind of "I" that one expects from "Western" discourses about self-experience, but that contravenes both dominant theorizations of Melanesian personhood and dominant theorizations of the Third World prostitute, figures who are respectively represented as constituted through relational networks or doubly dispossessed of self-determination by gender and economic structures. (Indeed, while ethnographers of Melanesia and feminist scholars of sex work have recently attempted to recuperate the agency of those they study, in this case, if one relies solely on Megeme's retrospective narrative, one must work hard to recuperate the structures that shape and give meaning to her apparent voluntarism.) Admittedly, Megeme also displays a cultural logic more familiar to ethnographers of Melanesia—an assumption that social action is constituted through reciprocity: she suggests that the act of giving—beer in this case—would bestow the giver with authority over her behavior. However, she undermines this logic at the very moment of positing it by belligerently asserting that nobody has, in fact, given her anything that would make her cede her self-possession. In a sense she is reiterating the rationale that informed her initial decision to become a *pasinja meri:* "my kin never give me anything"; therefore, she owes them nothing, and certainly not her submission.

It is also possible to see a fair amount of passivity in these events: Megeme allowed herself to be picked up by strangers and taken to the Bomana cemetery for sex, and she simply acquiesced when the policeman decided to take her home with him. Moreover, hers is an ambivalent "possessive individualism"—at once gleefully audacious and gloomily bitter, as if she has been coerced into acting as a "free agent," but is now embracing this mode of being, if only to defy those around her.

Reflecting on Female Agency: Retrospective versus Prospective Cases

When women talk about how they came to live as *pasinja meri,* many of them cite decisive moments in which they felt so disappointed by and angry at their kin that they deliberately chose in one fell swoop to ruin their families' chances at obtaining bridewealth for them, to bring shame upon their families, and to use their sexuality for their own purposes. The vignettes that started this chapter all came from retrospective narratives that made the act of becoming a passenger women appear intentional, decisive, and abrupt. However, given the "agentive ethos" of Huli women—that is, the inclination to narrate their lives in a triumphalist language of self-determination—and given a literature on sex work that tends to emphasize women's lack of agency, it is important to treat passenger women's retrospective narratives with caution. As Ortner reminds us, "The dominant often has something to offer, and sometimes a great deal. . . . individual acts of resistance . . . are often themselves conflicted, internally contradictory, and affectively ambivalent" (1995: 175–79; see also Abu-Lughod 1990). In this case, losing one's reputation as a *wali ore* (a good woman) is a heavy price to pay, and one might thus expect that women's "decisions" to become *pasinja meri* are not as calculated and resolute as they often represent them. The process of becoming a *pasinja meri* may be more gradual, circuitous, and conflicted than women's narratives suggest. Here the researcher confronts the methodological limitations of retrospective life history narratives. While social scientists have long acknowledged the motivated, constructed, and partial nature of retrospective narratives, this recognition does not make the recuperation of past events and processes any easier.

The younger Mangobe sisters, discussed briefly in the introduction, thus serve as a fortuitous and useful prospective case study of the possible paths some women follow on their way to becoming passenger women. From the same family, close in age and experience (although not in temperament), both of these young women slipped in and out of the category of *pasinja meri,* sometimes taking steps that they knew would damage their reputations and sometimes attempting to retrieve the moral status of *wali ore.* I knew both of them from the very start of my fieldwork, lived with one or both of them for long stretches of time over the course of two years, and thus observed their actions, discussed with them their motivations, and heard the way other people described them. Their stories provide more nuanced and temporally sensitive accounts of the various factors that predispose women to act in ways that lead to being labeled *pasinja meri,* as well as the actions they can take to either counter or reinforce this label.

Birime and Lirime Mangobe—both in their late teens or early twenties—were the youngest of five sisters. They had no biological brothers, which was already a strike against them: it meant that they had no one in their immediate family to discipline them, and so, according to Huli dogma about female development, they were more likely to be willful and easily led astray. The story of how their father had killed his daughter, Pugume, the third of the five sisters, was told to me within my first week of fieldwork. While there were various theories about this incident, Lirime and Birime subscribed to the idea that their father—old and infirm— knew that he would not live long enough to "eat" the bridewealth of his younger three daughters: Pugume had abandoned him to go to Mt. Kare with her mother, and the last two—Lirime and Birime—were too young for marriage. Lirime and Birime insisted that he had wanted to kill all three of them so as to punish their mother for her disloyalty and to prevent her from "eating" the bridewealth to which he himself felt entitled. However, he only managed to kill Pugume.

It was Lirime who found the body, sprawled out beside the bushes where she had draped her wet laundry, her head nearly severed by an axe. From a distance, Lirime thought her sister had fallen asleep by the side of the creek. When I asked her how this incident had affected her, she stated that she no longer liked old men: they were smelly, wheezing, *jelas* creatures who only wanted to "eat bridewealth." Moreover, she was angry that none of her kin had demanded compensation from her father's relatives for the murder of her sister. Indeed, this is one of the structural problems with a murder committed by the victim's father (which by all accounts is quite rare): the victim's father's kin cannot demand compensation because they would have to sue themselves. (The victim's mother's kin can demand compensation from the father's kin.) In this particular case, Pugume's mother's brothers lived quite far away and could not effectively threaten tribal warfare and did not pursue compensation. Lirime resented that her sister's murder had no political repercussions, and she bitterly protested that her mother's brothers didn't deserve any of her future bridewealth and were not going to get any. (Here, I would point out that Lirime's story so far parallels the model I have described for *pasinja meri*, although in her case the trigger incident was not her own rape, but her sister's murder.)

Both Birime and Lirime had lived outside of Huli territory, and this fact also was used by people in the community to cast a dim light on their characters. Birime was boldly flirtatious and boasted openly about having lived in Port Moresby, evidence for others that she had been negatively influenced by city ways. Like Birime, Lirime had been asked by relatives in Port Moresby to come work as their babysitter, but knowing that she was already gossiped about for having lived outside of Huli territory, she gave the plane ticket to someone else. (People covet tickets to the capital city, so this was a remarkable step to take.) Lirime, unlike Birime, was known to be strong, hardworking, and rightfully proud of her skills as a gardener, but people found her large stature and the teasing glint in her eye unnerving. My field assistant called her a *"rough meri"* (a woman who is too fierce). For example, it was widely known that Lirime had threatened to kill her older sister's children. She was furious that her sister, the second born of the five, was happily bearing children for a man who had given only a third of the expected bridewealth (her sister's own complacence about this situation was attributed to her "husband's" powerful love magic). Her reputation as "rough" masked a quite sensitive nature, however: when I mischievously (and tactlessly) told her of my field assistant's comment, she was obviously hurt.

When I first arrived, the reputations of both young women were on a downward trajectory—although I was not initially aware of this—and my presence did not help. I first lived with Tamu, the oldest of the sisters, and the only one who was irreproachably *wali ore:* she was married; she had three little boys who slept in the men's house; she never went to town and rarely to the local market; she worked in her gardens everyday; she supported her husband's political and economic interests; she never bought clothes, cigarettes, or small items of food for herself; and she went to church every Sunday. When I moved in, she invited Birime and Lirime to live with us in order to help me learn Huli and to accompany me wherever I went. Lirime's theft of my umbrella, and the subsequent minor court case, did not help her reputation. Nor was it helped when we were all evicted for the menstrual pollution of Tamu's youngest son. During that village court case, a number of men argued that it was Lirime and Birime who were to blame since they were known to flirt with men, go to Tari town quite frequently, occasionally attend bush discos, and then *"go insait long banis"* (literally, go inside the fence) of morally upright men like the complainant.

After our eviction, Birime and another young woman were caught having a romantic, perhaps sexual, tryst with two young men while the rest of the community was away at a funeral, a not unusual occurrence since funerals are one of the few events that throw many people together, making it possible for young people to sneak off without being missed. That she had accepted about US$3 from one of the young men was held up as proof that she was a passenger woman (she was also mocked for accepting so little), and the ensuing court case turned out to be a pivotal moment in her life. As it happened, the two young men were from the same clan, and it was agreed by all parties that it would be too costly for this clan to provide bridewealth for both young women; at best they could marry one and give *nogo tauwa* for the other. Birime immediately volunteered to be the one who got married, but she was flatly told that she had spoken out of turn. Who was she to direct the proceedings of the court case? As the case went on, in front of hundreds of people, it became clear that if the clan agreed to give bridewealth for one of the girls, it was definitely not going to be Birime. Moreover, everyone assumed that she had been the ringleader for the tryst. Finally, one well-respected man stood up and yelled:

. . .

Birime, you're not a quiet girl who stays in the *anda* [at home]. You go around and fuck lots of men. You told the other girl "let's go," and for that reason if the two boys go and die, you will have to pay compensation. *(Birime, I tambone andaga perene ndo. Agali tangama ibaga piaga harigoni. Ani puwa wali mendego "mba" laritagoni, ogoni naga igiri ogo labo pu hama bitagola I homole pere.)*

. . .

In other words, if the case was not settled and a tribal fight broke out because of it, and if the two young men were injured or killed during this tribal fight, then Birime would be held to blame because she was perceived to have lured the other young people into the assignation. She would be responsible for paying compensation for the young men. Few people really believed that this dispute would result in a tribal fight, and it wasn't likely that anyone would really have demanded compensation from Birime had a tribal fight taken place; nevertheless, this rhetorical strategy was an effective way of humiliating Birime and discursively constituting her as a promiscuous woman who was capable of corrupting others and creating rifts in the community. Yes, many people agreed, Birime was a *"tanga bubu"* (a person who fucks); indeed, *"ibu agali turia ayu tege tanga ka hayatagonigo"* (she goes around and fucks five men a day). The male kin of the other young woman argued forcefully for her marriage and implied that they would, in fact, be willing to wage war if bridewealth was not given for her, but no one stood up for Birime and demanded marriage. Not one of her male relatives even demanded *tauwa*, thus effectively announcing to one and all that they no longer considered her their sister. After this court case, Birime engaged in a number of other sexual liaisons, occasionally attended bush discos and *dawe anda,* and then ran away to Mt. Kare, where she was said to be living with a man and helping him look for gold.

Lirime, for her part, moved with me to my new household after our eviction, but stole money from me and was again evicted. She then moved in with a man who subsequently refused to pay bridewealth for her. I practically begged to be taken to the village court case about this situation, but her male relatives were so disgusted with her behavior that they themselves refused to go. Shortly after, Lirime left this man and moved back in with her mother. It was at this time that I had to leave the area after testifying about the fight between my host and his wife, and I was therefore no longer in direct contact with either young woman. I had been especially friendly with Lirime (and was never quite exciting enough for Birime, who seemed to expect much more outrageous behavior from a white woman), but whenever I asked about her, people expressed surprise and some disapproval that I would take an interest in someone who had stolen from me and who was a *pasinja meri.* Indeed, everyone assumed that she was, in fact, living as a passenger woman: I was told repeatedly that she had independently hopped on a PMV bound for Mendi and was surviving through the sale of sex. In fact, it turned out that she had stolen money from me because she wanted to extricate herself from the community where her reputation was irretrievably lost. She only wanted bus fare to Komo, a small government station south of Tari, where a male cousin had agreed to take her into his household. When this plan failed she approached a half-brother, the son of another of Mangobe's wives, who worked as a policeman. This man was known to be domineering, but he lived quite far from Tari, and she persuaded him to make her part of his household. There she reinvented herself as a completely obedient half-sister, spent her days in her peanut and sweet potato gardens, and always asked her half-brother for permission to go to certain places or to associate with certain people (including me).

Lirime and Birime conform in some ways to the pathway I have proposed for passenger women, but they also problematize this model, particularly women's assertions that they deliberately take up and embrace this subject position as an impulsive act of revenge. True to my model, they had witnessed brutal violence toward a female relative, which had then gone uncompensated and unavenged, and, at least in Lirime's case, this incident provoked a desire to retaliate through the denial of bridewealth to her kin. Nevertheless, although Lirime was more openly angry about the aftermath of their sister's murder, she made a concerted effort to recuperate herself as a *wali ore* after a tentative, and probably frightening, foray down the passenger woman path. Indeed, Lirime acted quite strategically: she knew, for example, that in order to salvage her reputation she had to get herself "under the legs" of her male kin, and she deliberately chose places far from her home community and men who were reputed to be strict traditionalists when it came to women. Birime too, after taking initial steps down the passenger woman path, quickly tried to backpedal, volunteering for a marriage she didn't really want in order to reestablish a *wali ore* status. She was not as savvy as Lirime, and her efforts failed miserably.

These more prospective cases suggest that the events that culminate in a woman's "becoming" a passenger woman are likely more tortuous than the accounts given to me by passenger women much later in time. Moreover, it is likely that women's "decisions" to embark on this path are not as deliberate as they often claim. What begins as an angry and retaliatory act may become more ambivalently evaluated, and women may even try to backpedal and salvage their reputations as *wali ore*. It may well be the case that many women take steps toward becoming *pasinja meri* and then manage to retreat when they realize just what it is going to cost them. Those women who go too far down the slippery slope may find themselves treated as, and then acting as, *pasinja meri*, whether that was their initial intention or not. As they are increasingly stigmatized by others as *pasinja meri* or *tanga bubu*, their attempts to reintegrate themselves may become ever less tenable.

Passenger women deny their kin the resource that women are most expected to subordinate to family and clan—their sexuality—and through this denial they claim it as an individual possession, a resource for themselves. In a structural sense, passenger women are simply responding to men's incipient individualism with an individualism of their own. Disappointed and angry at the failures of relationality in the modern context, passenger women remove their bodily capacities from the web of kinship in response to what they see as an analogous refusal by kin, men in particular, to perform their traditional obligations. Of course, while many women express discontent with men's individualism or with being treated *"olsem maket"* (like a market good), not all of them choose to become *pasinja meri*. Rather, specific moments of crisis—such as unavenged rape or the murder of close female kin—bring the failures of the bridewealth system into glaring relief and inspire an anger so overwhelming that it triggers the desire to spite one's kin and repudiate the system altogether.

Specifically, women engage in an embodied "negative agency." Like other women who physically disrupt village court proceedings, refuse to garden, or lop off their fingers, *pasinja meri* refuse to use their bodies for the purpose of genealogical reproduction and the social circulation of wealth and debt. Indeed *pasinja meri* act precisely within existing categories and discourses; they simply choose to disrupt every single one: Women should be "fenced in"? *Pasinja meri* hop on PMVs and run away. Women should be "for bridewealth"? Passenger women *guap guap nating* (have sex with no purpose) and keep any money they get for themselves. Women should not engage in sexually insulting or provocative language? *Pasinja meri* flaunt their public use of *hege* (curses), *mege* (insults), and *pobo bi* (sexy talk). Thus the agency exhibited by passenger women—while overwhelmingly seen as a transgressive departure from "traditional" femininity—both stems from and responds to constructions of gender that define women as able to influence the social field through bodily disruption.

This analysis of how some women come to "be" passenger woman may seem unduly voluntaristic; that is, I largely represent women as *choosing* this pathway (and not for economic reasons). Thus, for example, self-identified Huli passenger women tend to have many sexual partners, but sometimes this is figured as a deliberate choice (not something necessitated by economic duress). Ogai, for one, said she always got nervous when a man wanted to be with her more than once; "one day, one man" was her policy because, as she said:

· · ·

Like, the first time I befriended [i.e., had sex with] this man, that same day he asked me to meet with him again. Oh, you're this kind of man [i.e., she felt he wanted to establish some kind of ongoing relationship.] Forget it. I went and had sex with somebody else. I don't use the same man for more than one day. I hate them. It's like this: I already left my husband. I was fed up with him, and so I left him.

· · ·

In other words, Ogai avoided establishing an ongoing relationship with any of her partners because she had no intention of entering marriage or any other sort of relationship in which she could not *"raun long laik"* (go where she pleased).

My emphasis on passenger women's agency may seem to contravene much recent scholarly research on sex work, which tends to emphasize the ways in which women are coerced into this niche because of shifts in global political economies, often precipitated by structural adjustment programs and debt servicing (Schoepf 1992, 1993; Farmer et al. 1996). However, while passenger women themselves tend to use a voluntaristic idiom — at least in their retrospective narratives — it is certainly larger economic changes that shape their experiences and their choices. Monetization of the economy results in male out-migration for wage labor, which is experienced by some women as a kind of physical and moral absence or neglect; likewise, the growing need for cash results in the partial monetization of bridewealth, which women sometimes speak of as a kind of commoditization. Moreover, the prospective cases of Lirime and Birime suggest that the causal pathway to becoming a passenger woman is more complex and less under women's control than their retrospective narratives might suggest. Stigma and the inability to revise socially costly choices certainly also play a part in some women's "decisions" to "become" passenger women.

CHAPTER 5

"Eating her own vagina"
Passenger Women and Sexuality

Barbara de Zalduondo has criticized studies of prostitution that examine in clinical, quantitative detail the sexual behaviors that people engage in, arguing that "the interpersonal dynamics in sexual relationships are not being captured by studies of sexual 'behavior' in which acts are privileged over the identities and feelings of the actors . . . There is scarcely a mention of the affective dimensions of sexual behavior in the literature on AIDS, especially in the world regions where heterosexual transmission predominates" (1991: 238–39). Informed by a somewhat different literature, but in many ways recommending a similar prescription, Margaret Jolly has critiqued the "undue focus on men and the perduring masculinist presumptions of Melanesian ethnography of sexuality and reproduction" (2001b: 177). As a response to these challenges, this chapter examines the affective dimensions and cultural meanings of passenger women's sexuality, bearing in mind Sherry Ortner's observation that "the intentionalities of actors evolve through praxis; the meanings of the acts change" (1995: 175). I begin by discussing what passenger women's sexual behavior initially means to them and those around them, and then—bearing in mind the variability of women's experiences—trace how their understandings of their sexual practices change over time.

"Eating her own vagina": Consumer and Consumed

Because female sexuality is conceptualized as a resource produced by and for a woman's family and clan, when Huli passenger women exchange sex for money they are seen as accepting compensation for something that does not belong to them. In other words, the money a passenger woman receives when she "prostitutes" herself is not conceptualized by her kin as a discrete payment to her for her sexual services; rather, she is seen as stealing a resource that rightfully belongs to them.[1] In fact, many Huli contemptuously say that when a woman accepts money for sex she is "eating her own bridewealth," "eating her own *tauwa*" (the compensation payment given to a woman's kin or husband in cases of pre- or extramarital sex), or, more viscerally, "eating her own vagina." The conceptual association between female genitals and bridewealth is metonymic in nature: a groom's family gives bridewealth primarily for a woman's reproductive powers, or at least this is the dimension of her personhood that is emphasized at marriage; thus, her genitals are, in a sense, where bridewealth comes from. Reinforcing this semiotic equivalence are certain taboos. For example, a woman's father and brothers should never eat her bridewealth pigs since this is considered akin to incest and is said to result in illness (Goldman 1983). In fact, this taboo also applies to the money a passenger woman makes from selling sex: for a woman's father or brothers to eat food bought with this money is considered comparable to their consuming her bridewealth pigs, which, in turn, is seen as equivalent to "eating her vagina." Bridewealth is the quintessential wealth payment that is meant to be distributed to others; it is intended to pay back families in the previous generation who helped to "make" the bride by contributing to her mother's bridewealth, and it is meant to forge ties for the future. For a woman to "eat her own bridewealth," then, is to engage in an act that is the epitome of perverse selfishness.

Moreover, the phrase "eating her own vagina" is analogous to one that Huli parents use to chastise young children who refuse to share or who do not adequately express gratitude for gifts from others: they are told that they will grow up to "eat their own shit." To eat one's own shit—as dogs and pigs are seen to do—is to be less than human, as well as disgusting. One becomes fully human by cultivating exchange relationships and by refraining from selfish consumption. What one has, one must give, so that others will also give what they have. To repudiate this moral and pragmatic imperative is to sever oneself from the most reliable means of security as well as to repudiate that which differentiates humans from beasts. And, indeed, people say that passenger women eventually pay the price of their selfishness; as the conventional discourse goes, *pasinja meri* selfishly spend money on clothes instead of helping others, they don't tend their gardens, their male kin won't build houses for them, and so one day they find themselves old, dry-skinned, infertile, and homeless, with no one to take care of them.[2] As one woman said, "A *pasinja meri*'s mother will always have pity for her, because she went through the pain of giving birth to her, but her father and brothers will abandon her. If she asks them for food or money, they will tell her to go eat the cocks of the men she has fucked." Thus, not only is a passenger woman's "sex work" a kind of theft; it is also a form of perverse, ill-fated consumption.

Passenger women are aware that they are thought of as both selfish consumers and items for selfish consumption, and some defiantly flaunt these identifications by employing a pseudo-code in which the names of desirable items of consumption function as acronyms that stand for something salacious. Fanta, the soft drink, for example, stands for Fuck and Never Think Again; Pepsi, for *Plis em pen, sutim isi* (Tok Pisin for Please, that hurts; thrust more gently); Cambridge (a brand of cigarette), for Come Along My Boy; Remember I Don't Get Enough. Sometimes *pasinja meri* will simply shout out the names of these items and then burst into cackles of laughter, glancing around to see who "gets it." One woman I knew would sit with other women at market and loudly spell out the Huli word for vagina (H.A.M.B.A.), which she thought was extraordinarily funny because she was using a Huli word, but shouting out English letters, and no one seemed to get it. This genre of joking is a disruptive discourse that violates expectations of restrained language in public places and infuses commodities with sexuality—and not just any kind of sexuality. To "fuck and never think again" about one's partner is certainly not the kind of sexuality deployed in the reproduction of kinship, the creation of relational persons, or the proud command of lengthy genealogies. Thus, this word play confronts people with the fact that *pasinja meri* sexuality can, like a consumable commodity, be used once and discarded. At the same time, passenger women also associate themselves with commodities that everyone finds seductive and wishes they could buy at will.

One of the more clever puns I learned from *pasinja meri* was *"auksen pamuk,"* a spicy play on the name of a common trade store good, Ox and Palm corned beef. Ox and Palm is the most expensive and, in many people's opinion, best-tasting brand of canned corned beef in Papua New Guinea. At that time it was also the best advertised: many trade stores in the area displayed the bright red posters of an ox next to a palm tree, and there were large billboards at the outskirts of many highland towns. Because of its price, few Huli people I knew actually bought Ox and Palm; in fact most people bought the cheaper canned mackerel instead of any corned beef at all. Nevertheless, everyone knew that Ox and Palm was a symbol of excellence (if only in the corned beef department). *"Pamuk"* is

FIGURE 13. Outside a trade store, men in traditional dress consume two popular commodities, Coca-Cola and cigarettes. Passenger women figuratively associate themselves with such consumable commodities, and are also more likely than other women to partake of them, which contributes to the perception of them as selfish.

the Tok Pisin word for slut or whore; some people use it interchangeably with the term *"pasinja meri,"* but most people think of it as a harsher term. *"Auksen"* (from the English word auction) is the Huli term for second-hand clothes that are bought in bulk from Australia and sold in local markets all over Papua New Guinea (cf. Hansen 2000). In the Tari area, most women aspire to selling second-hand clothes as the best and most presti-gious way (other than having a job) of making money.[3] Selling used clothing is profitable: the clothes don't rot like produce does; there is less competition, since there are no used clothing stores in Tari; and the items available are the desirable Western ones—jeans, T-shirts, sweatpants, and so forth. Thus the hidden meaning of the canned corned beef, Ox and Palm, becomes *"auksen pamuk,"* or second-hand whore. The name of the most coveted corned beef becomes a code word for the most stigmatized female behavior, a behavior which in fact is yet a better way to make money than selling second-hand clothes and enables *pasinja meri* to buy the expensive brand of corned beef that others cannot afford.

"Partibility" and the Un-making of Relations

Many passenger women readily agree that what they are doing is a kind of theft from their kin—indeed it is exactly this logic that motivates many of them. However, they argue that their kin have forfeited custody over their sexuality by engaging in acts equally, if not more, selfish and venal than passenger women's exchange of sex for money. Some passenger women also talk about their initial acts of illicit sexuality as analogous to, but less extreme than, suicide. "I was so angry that I wanted to kill my-self, but instead I went and passenger-ed around," was a phrase often used by passenger women I interviewed. Since rates of female suicide are quite high among the Huli, the assertion of a desire to kill oneself should prob-ably be interpreted as more than just a rhetorical expression of anger. In-deed, I took women to mean this phrase quite literally: that they did, in fact, see illicit sex and suicide as somehow analogous acts, and that both were tenable responses to rage.

Marilyn Strathern's concept of partibility is useful at this juncture for making sense of this seemingly strange equivalence. As was discussed in the introduction to this ethnography, Strathern (1988) has argued that the Melanesian person is "multiply authored" or "multiply caused"; that is, the person is "made" through the gifts, actions, and substances of other persons. Thus, the person's seemingly unified and autonomous body is a historical precipitate of previous acts and relationships, and the person likewise has social effects through his or her partibility—through the wealth objects and bodily substances that he or she gives to others. Through an ongoing logic of generative synecdoche, persons give them-selves away (or are given away) to others by giving away parts (wealth objects, bodily substances) of themselves. Bridewealth marriage, then, can be seen as an act in which a woman's family gives away some of their reproductive potency as it is embodied in her vagina. Of course marriage is more than that, too: a woman's affines also receive "her hands" (her productive labor), her breasts (her ability to feed and nurture), her mind (her ability to strategize about the management of resources, although this aspect of her personhood is more culturally muted), and so on. The point, of course, it not that a group is giving away parts of a woman, but that these parts represent capacities within her that have been "made" by them and are therefore aspects of them.

To the extent that scholars of Melanesia draw on the concept of partibility, they typically assume that it works "positively" to generate and sustain relationality; however, the phenomenon of passenger women suggests that partibility can work "negatively" as well—that is, it can unmake relations. A passenger woman's personal acceptance of a payment for sex is seen as equivalent to her deliberate removal of her vagina (her reproductive energies) from the web of kinship. Rather than be transacted as an aspect of clan potency, she severs herself from the social body. From this perspective, then, it is not surprising that women draw a parallel between suicide and paid sex: both are the deliberate withdrawal of bodily capacities from relationality—the former the removal of the whole body, and the latter the removal of the reproductive body. Indeed, Huli women use the same idiom to explain incidents of finger-lopping, invariably saying that they were so angry that they wanted to kill themselves, but instead chopped off a finger and threw it at their opponents. Like finger-lopping, what looks like "prostitution" (that is, the exchange of sex for money) is said by passenger women to be a lesser alternative to suicide—that is, a reduction of clan potency through destruction, injury, or excision of the individual body or its parts. Put in other terms, when one's personhood is defined as encompassed by others, one powerful mode of agency is to make "partibility" literal—simultaneously amputating one's self from encompassing projects and "giving" others a useless version of one's self (a corpse swinging from a rope), or parts of one's self (the tip of a finger, cut off and thrown at the other in rage).

Delight and Disgust

Given this range of relational and bodily meanings, it is perhaps not surprising that passenger women's initial experiences of sex outside of the bridewealth system are not usually framed by them as "sexual" (i.e., as sensual or erotic experiences). Their affective desires at these pivotal moments are not oriented toward the male sexual partners they have at hand, but toward those persons whom they feel have betrayed, disappointed, or exploited them. The one desire they do express is to make these persons angry in return, and the exchange of sex for money is a very effective way of accomplishing this goal. As time passes, however, the personal meanings of their sexual liaisons change: the intention to outrage and humiliate kin or husband is satisfied, and they become more oriented toward their sexual partners, the money they can demand, and their own bodily experiences. In other words, their acts of illicit sexuality become less about the relationality of kinship—or, more accurately, its repudiation—and more about their own individual desires, whether for love, pleasure, autonomy, money, or the power that comes with being desired.

As one would expect, women express a range of attitudes toward the sex they experience as *pasinja meri*.[4] Some, for example, frankly describe the pleasure they have experienced since becoming passenger women and say that they choose their sexual partners to some extent for their physical attractiveness and the anticipation of sexual enjoyment. As Kame said:

· · ·

I get sexual feelings. Sometimes no. Some men I don't like. Some I like. Some don't do it right. They do it too fast and then I don't feel anything. If they do it nice and slow and I get lots of feelings, I like that. I think to myself, "Next time I'll have sex with that one again!" Old men, I don't get feelings. Old men are not strong and their penises are limp. Really! We have to work to make them hard. I get fed up with that. The limp ones, we have to work and work and work to get them hard. Please! It takes time! Forget it—go away! . . . When they touch me here [points to nipples], aiii! My feelings—altogether something else! Really high. Now please! "I'll just lie back and you do it!" And sometimes men suck on your nipples. That policeman I told you about, he did that, and aiii-o! When babies have sucked on my nipples, it's never been like that. This was something else! Really good. I was really turned on! I just lay back and thought to myself, "Give it to me. Do your work. Satisfy yourself." . . . When we kiss, I don't feel anything, that's just eating each other's mouths.

· · ·

Similarly, Megeme once observed that "people only think women don't feel desire because it's not visible the way a man's penis is." She herself loved that feeling of an erect penis inside her, she grinned, squeezing my arm firmly with both her hands in an attempt to demonstrate what it was like. On another occasion, when I asked her whether she enjoyed sex with men who paid her, she asserted that even the Bible (the ultimate authority according to her, though nevertheless open to idiosyncratic interpretation) showed that women had lots of sexual desire. As she explained it, the Bible employs "parable talk" (i.e., metaphorical or cryptic language) when it tells of the fruit that Eve was persuaded to eat by the serpent. What really happened, she claimed, was that Eve had sex with the serpent and enjoyed it so much that when she saw Adam's penis she wanted to try it too, and so she seduced him. As Adam became aroused, his semen began moving down from his brain into his penis, but God caught them before he could actually ejaculate, and a ball of semen got caught in his throat, making it look like he was in the middle of swallowing something (thus the metaphor of fruit, and thus Adam's "apple"). Since Eve is the mother of all women, Megeme explained, other women must be like her—they like sex.

Most self-identified passenger women, however, were reticent to talk about their bodily experiences, their thoughts about sex, or whether their experiences of sex as passenger women were different from those they'd had with previous husbands or *lawini* (romantic interests). And most were more ambivalent about sex than the above quotes would suggest. Indeed, the above observation was quite uncharacteristic for Megeme, who usually grimaced when I asked her about sex and described it as dirty and disgusting. She always carried a small towel or baby diaper, she said, and insisted that her partners dry off her genitals after the act—she herself couldn't even look at her own genitals after sex, let alone wipe them dry. Men were the ones who wanted it, she sniffed, and so they should be the ones to clean up afterward. Many women expressed a similar aversion—not so much for the act of sex as for sexual fluids (cf. Herdt and Stoller 1990).

This aversion suggests that women, or at least some of them, internalize dominant Huli discourses that describe female sexual fluids as *ngubi* (smelly), dangerous, and polluting. Indeed, a few women asked me why men would pay for something that they knew was dangerous to them, and two women I interviewed said that they had given money to men after a sexual act—not as payment for a man's sexual services, but as compensation for having "damaged" him. Tiago, for example, spoke guiltily of the time she'd agreed to have sex with a young man who approached her on the road (and by young she seemed to mean late teens or early twenties). She'd had misgivings even as she agreed to the liaison because the man was "not married and didn't have children." In other words, as a never-married man whose body had not yet, as passenger women often say, "get used" to sex, he was more vulnerable to the dangers of her body. (Passenger women often use the English phrase "get used"—as in being habituated to something—to describe whether a man's body is either vulnerable or inured to the dangers of female sexuality. And, in general, they prefer to have sex with married men who have children, since a man's fertility indicates both that he is healthy and that his body has been "broken in," as it were, by sex with his wife.) In recalling the incident, she surmised that it must have been his first time because he did not seem to know what he was doing. When it was over his penis was swollen and scraped, and Tiago blamed herself, saying that he was too young for sex, while her vagina was "the big vagina of a woman who already has children." Her vagina was just "too strong" for him, she declared, and so she gave him 5 kina (about US$3 at that time) because, as she said, "I damaged him" *(Mi bagarapim em)*.

Nevertheless, even while subscribing to the dominant idea that the bodies of men—especially young men—are vulnerable and those of women are dangerous, passenger women also consider alternative, counterhegemonic propositions. Many assert, for example, that men's sexual fluids are also "hot" and dangerous, and they express concern that their exposure to many men's semen will prematurely age them, dry out their skin, or make them weak—anxieties that mirror men's about female sexuality. Complicating such discourses still further, Tarali insisted that excessive semen from one man (one's husband) was polluting, but that small amounts from many men actually made women healthier. As she said in response to my question about whether semen was potentially polluting, or whether it might age a woman or dry her out, "Now, women who passenger around, they use all sorts of men, and so their skin can't be damaged. Their skin gets nice and fat. [Why?] Well, think about it— the semen from all sorts of men goes inside them. That means they can't have children, so instead the semen makes their skin fat." In this conceptualization, far from being dangerous, men's sexual fluids are innately life producing. However, in order for a fetus to form, a woman must accumulate the semen of one man inside her through repeated sexual acts. Since passenger women accumulate small amounts of semen from many men, but not a critical mass of semen from any one man, the semen's generative power works to enhance passenger women's health. Tarali's assertion was likely informed by, and intended to contradict, the common contention that passenger women get *"sik gonolia"* (the blanket Huli term for all sexually transmitted disease) because the different seminal fluids in them form a chaotic mass of heat that causes disease. Here, then, Tarali was less concerned with undermining received notions about the dangers of female sexuality and more concerned with contesting the stigma associated with the sexual practices of passenger women.

One aspect of their sexual experiences that many *pasinja meri* are less reluctant to talk about, again with frank protestations of both delight and disgust, is their partners' requests to try sexual practices that women consider nontraditional and somewhat outré—specifically, allowing men to gaze at or touch their genitals and oral sex (with either partner as recipient).[5] The few men with whom I felt comfortable discussing this issue also characterized these practices as nontraditional and explained that men who migrate out of Huli territory often learn about them from pornographic videos, magazines, and playing cards, and associate them with both modern and white masculinity (since, as they pointed out, the bodies seen in these visual representations are usually white). Indeed, more worldly Huli men deride "traditional" sexuality as *"olsem pig na dog"* (like pigs and dogs), by which they mean that it is oriented solely toward vaginal penetration and reproduction, and is not concerned enough with aesthetics, erotics, and *"kainkain style"* (all kinds of styles). Interestingly, it is usually women who use the phrase *"olsem pig na dog"* to disparage male promiscuity in the contemporary context and to contrast it with an idealized past in which men were properly self-disciplined and ascetic (see also Zimmer-Tamakoshi 1997). Men these days (say women) *"guap guap nating"* (literally go up, go up nothing; have sex for no reason or with no purpose). A "nature/culture"—or at least animal/human—antinomy is at play in both these rhetorical deployments of *"olsem pig na dog"*: in one, men are inappropriately animal-like because of their excessive lust; in the other, wives are inappropriately animal-like because they resist stylistic innovations that would make sex more than an act of reproduction or bodily release.

And, in fact, wives are often reluctant to try such nontraditional sexual behaviors—perhaps primarily because they are associated with *pasinja meri* (i.e., only a whore would do that). Being a *wali ore* (good woman) is associated with the work of reproduction and child rearing; *wali ore* are the mothers of children, not the erotic partners of their husbands. Self-identified *wali ore* see such sexual experimentation as contravening both proper masculinity and proper femininity: men are supposed to exercise proud self-discipline over bodily desire, and women are supposed to protect men from the dangers of female sexuality. (Indeed, some older married women I interviewed objected to family planning on these same grounds, arguing that the Huli sense of themselves as a moral people was bound up in men's self-disciplined dedication to strict rules of sexual avoidance. The desire to use artificial contraception—which, as advertised, allows people to have sex whenever they want—was thus perceived as an admission that men could no longer discipline their sexual desires, which was tantamount to forfeiting moral, and thus cultural, worth.) Thus, *pasinja meri* become the medium through which men experiment with these practices. Self-identified passenger women, again as one would expect, express varying opinions about their forays into new sexual territory. Many say they refuse to engage in oral sex, citing anxieties about pollution or flatly stating that "mouths are for eating and genitals are for sex." Most, however, are quite willing to let men look at and touch their bodies, or to try different sexual positions (as long as they involve vaginal penetration), saying that these things take little effort and are often pleasurable.

The Extortion of Desire

More prominent than any discourse of bodily delight or disgust in passenger women's observations about sex is a discourse of sexual power—a theme I came to think of as "the extortion of desire"; that is, the potency passenger women feel in the face of a man's naked want. I begin my exegesis of this "extortion" with a well-known Huli myth that, while playful, nevertheless captures the Huli construction of sexual desire as a kind of weakness that can be exploited by its object.

. . .

Once there was a woman named Bebego Wane Pandime. There was also a man whose name was Gambe Kogo Ralu. Bebego Wane Pandime lived alone on her land, and Gambe Kogo Ralu lived alone on his land. One day Gambe Kogo Ralu was out walking during the dry season and he became very thirsty. He spied two *keromi* fruit (red fruit the size of small papayas which grow on vines that coil around trees). He was extremely happy. He climbed up the tree and grabbed the two *keromi* fruits and held one in each hand. Suddenly he heard a voice say, "Gambe Kogo Ralu, it's the dry season, and you must be thirsty. What kind of fruit are you trying to pick? Those are my breasts you've got in your hands, and I want them back." Bebego Wane Pandime then yanked her breasts out of his grasp. Gambe Kogo Ralu was very angry and embarrassed, and as he climbed down the tree he muttered to himself, "How can I get even?"

One day Bebego Wane Pandime went to her garden. Her house was on one side of a river and her garden was on the other side. A huge rainstorm came, flooded the river, and swept the bridge away, leaving her stranded. She followed the river downstream looking for a place to cross and finally found a beautifully constructed bridge—not just a foot bridge, but one with handrails as well. She had one hand on each handrail as she made her way across the river. Then she heard a voice yell out, "Bebego Wane Pandime, you think you're crossing a bridge, but now I'm taking my arms back!" The handrails suddenly disappeared, leaving Bebego Wane Pandime balancing precariously on the bridge. "This bridge is my cock, and I'm taking it back," Gambe Kogo Ralu yelled out again. Bebego Wane Pandime plunged down into the middle of the river. The flooded river swept her away and threw her onto shore far downstream. Feeling cold and ill she shivered miserably as she made her way home.

She arrived home thinking that she would light a fire, but all the embers in the hearth had died. She looked through the ashes and could find only one tiny burning ember. She blew and blew on it, but couldn't get a flame to come up. She blew and blew with all her might. Then she heard Gambe Kogo Ralu jeer, "Bebego Wane Pandime, you're cold and trying to light a fire. Well now I'm taking my cock back." He then removed the one red ember. The poor woman didn't know what to do. She went to sleep cold, shivering, and hungry.

One day Gambe Kogo Ralu went on a journey. He walked on and on, and on the way a huge rainstorm came. The rain soaked him to the skin, but there was nowhere for him to get out of the rain. Then he came upon a beautiful house with tall house posts. So he went inside, put down his string-bag and his axe, and then began rubbing sticks together very quickly and made a huge fire. He rubbed and rubbed and rubbed and started a huge fire. He fed it with sticks until it was blazing, and then he fell asleep. As he was dozing off, he heard the voice of Bebego Wane Pandime jeering, "So now you think you're cozy and falling fast asleep," and then she removed her two legs. Suddenly the house vanished! The house posts had been her legs, and the nice dry roof had been her grass skirt. Gambe Kogo Ralu was left to be drenched in the pouring rain. He was furious and shouted, "Bebego Wane Pandime, you've tricked me and really treated me badly now!" Then he thought to himself, "But what can I do in revenge? We've both tricked each other and treated each other badly, and neither of us has won, so what should we do? Let us forget all this and get married." And so they did.

•   •   •

This story never fails to elicit gales of mirth at the moments of salacious revelation: he thought he had fruit in his hands, but it was her breasts! She thought she was blowing on a glowing ember, but it was his cock! Sexual desire, while figuratively concealed, is depicted in this narrative as something that feels like excruciating need: his penis is a bridge when she is desperately stranded on the wrong side of the river, her genitals are a toasty fire when he is soaked to the skin. These metaphorical scenarios suggest that sexual desire is an inevitable but potentially humiliating weakness. Heterosexuality is both a kind of complementarity—the ability of one gender to meet the needs and desires of the other—but also a kind of combat fought through the manipulation of desire: whoever is able to put the other in a position of abject desire (i.e., must have the fruit, must use the footbridge) is the winner. And this is the way passenger women often talk about their partners—whether these partners are long-term boyfriends or something more like customers.

It is acknowledged by men and women alike that in the game of love it is not a level playing field, for among the Huli it is men who are considered the epitome of beauty and that which is desirable (Glasse 1974; Goldman 1983).[6] As in many New Guinea highlands societies, a person's appearance—often referred to as their "skin"—is thought to reflect his or her internal moral state (A. Strathern 1977; M. Strathern 1979; O'Hanlon 1989). Since men are both "naturally" and ritually more pure than women, they are also literally more attractive—that is, they can attract the attention, desire, and goodwill of others—which, in turn, makes them effective social actors. Further, men can display and enhance this attractiveness through self-beautification. Thus, it is little boys whose appearances are carefully attended to by kin, and, during ritual celebrations, it is men who slick down their bodies with oil; paint their faces with bold yellow, black, and red paint; and don the long woven aprons that cover them in the front, but provocatively provide glimpses of their thigh and gluteal muscles from the side.[7] What woman could resist a man whose skin had a rich rubicund glow and whose head was emblazoned with a wig of bedazzling bird-of-paradise feathers? older men asked me. Seeing such men walk around town, I myself was arrested by their aura of fierce self-possession, as well as their greased up hamstrings. Women, by contrast, are not considered "naturally" beautiful and pure in the way that

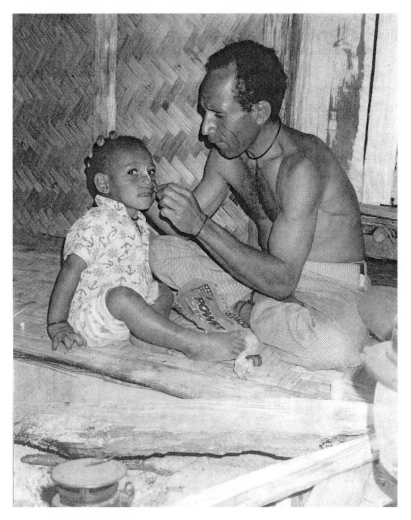

FIGURE 14. Ato decorates the face of his sister's son with traditional Huli colors, red and yellow. Huli men are taught at a young age that they are the gender that should attend carefully to physical appearance and beautification.

men are; their skins are duller and they are *ngubi* (smelly). They are less desirable.

Dominant Huli discourses about masculinity also emphasize men's *hongo* (strength, moral fortitude), self-discipline, and control over desire, including romantic and sexual desire (also see Johnson 1981). For a man to concede that he wants sex for purposes other than reproduction—let alone that he is willing to pay for it—is thus to admit that he has relinquished the sexual self-discipline expected of proper masculinity. Not surprisingly, then, passenger women interpret men's readiness to pay for sex as a testament to their powers of attraction. To get a man so aroused that he loses the moral strength and self-control that is a defining characteristic of Huli masculinity is a source of pride, and it is in this way that payment for sex with women is a kind of extortion. While Western discourses often (though certainly not always) construct desire as active and agentive, and being desirable as passive, and thus supposedly not agentive (e.g., the power of the desiring "male gaze" versus its object), among the Huli, to be desirable is to gain potential efficaciousness. Indeed, perhaps nothing feels more agentive than removing someone else's self-determination from them by putting them at the mercy of desires that you yourself have inspired. And, according to passenger women, men's willingness to pay for sex is an indication of such desires; thus, Megeme explicitly boasted that by getting men to pay for sex she was *"daunim man"* (literally, downing men; subjugating them; see also NSRRT and Jenkins 1994: 102–3).[8]

Passenger women derive much pleasure from titillating men and eliciting their desire.[9] Megeme, for example, once dragged me around Tari town trying to point out the men who got erections just from seeing her walk by (or so she claimed). She explained matter-of-factly that Huli men liked to wear second-hand, imported trousers, but that they didn't wear underwear, and so it was easy for her to see their erections. She also boasted that men had told her that they liked having sex with her because her vagina wasn't *"ngubi"*—it was *"swit"* (pleasant, good-tasting)—and Megeme was determined to keep it that way by spending part of her money on deodorant sprays which she used "down there." Other passenger women, although not as crude (or analytical) as Megeme, also gloated that men found them desirable, and often exhibited a gleeful and triumphant fascination with male desire. As Kame said, "I just reach out and touch his penis, and it gets hard just like that. Sometimes I get them all hot and then I run away. They say, 'Hey, I've got an erection, let's go do it,' and I'll say, 'Buy me first. If not, piss off!' That's what I say."

Thus, although the commoditization of female sexuality is clearly taking place—that is, passenger women exchange sex for money—it is described by many passenger women as an empowering transaction; it shows that they are so desirable that a man's *hongo* deserts him and he is willing to part with cash. Of course this sense of empowerment is solidly embedded in a complex web of local meanings. Thus, for example, pas senger women might not be so taken by men's desire if women were not said to be made of such poorer stuff than men. Likewise, money does not have quite the same meanings as it does in the West (Akin and Robbins 1999): the potential for money to be "dirty lucre" is not inherent in the cash form and does not automatically sully those who exchange themselves for it. Indeed it is important to keep in mind that while passenger women are stigmatized, much as prostitutes or sex workers are elsewhere, it is not because they forfeit their dignity or female purity for money (Wardlow 2004). Rather, it is because they are seen as repudiating their kin by refusing to play their prescribed female role in the bridewealth system. Passenger women's interpretation of "commoditization" also contradicts dominant Western assumptions that the person who has the money to pay is the one in the position of power; from their perspective, the willingness to pay is a weakness which both indicates and enhances the power of the "seller." Not surprisingly, then, passenger women are usually adamant about discursively positioning men, not themselves, as the desirers and instigators—in Huli, the *tene,* or cause—of sexual encounters.[10] As Ogai said in response to my question of whether she enjoyed sex: "Like, if the man wants it, we go and take care of their worries. As for lust, I don't think so. This is what I think: 'Man, you really wanted me to go with you,' I say this to them. 'Only because of you, because you will be happy, I went with you.' Really I say this to them. 'You yourself wanted to be happy. You wanted a woman and so I came to you.' "

Of course it is important to be cautious in interpreting passenger women's assertions about money and male desire. For one, it is difficult to know whether such assertions have much purchase in the wider population. Do men, for example, understand paying for sex as a failure of *hongo* or a concession to female desirability? (As is discussed below, other women do.) Perhaps more important, it pays to be wary of attributing too much interpretive force to local cultural logics; that is, I would not want to be taken to mean that the commoditization of female sexuality isn't really taking place among the Huli—despite the exchange of sex for money—because gender and money mean something different there. While gender and money are, in fact, constructed differently, important in making these local meanings sustainable is that Huli society is not (yet) fully monetized; there are not (yet) landless Huli peasants; and women are not (yet) impoverished by national and global economic structuring.[11] In other words, one cannot disentangle semiotic structures from material structures, and it would likely be difficult for Huli passenger women to sustain a sense that they are in a position of power if their economic circumstances were more perilous. Nevertheless, while it may eventually be the case that Huli passenger women will act from a position of weakness defined in economic terms, at the present moment weakness is defined more in terms of a gendered politics of desire in which men are the losers (and not always graceful losers, as will be seen).

That other women share this model of desire can be seen in the fact that *pasinja meri* often find themselves called upon to act as experts in *hubi bi* (literally, trap talk; love magic)—spells that can be put on food, cigarettes, Coca-Cola, betel nut, or any other consumable and then given to a male "beloved" so as to coerce his affections. Because women are not thought to be naturally beautiful, it is suspected (by men) that they regularly resort to *hubi bi* in order to cultivate male ardor and attachment.[12] And while I gloss *hubi bi* as love magic, it is not a "loving" act; like any kind of sorcery or magic, it is an act of aggression, but with the intention of forcing the affections of the target. Thus, while women talk about *hubi bi* as a means of securing the men they love, they also say that *"hubi bi save daunim man"* (love magic subordinates men). Indeed, women who relentlessly pursue powerful *hubi bi* come to be called *"kaupi wali"* (bitter women)—a nickname I was jokingly given for asking so many women about *hubi bi*. Women's stories of *hubi bi* triumphs are met by other women (as long as they are not strict Christians) with expressions of both glee and contempt: "He thought he was such a 'strong' man, but *'hongo nahe'* [he's not strong]," women say. *Hubi bi* is said to work through sexual desire; it makes men *"tingim bol tasol"* (think only about/with their penises); lust is used to create an emotional attachment. Thus *hubi bi* victory stories also often elicit raucous crows of: *"Em hangamap pinis!"* (he's hung up, trapped), a sexual innuendo implying that the *hubi bi* spell has snared its target, but also that the man's penis "is snagged in the woman's 'hole' " *(hangamap long hul bilong meri).*[13] Since *pasinja meri* are thought to have had many a man "hung up" in their "holes," other women often assume that they have special techniques for capturing the desires (and economic resources) of men. (Thus a certain grudging admiration of passenger women exists alongside a discourse of contempt for their selfishness and promiscuity.)

Pasinja meri are also thought to be more conversant with love magic because they are usually well traveled. The Huli assertion that physical aggression is morally superior to sorcery as a form of combat means that people self-consciously distance themselves from knowledge about magic and assert that to attain effective magic (of any kind), you have to go elsewhere, or at least buy it from individuals from elsewhere. Thus, passenger women's *hubi bi* is often considered superior to the homegrown variety simply because they bought it or learned it while they were living outside of Huli territory. Megeme, for one, was so notorious for her travels and her sexual liaisons that many women pleaded with her to share her knowledge. Megeme initially insisted that she had no special knowledge at all and that it was simply because her vagina was "sweet" that men liked to be with her. But, as Megeme tells it, women persisted in badgering her to reveal her secrets, and so finally, out of impatience and a malicious impulse to take advantage of women who were so willing to be suckers, she began making up love magic. She would order women to bring her special types of stones, plants, and pieces of writing paper; write whatever came to her on the paper; wipe her own underarms with the stone; wrap the whole thing up in a package of leaves; instruct the women to run the package under their legs (thus symbolically making the male target "under the legs" of the woman); and then direct them to place the package at the top of the door frame (again so that the male target would be "under the legs" of the woman as he walked through the entrance to her house). She adopted an exacting air and fabricated elaborate injunctions and taboos about using certain kinds of soap and washing at certain times of day. And then, she said, her spells began to work. One after another, women came to her with extra money and gifts to express their gratitude for the resounding success of her magic. Eventually Megeme came to believe it herself; perhaps, she smiled, she did in fact have some kind of attractive power that she was able to put in various objects or spells.

Condoms and the New "Sexual Antagonism"

While passenger women are proud of their desirability and their relative worldliness, they are also careful not to flaunt these qualities too publicly, for men are said to resent and punish *pasinja meri* for such *bighed* behavior (see also Zimmer-Tamakoshi 1993b). Tales about the violent comeuppance of *pasinja meri* who overstepped the line were easy to come by in Tari, and when I asked a group of nurses at Tari Hospital about the high homicide rate of Huli women, they flatly opined that those women who were not killed by their husbands were *bighed pasinja meri* who were probably killed by men they had resisted. Many of the passenger women I interviewed had been raped, and passenger women were quick to say that the same men who paid them for sex could at a later time attempt to punish them for this payment. They articulated a number of reasons for men's antagonism. The two most prominent, and related, reasons were women's presumption that they could exercise choice over sexual partners, what Gail Pheterson (1993) has called "the right of refusal"—that is, the right to reject a potential sexual partner for any reason—and (rarer, because Huli passenger women tend to be quite careful about this) women's open attempts to elicit male sexual desire through visual display or erotic talk.

Huli passenger women frame their sexual practices as acts of autonomy and freedom; *"Mi raun long laik"* (I do as/go where I please) is a phrase commonly used by passenger women to explain how they differ from other women. From their perspective, this freedom includes choice of sexual partner: no man has paid bridewealth for them, so no man has claims on them, they say, (and if a man has given bridewealth for them, as is often the case since many are on the run from husbands, they expediently assert that their husbands have done something to forfeit their claims). In contrast, according to some men, passenger women are women who belong to no one, and should therefore be available to anyone. They are "loose," as some men say—not in the North American sense of being sexually available, but in the sense of having cut themselves loose from their social groups; they are adrift and thus should be there for the taking.

Moreover, they are the women who have the least right to a sense of self-worth and self-determination. So ignominious a person should not feel entitled to reject whomever she pleases, and yet passenger women are the ones who most display these characteristics. Indeed, some passenger women observed that as long as a woman doesn't resist rape, a man will often give her money afterward anyway, suggesting that it is women's sense of entitlement to sexual choice, more than giving money itself, that angers men. This resentment seems to be exacerbated if a passenger woman is perceived as overtly attempting to provoke male desire through her dress, body language, or verbal communication. As was found in one nationwide study of sexual practices, "The most common reason given by men for punitive sex in this study was to teach the woman not to be sexually arousing" (NSRRT and Jenkins 1994: 104). Among the Huli, women's blatant attempts to arouse men are interpreted somewhat as *hubi bi* is—as an attempt to undermine male self-determination. Thus, for example, a number of passenger women explained that they would certainly engage in *pobo bi* (literally, hot talk, sexually arousing talk) once they had agreed to have sex with a man, but not before, since this could be construed as a kind of boastful sexual bravado and as an attempt to *daunim man* (subdue a man).

Megeme, for one, had just barely escaped being gang-raped on one occasion for titillating and then rejecting a group of men. As she explained it, she had gone to a party in Lae (the second largest city in Papua New Guinea) where at some point during the evening she found herself gyrating over a young man from another highlands cultural group while doing her "sexy dance" (his party claimed that she had straddled him, and she claimed that he had crawled under her). The young man's compatriots accused her of "polluting" him, but she asserted that the real cause of their anger was that she had aroused them and then refused to have sex with them. They attacked her as she left the dance, but the confrontation quickly became redefined as an ethnic conflict when some Huli men from the party came to her rescue. She later had sex with some of them as a way of thanking them, thus positioning her female body as a site of masculine, ethnic struggle. That she, a Huli woman, refused to have sex with ethnically other men, but agreed to have sex with Huli men made her promiscuity less problematic for them.

Not only does this case demonstrate the potential dangers of being perceived as deliberately eliciting and then rejecting men's desire, it also suggests that anger about *pasinja meri*'s presumption of sexual choice may have as much to do with relations between men as with *pasinja meri* themselves. These tensions are more often about class than about men's ethnic or cultural group identification. Because *pasinja meri* do usually choose their own sexual partners, and do, for the most part, choose men who can afford to pay them, they come to both symbolize and reinforce emergent class differences between men. Indeed, older men with money tend to take a more indulgent and humorous tone when talking about passenger women, while the "grassroots"—a term often used by the Huli to refer to young men who have traveled outside Huli territory, have an acute sense of economic disparities, and are without a source of income—express the most antagonism toward *pasinja meri*. Thus, hostility—and consequent violence—toward *pasinja meri* may largely be about the role that they play in symbolizing the marginalization of men with less access to cash. That it is stigmatized women who cause these humiliations of class (Errington and Gewertz 1998) only exacerbates this antagonism.

The concept of "sexual antagonism" was once so common in the literature on Papua New Guinea that it was often treated as a given, rather than as a dimension of social life that required exegesis. Then, in an influential article on sex and gender in Melanesia, Herdt and Poole (1982) critiqued the notion of "sexual antagonism," demonstrating that it had been used to describe an immense variety of gendered phenomena in different cultural areas of Melanesia. Ethnographers were often not talking about the same thing when they used the term. Herdt and Poole concluded that "throughout some fifty years of New Guinea studies, only a few seminal ideas seem to have remained vital in explaining 'sexual antagonism' in the region" (23). One of these was that "in terms of individual gender identity and erotic organization, it may be that men are motivated to be hostile toward women in order to achieve and sustain their individuation and separateness as male persons in the cultural context of what males must do to be 'masculine' " (24). In other words, the existence of something that could legitimately be called sexual antagonism was due to the sociopsychological requirements of men—particularly the requirement that men become warriors. They also suggested that "for men in particular, sexual relationships were often a convenient idiom through which to register their concerns about cultural vitality and masculine identity in the wake of pacification . . . The fact that *male* ethnographers had dialogues primarily with *male* Melanesians—concerned to maintain control over their own destinies and societies—transposes the nature of our ethnographic materials on 'sexual antagonism' " (9; their emphasis). In other words, "sexual antagonism" has as much to do with male anxieties about modernity—particularly when these anxieties surface in dialogue with persons who appear to embody and control modernity—as it does with anxieties about women. While anthropologists have since been cautious about employing the concept of sexual antagonism, it seems appropriate to redeploy it here since men's ambivalence about passenger women, and their sometimes punitive acts against them, signal an anxiety about modernity, specifically the fears that some men have greater access to it than others and that this access is symbolized by access to passenger women.

While the concept of sexual antagonism was used in the past primarily to describe male fears about women, passenger women's discourse about *daunim man* (subduing men) and their anxieties about male resentment suggest that this antagonism and ambivalence is bidirectional. One way that passenger women express these anxieties is in their discourse about condoms, which is largely negative and fearful in nature. In the course of my interviews with passenger women, I decided to engage in condom distribution. This decision was not undertaken lightly. There were many reasons not to give out condoms: my reputation as a "good woman" (more or less) could have been damaged, putting me at greater risk for sexual violence; I was informed by my field assistant and others that I could be designated a *tene* (a contributing cause) of premarital sex, and thus taken to village court and sued if the young people in question were caught using condoms that could be traced back to me; condoms were usually given out by Tari Hospital staff, who (at that time) preferred to make them available only to married couples as a form of contraception and who therefore might not have approved of my more "promiscuous" distribution policy; and then, of course, there is the ethnographer's anxiety about intruding on the scene that he or she should be trying to observe and interpret, not influence. Ultimately I decided to distribute them only to men who attended *dawe anda* (discussed in the next chapter) and *pasinja meri* who already knew what they were and wanted them—admittedly a very conservative policy; others in similar situations chose a different path (Hammar 1996a, 1996b). I also gave them to my male field assistant, who knew better than I how to be judicious in their distribution.

As it turned out, many passenger women refused them, declaring that men deliberately leave condoms to rot inside women in order to kill them (see also Hammar 1992, 1996b).[14] As one woman said:

. . .

I'm afraid of condoms. It's like this: some men will remove them inside us. Then if we get sick and are in pain, people will say, say behind your back, "Oh, that woman was looking for *raun* [literally, around; sexual mobility], and now she's paying for it. You passenger women look for freedom, and you find pain." That's what they will say. Me, if a man says, "Let's go have sex," and we go to the bush and he takes out a condom, I say, "Ai-o! I don't like those things. I don't have a disease. I am a mother with children. If I were to go, if I were to go get married, I would get pregnant. If you think I'm a *raun-raun* woman [a woman who goes around, a passenger woman] and you think I have a disease, you can go to the hospital and check for my name. My name isn't there."

. . .

Condoms here are clearly associated with having a disease; thus, agreeing to their use is equivalent to admitting that one is diseased, and thus that one is a prostitute, a semiotic chain of association found in many areas of the world. But they are also conceptualized as a weapon that men can use against passenger women. What is touted as a means of protection is actually an instrument to punish passenger women for their autonomy and promiscuity. Thus, among those women who knew what condoms were (and there were quite a few who did not), many wanted no part of my little distribution plan. Almost every woman I spoke with—*pasinja meri* and not—said that they knew, or knew of, a woman who had died because a condom got stuck in her and either rotted or prevented her from expelling "bad" fluids. Death was the primary association that many women had with condoms.

Women said that men deliberately eased the condom off while the penis was still in the vagina, leaving it there to fester, though some less suspicious women conceded that this might occur accidentally. Women rejected my suggestion that they might be able to feel whether this had happened, saying that men would be sure to leave it in too deep to be felt, and the idea that they could use their fingers to check was greeted with dismay and disgust, an indication of women's internalization of discourses about the dangers of sexual fluids, both male and female. Men's behavior, not surprisingly, was said by passenger women to be motivated by *"madane."* Men were thought to resent the fact that women gained money through their sexuality and that women now seemed to consider their vaginas "good things." Even the one or two *pasinja meri* I interviewed who claimed that they consistently used condoms made such assertions. They managed their fear by checking the man's penis after sex to make sure the condom was still visible. Men, for their part, although on the whole much more positively disposed toward condoms, sometimes said that *pasinja meri* refused to use them, and asserted that this refusal was again motivated out of *"madane";* namely, they asserted that *pasinja meri* resented their stigmatized social position and therefore wanted to infect men with *gonolia*. (It is important to note that most passenger women, even those who were afraid of condoms, said that if a man wanted to use condoms, then they would; it was "up to the man," again a finding that accords with studies in other world areas.)

The commodity logic of prostitution is only slowly and uneasily becoming naturalized among the Huli. On the one hand, that *nogo tauwa* is given for the "theft" of a woman gives the exchange of sex for money a kind of plausibility. On the other hand, *tauwa* is meant to be given to a woman's kin in public, not to the woman herself in private; *tauwa* is compensation for transgression against a woman's family, not a fee given to her as an individual. In order for the exchange of sex for money to make sense, a woman's sexuality must be conceptualized as an individual capacity that she may use as she sees fit; however, female sexuality is not conceptualized this way. Indeed, bodies—male or female—are not understood this way. Thus, when a person is injured in a domestic quarrel or tribal fight, his or her family will likely demand compensation from the assailant(s), but the victim does not keep this money. That he or she usually distributes the cash or pigs is an acknowledgment of his or her individual violation; however, these must be distributed among his or her kin as compensation for damaging or weakening them through the injury of one of their members. Sex with a woman outside of bridewealth marriage is similarly conceptualized as a kind of unsanctioned drain on clan resources.

Thus, Huli people—both men and women—express not only disapproval about the exchange of sex for money, but also puzzlement. Men, for their part, will sometimes say that they don't see why a woman should receive money when she is not cooking for a man, raising his pigs, doing his laundry, or planting a garden for him—in other words, when she is not performing any kind of work. Sex, they say, is not work—at least not the kind of sex passenger women provide; only sex in the service of reproduction and sanctioned by bridewealth counts as work (Nihill 1994). Moreover, men scoff, "Do these women think their 'things' are good things?" In other words, since women's genitals are *"samting nogut"* (something no good), it is illogical for passenger women to expect money for them. Admittedly, men also acknowledge that it is quite pleasurable and liberating to have sex that is not geared toward reproduction, not necessarily embedded in a relationship, and free of the genealogical weight of bridewealth and marriage (also see LiPuma 1999). But this does not mean that men's assertions about the illogic of paying for sex should be dismissed as disingenuous; many men articulate a kind of cognitive dissonance about passenger women in which they see the logic of paying for something that is pleasurable, but also see the irrationality of paying for something that produces nothing and that may be polluting to boot.

One way to think about this dissonance is in terms of an acute symbolic tension between female sexuality as a force of production and female sexuality as an object of consumption. Both of these conceptualizations are culturally elaborated in myths, songs, and *mana* (customary knowledge). Indeed, both are cleverly captured in the folktale about Bebego Wane Pandime and Gambe Kogo Ralu: there the metaphors for female sexuality—particularly fruit and fire—show it to be both a powerful nurturant force and a site of individual pleasure and consumption. Nevertheless, it is the productive aspects of female sexuality that are dominant and accorded moral value (in discourses about bridewealth, in myth, in traditional lessons given to newly married couples about the management of sexuality); that is, female sexuality is most often spoken of as a bodily energy that can be mobilized—when appropriately "fenced in" by bridewealth and taboos—to make other persons.

Increasingly this antinomy is partitioned off, with the productive aspects of sexuality accorded to *wali ore,* and the consumption aspects accorded to *pasinja meri.* Thus, people often assert that passenger women are infertile—that they have lost the productive aspects of their personhood—not because of infection, but because no one has given or received bridewealth for them. Similarly, it is often said that they are lazy and refuse to do the work expected of women; thus, when asked if they would consider marrying a passenger woman, many men scoff, "What would I eat, her vagina? She would never garden or cook for me." (Nevertheless, some men do, in fact, take passenger women as third wives, citing a range of reasons—love, sexual pleasure, and negligible bridewealth being foremost among them.) Thus, while passenger women forge personal meaning out of their sexual liaisons—revenge, conquest, autonomy, pleasure, and sometimes love—they have difficulty imbuing these meanings with moral value and are stigmatized and sometimes punished when they push these oppositional meanings too far.

CHAPTER 6

"When the pig and the bamboo knife are ready"

The Huli Dawe Anda

The first *dawe* song I heard was performed by Lirime Mangobe only a few weeks into my fieldwork. I had my tape recorder out and was trying to elicit genres of song or storytelling other than the Christian hymns — "*Jisas i namba wan . . .*" (Jesus is number one) — women were so eager to sing for me. I didn't know what *dawe* songs were at that time, and when I asked Lirime to translate, she became embarrassed and refused. It turned out to be a poignant chant of loss in which she mused that when she saw Air Niugini planes flying overhead, she would always think of me. As probably happens often to ethnographers in the field, she was already anticipating my absence when I was feeling that I had just arrived. When I later played the tape for my female field assistant and asked her to help translate this and a few other *dawe* verses, she adamantly refused, saying she was not "that kind of woman," and in any case would not understand the metaphors or esoteric vocabulary used in *dawe* songs. My male field assistant was equally appalled, and likewise refused to translate Lirime's songs on the grounds that women "didn't know" such songs, let alone sing them. He worriedly warned me not to let other men hear the tape since Lirime's apparent familiarity with this genre of song would only worsen her reputation. She might be barred from seeing me for fear that she would teach me "bad things" about Huli culture. Although Lirime's verses contained no sexual content, the fact that she had used the *dawe* form was enough to taint them with an air of illicit sexuality.

Much later in my fieldwork, after interviewing a number of women who regularly attended *dawe anda,* I finally understood just how shocking it was that Lirime—a young, never-married woman—knew songs of this genre and was, in fact, quite adept at composing her own. When I spoke with her about my field assistants' reactions, she vigorously denied that she had ever attended a Huli *dawe anda;* rather, she had learned these songs when living with Engan kin at Porgera, who, she said, had a similar ritual of singing courtship songs, using roughly the same meter and melodic structure. Unlike the Huli, she said, Engan men *and* women sing *dawe* songs. Also unlike the Huli, Porgeran *dawe anda* were not *"haus guap"* (literally, houses for going up; houses for fucking); she was distressed that what had been a fun and only faintly illicit pastime among the Enga had so much worse implications back in Tari.

In this chapter, I discuss women who attend *dawe anda* as a kind of subset of *pasinja meri,* and Huli *dawe anda* (literally, courtship house) as courtship rituals that have become, to some extent, *haus guap.*[1] *Dawe anda* are an important feature of the current sexual landscape among the Huli, for they are the one place where extramarital sex, often in exchange for money, is localized and institutionalized. In general there is no one place that one can go to purchase sex in the Tari area, and the sexual liaisons of passenger women are quite dispersed.[2] Indeed, finding a space where "prostitution" can take place is a substantial obstacle. It is rare to find women living alone or in a situation where romantic or sexual partners can unobtrusively visit. And, since all land is owned by particular families—and is usually surrounded by deep trenches and thick bushes—finding a private space to have sex can be quite difficult. *Dawe anda* are an important exception: they are houses, usually located far from roads (and thus far from interference by the police), where men can go to meet women and have sex with them (although this is not all that takes place at *dawe anda,* and for some men is not the reason they attend). Like other passenger women, women who attend *dawe anda* have often fled their marriages and have embarked on a way of life that includes exchanging sex for money; however, they are more stigmatized and usually have fewer options than other passenger women, for reasons to be discussed later in the chapter.

The *dawe anda* itself is a paradoxical site. Some men claim that *dawe anda* are the most authentic of remaining Huli rituals, and others claim that they are a profound corruption of a traditional practice. Indeed, men assert both of these descriptors to explain why they do or do not participate in *dawe anda:* some explain that they participate because it is the one remaining venue where men can exercise their skills in the figurative dimensions of Huli language that are being lost as Tok Pisin and a more stripped-down, instrumental mode of Huli become predominant; others disparage *dawe anda* as *"bush kanaka"* (rural, unsophisticated) and *"samting bilong tumbuna"* (an outdated, ancestral practice); some maintain that they have never attended because of the disreputable innovation of paying for sex at *dawe anda;* and others eagerly attend for exactly that reason. Some men speak of the *dawe anda* as the site of an expressive male art form, and others claim it as a site of resistance to "modern," emasculating institutions, such as the Christian church. And, perhaps most paradoxical, although men pay for sex at the *dawe anda,* they joke that the women are "free food."

Dawe Anda: Then and Now

Traditionally the *dawe anda* was a cultural institution that enabled married men to find additional wives. Never-married and newly married men were not allowed to attend—and this is still the case—since the overtly erotic atmosphere was thought to embarrass and pollute them. Whether young, never-married women attended *dawe anda* in the past is unclear: some older women I interviewed asserted that it was a legitimate arena for a young woman to find a husband if she and her family didn't mind her being a second wife, but other women claimed that only divorced or widowed women ever attended *dawe anda* and that *dawe anda* have always been places restricted to bodies that have become habituated to sex, whether those bodies are male or female. At the time of my fieldwork almost all the women who participated were divorced, widowed, abandoned, or on the run from husbands. Of the very few young, nevermarried women who were to be found there, most were said to have first attended at the insistence of their mothers, who wanted to punish husbands and other male kin for abandonment, adultery, or refusal to provide economic assistance.

Ritually and aesthetically the *dawe anda* does not seem to have changed much from the past. Now, as in the past, men and women gather at night in a well-secluded house where the men form competitive singing teams and vie for the women. The women sit together on one side of the house, while the teams of men take turns serenading each individual woman with chants that employ cryptic erotic metaphors and list the names of geographic places associated with each woman. When a woman decides which man she wants, she goes and sits next to or behind him. Only after a woman has made a definitive choice are the singing teams supposed to move on to the next woman, and theoretically the teams could sing all night until each woman has made up her mind.

Dawe anda are still sites for inventing clever courtship songs, and they still serve as arenas for finding marital partners (if a man is willing to marry a passenger woman), but they are also somewhat like brothels. A man with some capital will have the house built, recruit *pasinja meri* from town or from other *dawe anda,* and charge an entrance fee for the men who attend. Men still sing the traditional songs in teams of ten to fifteen, and compete for the women, but at the end of the night couples go have sex in the bush outside the *dawe anda*—a radical departure from past practice (according to the older *dawe anda* men I interviewed). While day-to-day gender relations among the Huli are characterized by physical and verbal modesty and distance, at the *dawe anda* men and women hold hands, play cards together, and *"diskraibim"* each other. To "describe" someone is to talk about someone's body in an insulting and/or sexualizing way, verbal behavior that in other contexts often leads to physical fighting, but in the case of the *dawe anda* is meant to be playful and flirtatious. The women who attend *dawe anda* are usually paid a small amount of money by the men with whom they have sex, and on slow nights they also receive food from the man who owns and organizes the *dawe anda*. However, this man is in no way a "pimp"; he does not arrange any of the liaisons and does not expect a portion of what the women are given by their partners. Rather, he makes his money by demanding "gate fees" from men and by selling food, tea, and cigarettes to participants. Whatever male *dawe anda* participants do—whether it is sex or just singing—is their own business, but he expects the women to carry out their role of "choosing" men during the *dawe anda* singing, so that the men will continue to attend.

The *dawe anda* encompasses a wide range of relationships and desires. In one survey conducted by my male field assistant, approximately half of the men present said that they were not there for sex, but rather because they enjoyed singing the traditional songs and being in the company of male friends in an atmosphere where sexual joking and physical affection with women were the norm. That they could tease the women, sit side by side with them, creatively compete with other men, and sing romantic, erotic, and insulting songs was reason enough for many to attend. Most of the women, on the other hand, fully expect that by the end of the night they will engage in sex, although some have steady *dawe anda* partners to whom they are sexually faithful and thus will not have sex if those partners are absent. While some men and women form long-term romantic and monogamous (within the *dawe anda*) relationships, other participants change partners nightly.

It is not clear whether *dawe anda* have always been stigmatized. Glasse (1968) briefly mentions "courting parties" in his ethnography of the Huli, but he does not characterize their moral status. My interviews with old women suggest that even in precolonial times an aura of the illicit surrounded the *dawe anda*. Certainly at the present moment, no upstanding young man or woman would consider attending one: young men fear being "polluted" through witnessing sexual acts or hearing sexual talk (or at least this is what older people say young men would and should worry about), and both young men and women fear ruining their reputations. Even many self-identified *pasinja meri* stay away from *dawe anda,* describing them as either too *"bush kanaka"* or *"gonolia pulap"* (full of STDs). *Dawe anda* are frowned upon by Tari Hospital staff as reservoirs for the spread of sexually transmitted diseases (although this does not prevent some male health workers from participating in them), and until it ran out of money to do so, the hospital paid the police to burn down *dawe anda* sites.[3] Not surprisingly, then, *dawe anda* sites come and go. Some last for a few months and are eventually forced to disband by disgruntled members of the community; some last longer, but repeatedly move from one place to another.

A Note on Methods

I never attended a *dawe anda* at night when the actual ritual of male singing and female choosing takes place. For reasons of safety I was very careful about establishing a reputation as a "good" woman during the early part of my fieldwork, and this precluded going to *dawe anda*. Later, when I expressed an interest in attending one, the Huli men I knew refused to take me, saying that I would be raped and robbed. In general people seemed shocked and disapproving when I expressed an interest in *dawe anda*. When I finally reached an agreement about going to one—an agreement that entailed hiring a number of body guards and the understanding that I might be subject to a court case should anything happen to us on the way to or from the *dawe anda*—a tribal fight broke out and the *dawe anda* I had in mind was suspended. My information is therefore based on interviews conducted with male and female participants at one particular *dawe anda* during the daytime and on tape recordings made by my male field assistant, who attended *dawe anda* at night.

The *dawe anda* where I conducted interviews may have been somewhat atypical. It was located on land owned by a prison just north of Tari town (though the prison officials had certainly not given permission for the land to be used this way). When the prison was first built, officials hoped that it would be able to supply its own food through having inmates maintain sweet potato gardens; thus, the government acquired a large amount of land from local landowners. However, when too many prisoners escaped during gardening sessions, this plan came to a halt and a large area of prison land fell into disuse, but was not returned to local people. Local men asserted that they were grossly undercompensated by the government when they gave up this land, and although few men I spoke with actually wanted to use the land for gardening, they resented having been cheated (as they saw it) by the government. Many, therefore, were happy that a tiny part of it had been reappropriated by them as a *dawe anda* site; indeed, some spoke gleefully about engaging in illicit and polluting activities on government land. Because this particular *dawe anda* was located on land belonging to, but unused by, the state, it may depart in some important respects from other *dawe anda*. For example, this *dawe anda* had been in place for almost a year when I arrived—longer than other *dawe anda*—primarily because most people felt that it was the government's responsibility, not theirs, to curtail any undesirable activities taking place on its land. Likewise, the man who owned this *dawe anda* freely permitted some of the women who attended to establish gardens near the *dawe anda* site, again asserting that in fact it wasn't really up to him; if the government objected to women making gardens there, then the government could do something about it. Allowing female participants to establish gardens at *dawe anda* sites is usually impossible since the *dawe anda* owner's wives, siblings, and other kin have claims to this land; that women could make gardens at this site gave them more security and meant that they were more settled than many *dawe anda* women, who move frequently from one *dawe anda* site to another. Finally, a number of the women at this *dawe anda* had recently been released from the prison, where most had been jailed for violating court orders demanding that they return to husbands from whom they had fled or that they pay compensation for injuring others. Fearing that they might be picked up by the police again, they hid out at the *dawe anda*. Thus, this *dawe anda* more than most may have provided a relatively safe haven for women who needed it.

Dawe Anda Men

The men who attend *dawe anda* are typically married and have at least a few children. Early in a man's life it is considered too polluting for him to go to *dawe anda,* while later in a man's life it is potentially polluting for him not to go. According to most men and women I spoke with, it is too dangerous for young, never-married men to have sex with *dawe anda* women, since young men's physical health and beauty is vulnerable and easily compromised by any sexual contact, let alone contact with women whose bodies have "get used" (as Huli say, meaning have gotten used to) many men and whose vaginas have become "strong" through sex and childbearing. A newly married man, who has presumably engaged in conjugal sex, is less vulnerable, but should be devoted to regulating his and his wife's procreation by following sexual avoidance taboos and other injunctions meant to ensure health, fertility, and social success. Thus, it is only when a man has had a few children that older men may urge him to attend *dawe anda,* for as one man (who had been treated for gonorrhea in the past, and at the time of the interview reported syphilis-like symptoms) put it, "The old men teach the young men that if you constantly sleep in the 'family house' and are always with your wife, then your wife's smell will ruin your skin and close your nose. So they tell you you should go to the *dawe anda."* Too much time spent in a wife's company, and in the domestic sphere more generally, gradually erodes a man's health and well-being (also see Jolly 2001b: 196). To have one's "nose closed" by a wife's "smell" refers both to the fact that women are considered *ngubi* (smelly) and that wealth and social success are said to come to men "through the nose" (Goldman 1983). A man's nose becomes closed—and his opportunities for obtaining wealth foreclosed—by constantly being awash in the smells of the domestic sphere: women's sexual/menstrual fluids, infants' feces, and rancid pig fat. While the various Christian missions have successfully promulgated the idea that the nuclear family house is the morally preferable way to organize social space, they have not succeeded in eradicating men's concerns or irritations about extended confinement with women in such spaces. Ironically, then, some men say that the church has made *dawe anda* more necessary, since many men no longer have their own houses to escape to.

As a man gets older, it becomes ever more acceptable for him—in his own mind and in the minds of other men, although perhaps not his wife's (or wives')—to attend *dawe anda.* This is primarily because his body is gradually becoming more "dirty" and polluted through ongoing contact with his wife (or wives). Men's and women's bodies are thought to be "joined" by marriage; the transfer of bridewealth pigs, as well as sexual contact, links them morally and physically in the joint project of reproductive work. And while women generally speak positively of this con-

jugal "permeability"—often imbuing it with an air of emotional intimacy—men take a darker view of the predicament. They too see themselves inextricably bound to the bodily processes of another upon marriage, but for them this means that their bodies inevitably become
tarnished. The only upside to reproductively induced aging and pollution—beside children—is that it eventually becomes pointless for a man
to guard fastidiously against those activities—such as *dawe anda* participation—that can sully him. Thus, Huli men often become more vigorously sexual as they progress through the life cycle and, in a sense, feel
they have less to lose.

This depiction of Huli masculinity and masculine embodiment corresponds to Robert Glasse's findings (1974). Challenging Meggitt's
(1964) classic dichotomy between Melanesian societies in which men
are "prudes" and those in which men are "lechers," Glasse asserted the
need for a more temporally sensitive model of masculinity. Meggitt had
asserted that the relative degree of "sexual antagonism" in Melanesian
societies was correlated with "the presence or absence of particular
kinds of men's purificatory cults" and with "the degree of hostility existing between affinally related groups" (1964: 206). In those societies
where men married women from enemy groups, it was more likely that
sexual pollution fears would be acute, bachelor cults would be manda-
tory, and there would be a greater degree of sexual antagonism; in those
societies where men did not marry enemy women, pollution fears
would be less pronounced and a more conquest-oriented sexuality
would predominate among men. Meggitt concluded that "we must dis-
criminate between at least two kinds of inter-sexual conflict or opposition . . . the one reflects the anxiety of prudes to protect themselves
from contamination by women, the other the aggressive determination
of lechers to assert their control over recalcitrant women" (221). Glasse,
however, urged the adoption of a more psychologically and develop-
mentally nuanced perspective. Specifically, he asserted that as Huli
men moved through the life cycle, they progressed from being acutely
anxious about sex to being somewhat licentious—in other words, from
"prudes" to "lechers"—but that this was not an automatic or easy tran-
sition; some men, unable to resolve the contradictions, either remained
bachelors for life or had marriages fraught with violence. To make his
case, Glasse analyzed the different kinds of decorative wigs that men
wore as they moved through the life cycle, and particularly the decreasing degree of care and fastidiousness that they invested in them as
they aged. As he put it:

The idea that I am advancing is that Huli attitudes towards their wigs contain contradictory elements. For the virgin, the wig is a symbol of his chaste virility; for the married man, it symbolizes his "fall" and his acceptance of a certain sexual liberty . . . How does this relate to the issues of male-female antagonism, and what interpretation can be found to replace that of Meggitt's? We have seen that Huli conceptions of masculinity and femininity are in strong opposition, but does this opposition entail actual hostility between men and women? The answer is complex, for it depends on the category of man we are talking about. . . . For the Huli, sexual antagonism is not the consequence of choosing a spouse from an enemy group. It instead stems from the conflict that men live with in trying to reconcile inherent contradictions in the construction of Huli masculinity. There is, in a way, a contradictory double imperative: one must stay chaste and one must reproduce. (1974: 83; my translation)

Huli men's discourse about *dawe anda* participation supports this argument. When a man is young and pure, it is abhorrent for him to besmirch his own beauty and social appeal by thrusting himself into a heavily sexualized environment like the *dawe anda*. But after he has already been sullied through the necessity of marital sexual reproduction, it is hardly worth worrying about additional insults to his body. Thus the *dawe anda* has probably long been an arena where older Huli men can express forms of sexuality, intimacy, and masculinity that contradict the gender avoidance of everyday life in other social arenas. And while older men are adamant in insisting that sex did not take place at *dawe anda* in the past, this innovation (if, in fact, it is an innovation) seems a logical extension of the symbolic place that *dawe anda* have long held in the male life cycle.

However, not all older married men attend *dawe anda*. Typically men who consider themselves good Christians and men who are more educated do not attend, sometimes expressing disdain for such "traditional" practices, but more often asserting fears of contracting *gonolia*. And even among those men who do attend, it would appear that a significant proportion of them are there for the sake of exercising their poetic creativity and enjoying the company of other men. A number of older men said, for example, that one can no longer parade one's rhetorical artistry in the village court arena, for the younger generation no longer understands or appreciates the metaphors, aphorisms, or analogies that demonstrate subtle moral or legal reasoning. However, the *dawe anda,* they say, is still a space where more traditional wit and creativity can be exercised. Moreover, some men attend *dawe anda* to enjoy the air of male camaraderie and the thrill of being desired by women, but have no intention of having sex. As one man put it, being a responsible father he wouldn't *angua tole* (jump over, disrespect and pollute) his wife and children by having sex at the *dawe anda;* however, it was "sweet to have something from far away suddenly come near" (i.e., to be able to entice a *dawe anda* woman to choose him), while "things that were too close at hand [i.e., a wife] made life bitter." Thus, for some men, *dawe anda* women serve primarily as facilitators of male camaraderie and as the means by which they demonstrate their powers of attraction (to themselves as well as others). (Of course it is women's duty at *dawe anda* to choose men and thus confirm men's desirability and powers of attraction; also see Allison 1994).

A wife's angry words, this man added, were painful—"like the deep wound in one's foot from cutting oneself with a spade"—but songs sung at the *dawe anda* were "sweet." He was also quick to tell me that wives didn't object when their husbands went to *dawe anda,* for they knew that "it was the law" that "a wife was for gardening, raising pigs, and having children," while a man could do as he pleased. And, he added, with a twinkle in his eye, he only went to *dawe anda* because he pitied his poor wife and wanted to find another wife to help her with her onerous duties. His wife was present during this little speech; indeed, she had a bald spot on her head from their most recent altercation, which occurred when she followed him to the *dawe anda* and publicly harassed him. Defeated and humiliated at the *dawe anda,* she had returned home, thrown his mattress into the fire, and ripped up his shirts. Clearly men's *dawe anda* participation is more controversial than men typically suggest.

Dawe Songs

As this man noted, the songs sung at *dawe anda* are "sweet." For a newcomer, *dawe* songs are remarkable because they express feelings about love and eroticism not openly articulated between men and women in any other arena. The often tender or bawdy content of the verses contradicts the characteristic daily interactions between men and women. Some are funny and ribald, some are wistful and romantic, and some are clever *"tok box"* (literally, boxing talk; insults) directed at opposing male teams or at women who refuse a particular man. However, only men are supposed to know, compose, and perform *dawe* songs. Thus, for example, it would be highly inappropriate for women at the *dawe anda* to respond to the serenading male teams with songs of their own. Indeed one man I spoke with delighted in the fact that when a *dawe anda* woman had chosen you one night, but rejected you on a later occasion, you could jeer at her through song and she had no verbal means of retaliation; after all, he said, "Women don't have songs" *(Ol meri nogat singsing).* [4] And most Huli women are not like Lirime Mangobe: they do not compose or sing *dawe* songs, even in the relative privacy of women's houses.

The songs themselves follow a simple formulaic and repetitive pattern that allows for metaphorical creativity on the part of the team leader, but also enables his team to join in once they know the first line. The subsequent lines are usually the same as the first, but different place-names are substituted. For example, a typical chant is:

> When the pig and the bamboo knife are ready, we two will go to that
>   muddy place, Tugu.
> When the pig and the bamboo knife are ready, we two will go to that
>   muddy place, Ibugu.
> When the pig and the bamboo knife are ready, we two will go to that
>   muddy place, Ibari.
> When the pig and the bamboo knife are ready, we two will go to that
>   muddy place, Langari.
> Yes, to Hiburi too.
> We will go to that muddy place, Hebari.

> *Nogo tapa la mandamanda biragola Tugu waru mbaliya.*
> *Nogo tapa la mandamanda biragola Ibugu waru mbaliya.*
> *Nogo tapa la mandamanda biragola Ibari waru mbaliya.*
> *Nogo tapa la mandamanda biragola Langari waru mbaliya.*
> *E o, Hiburi nde.*
> *Hebari waru mbaliya.*

Here, the pig is a metaphor for the women present, the bamboo knife is a metaphor for the men, and the singers are asserting that when the other team begins to pair up with women for sex, they will instead go home with the woman being sung to (a suggestion of a deeper commitment to her). This pair of metaphors—pig and bamboo knife—is a standard one that everyone would be familiar with. A similar metaphorical pair is pig/killing stick :: woman/penis. One standard verse, for example, translates as, "You said come here and we will kill a pig without even bothering to see if it's the proper kind of stick for killing pigs." In other words, the men are so aroused that any type of penis—big, little, fat, thin—will be adequate for having sex. Once the first place-name in the verse is articulated, the subsequent string of names that refer to that same place is usually known by the rest of the singers. Moreover, the place-names are usually alliteratively related, making the order easier to remember: Tugu, Ibugu, Ibari, Langari, Hiburi, Hebari. Another salacious example is:

> Oh girlfriend from Ti, I will romance you with dundu grass so let's go.
> Oh girlfriend from Tindai, I will romance you with dundu grass so let's go.
> Oh girlfriend from Ibanda, I will romance you with dundu grass so let's go.
> Oh girlfriend from Eganda, I will romance you with dundu grass so let's go.
> Yes, and Pagua too.
> Yes, from Palena I will romance you with dundu grass so let's go.

> *Ai, wandari lawini Ti dundume lawilo mbaliya ta.*
> *Ai, wandari lawini Tindai dundume lawilo mbaliya ta.*
> *Ai, wandari lawini Ibanda dundume lawilo mbaliya ta.*
> *A, wandari lawini Eganda dundume lawilo mbaliya ta.*
> *E o, Pagua nde.*
> *E o Palena dundume lawilo mbaliya ta.*

Dundu grass is a rough, durable grass often used to scrub pots, so the singer here is boasting that he has what it takes to scratch her itch, as it were. Again the place-names are alliteratively related, making the memorization relatively easy: Ti, Tindai, Ibanda, Eganda, and so on. The metaphors for sex are not always so aggressive or ribald; some are poignantly erotic:

> When the stars fall down on the trees [an image denoting frost], we will put down our bows and go back to Alu.[5]
> When the stars fall down on the trees, we will put down our bows and go back to Hapialu.
> When the stars fall down on the trees, we will put down our bows and go back to Hiruma.
> Yes, and to Kurube too.
> Yes, we will put down our bows and go back to Ereba.

> *Pibiya iriani laragola Alu wangale yuwa hole ngaba.*
> *Pibiya iriani laragola Hapialu wangale yuwa hole ngaba.*
> *Pibiya iriani laragola Hiruma wangale yuwa hole ngaba.*
> *E o Kurubu nde.*
> *E o Ereba wangale yu pe hole ngaba.*

Here the image of falling stars is a metaphor for orgasm, and the bows stand for the aroused and ready penis. While the metaphor for male desire here is again that of a weapon, this time it is more romantically deployed. And, in fact, many of the *dawe* songs are not overtly sexual at all, and instead are quite wistful and tender. For example, "Daughter of the pine trees, even if you have had many lovers, you must come to me, your very first beloved" *(Kuraya wane, I lawini tewali hayagua yamali ala wini kabaria ibabe).* Similarly, an image repeatedly used in *dawe* songs is that of cirrus clouds, which are meant to evoke feelings of longing and nostalgia:

> You may feel sorrow later for your later lovers, but when you see the cirrus clouds hovering over Kiya you will think of your very first lover and feel crazy with grief and desire.

> *Mani lawini naga taramanigo; ala lawini naga tara Kiya alungi hondowa lulu baria yarata.*

This particular song fell apart after a couple lines because in fact the men on the team did not know the proper string of place-names that follows Kiya. While the place-names may not be of particular interest to the reader, they are crucial to a successful *dawe* song. For one, they should be specific to the woman being sung to, so they sometimes require a man to do some research—particularly since the women who attend *dawe anda* are often unknown to the men and come from far away so as to avoid running into their husbands or brothers. Second, as much of the ethnography of this region shows, place is an emotionally charged, highly meaningful dimension of identity. Thus, for example, Huli *dindi malu* (land genealogies) are as much about places as they are about ancestors, and mourning songs lead the listener through a landscape in which the deceased gardened, hunted, and gathered mushrooms or pandanus nuts. Like these two oral genres, *dawe* songs also emphasize the intimacy of place. Indeed, one quite eloquent woman who regularly attended *dawe anda* said that when she heard the men singing about all the various places associated with her life, she felt that they were touching her body with their songs. Thus, place is not only emotionally charged in this context, but also eroticized and imbued with phenomenological force.

While *dawe* songs use standardized themes and metaphors, they are also temporally sensitive. Thus, a night at the *dawe anda* is not just a recitation of a standard repertoire. Songs should be tailored for the specific woman in mind, and the best *dawe* singers are able to quickly and wittily respond to the moment—reminding a particular woman of how she behaved at a previous *dawe anda* and responding to insults sung by the other team. Thus, no string of *dawe* songs is exactly the same. They usually start with a description of the men's journeys to the *dawe anda,* often claiming that they were soaked by the rain, even if in actuality there was no rain that night. This characteristic makes them similar to Huli folktales, which also often begin with journeys and in which rain indicates entry into an extraordinary and transformative realm. The fact that *dawe* songs use a narrative convention also seen in myth suggests that the *dawe anda* is permeated by what Victor Turner (1969) called the "subjunctive" mood of sociocultural process—the mood of maybe, might-be, as-if, and fantasy. Thus, as soon as the singing starts, one is drawn into a space where there is a sense that anything can happen.

Once the journey has been described, the men will often sing about women who they were hoping would be there, but have either not yet arrived or are not at the *dawe anda* that night:

> Oh no! The *mbi* insects are crying out [it's almost night time] and it's too dark to see the *pawa* trees at Wanda [Eganda, Iriabi, Ekopia].
> Yes, at Kewa too.
> Yes, the *ne* insects are crying out and it's too dark to seen the *pawa* trees at Kayabi.

> *Aya ayali! Wanda pawa nahandabe hayago mbi lole biniya.*
> *Aya ayali! Eganda pawa nahandabe hayago mbi lole biniya.*
> *Aya ayali! Iriabi pawa nahandabe hayago mbi lole biniya.*
> *Aya ayali! Ekopia pawa nahandabe hayago mbi lole biniya.*
> *E o, Kewa nde.*
> *E o Kayabi pawa na handabe hayago ne lole biniya.*

Here, the men are saying that they were waiting for a particular woman from Wanda (Eganda, Iriabi, Ekopia), but it is now night and they still don't see her. Along similar lines, but more erotically charged:

> Oh no! I am wearing lots of erect, high-flying feathers from Hawi [Handale, Hibulu, Handabe], but I'm putting them down.
> Yes, and from Tindupe too.
> Yes, I have readied my Tandapi bow to fire an arrow, but where should I put it down?

> *Aya ayali! Hawi ega puri yeri pitogo ibiria haro.*
> *Aya ayali! Handale ega puri yeri pitogo ibiria haro.*
> *Aya ayali! Hibulu ega puri yeri pitogo ibiria haro.*
> *Aya ayali! Handabe ega puri yeri pitogo ibiria haro.*
> *E o, Tindupe nde.*
> *E o, Tandapi wangale pange yanga pitogo agoria ibiria hoabe?*

Here the upright feathers and readied bow stand for arousal, but since the man does not see the woman he desires, his arousal is fading fast. He wonders where he can direct his erotic energy before it is too late. Somewhat more insulting is:

We usually use good leaves to roast our pigs, but this time I am bypassing
   those leaves and using worse ones from Liwi [Lubalu, Nagalu,
   Nagabi].

Walu payame tawaga piago Liwi[Lubalu, Nagalu, Nagabi] yauama tawa ariba
kabago.

This song contrasts two different kinds of leaf used to line the earth ovens
in which pigs are cooked. Since the woman a man desires (the good kind
of leaf) is not available, he will have to settle for a worse one. This song
would usually not be directed at a particular woman, but perhaps toward
a group of women who have all come from the same general area, and it
would be meant more to tease than to offend them.

When a woman is reluctant to choose a certain man, the teams will
confront this predicament through song. Sometimes they will urge her
directly: "Dundu's daughter from Peri [Piagole, Ibai, Aluya], your heart
seems to be sitting sideways [i.e., you are undecided], so just come to us"
(Dundu wane Peri [Piagole, Ibai, Aluya] yamali piru andelo piriama ibube).
Other times, if it is late and the men are getting frustrated, they may insult her: "Oh no! The pig lice from Liwi are biting us; let's just leave" *(O*
ayali! Liwi nogo himi urume narago mbaliya). In other words, this is a
waste of time and, moreover, you are giving us lice. While female choice
is a marked theme in *dawe* rituals—female choice, after all, is what gives
the competition between the teams of men its spice—women are expected to choose, and tempers boil over when the women become preoccupied with talking to each other instead of being attentive to the men.
Many of the *dawe* songs suggest that it is the men, as a team or corporate
group, who are ultimately in charge: "We'll just build a fence around
these wild pigs from Maneba [Kera, Kawara], and the two of us will go"
(Nogo kagua naga Maneba [Kera, Kawara] hagiria pialu mbaliya ta). In
other words, the men will use their *dawe* songs to fence in these undisci-
plined women, carrying out in this arena exactly what men are meant to
do in other social arenas.

While many of the songs are like serenades directed toward individual
women, equally important to the men are the barbs and insults one team
directs at the other. Indeed, some men assert that the women are there
primarily to facilitate a rollicking rivalry between the men. Sometimes,
however, the verbal jousting can go beyond the bounds of fun and
threaten to escalate into blows. (It is perhaps for this reason that at many
dawe anda, alcohol is, contrary to what one might expect, forbidden.)
One of my female field assistants told of an incident in which her husband, who was from another area of Papua New Guinea and who didn't

speak Huli, decided to go to the local *dawe anda* to see what it was all about. Not realizing just how inappropriate it was for her to be there, he agreed that she could sit outside the actual singing area and sell cigarettes while he was inside. Suddenly she realized that a visiting Huli politician was singing about her: he was citing all the names associated with her father's land, and he sang that "government people should go with government people; *kanaka* with *kanaka*," meaning that since he worked for the government and had learned that she had once worked as a secretary in a government office, she should be with him, not with her husband. The other team responded that she was a married woman and that he should choose another one to serenade. He sang back that he wondered just how much bridewealth her husband had given, and how much of this he would have to "replace" in order to get her—"Would it be eight men or eight pigs?" The "men" and "pigs" in this verse referred to Papua New Guinea currency: the face of the first prime minister, Michael Somare (the "men" in this verse), is on 50K notes; the head of a pig is on 20K notes. By this time the local men were feeling somewhat put out by the visiting team who so boldly sang of seducing the wife of a man they considered one of their own; moreover, they felt the singer was deliberately humiliating them by implying that as a politician he had plenty of "men" and "pigs" (i.e., cash) at his disposal. So they retorted that her husband was also a government employee, not a *"kanaka,"* and that he too was quite familiar with "men" and "pigs." Worrying that a fight might break out, someone finally informed the husband what all the singing had been about, and he angrily took his wife home. This incident is a good example of how quick-witted singers can compose clever verses on the spot, as well as how the competition between the groups of men can quickly overshadow any interest in the woman who is supposedly the subject of song.

To the extent that men use their monopoly on *dawe* songs to determine and define the atmosphere and course of events during any particular *dawe anda* evening, *dawe anda* can be considered a "male sanctuary," somewhat in the sense that Donald Tuzin has discussed (1997). Analyzing the demise of the Tambaran male cult among the Ilahita in Papua New Guinea, Tuzin concludes that while the cult was, in fact, an instrument of patriarchy, its collapse has, if anything, led to the deterioration of gender relations among the Ilahita. Tuzin provocatively (and quite controversially) suggests that "masculine sanctuaries" which exclude women "exist both to protect men from threats to their ontological validity and sense of phallic adequacy and to protect them and others from the grim consequences of having those pretensions exposed as self-serving illusions" (191). In other words, the male psyche requires cultural institutions that create and sus-

tain an illusion of male potency, and thus organizations that appear to dis-
empower women by excluding them are actually to women's benefit.
While this argument can be (and has been) critiqued in a variety of ways,
my concern here is only to suggest that "male sanctuaries" may not require
women's physical absence, as Tuzin suggests. Indeed some "male sanctuaries" may serve the purposes proposed by Tuzin through women's very
presence—albeit a particular kind of presence.

It may be somewhat of a stretch to compare the Huli *dawe anda* with
the Ilahita Tambaran, since Huli social life (male or otherwise) did not
and does not revolve around the *dawe anda;* the *dawe anda* does not play
a role in Huli cosmology, nor, to my knowledge, is it founded on any secret male mythology; and, finally, women are not excluded from the *dawe
anda,* and indeed are crucial to it. Nevertheless, *dawe anda* are a kind of
sanctuary for married men, and they are linguistically structured so that
the women play a very specific role—that of appreciating male competition, being seduced by sung enticements, and eventually choosing men
(supposedly) for their worth. Indeed, fights occasionally break out when
it is discovered that some men have paid women in advance to choose
them, for the delight of the *dawe anda* is the sense (illusory in some cases,
not in others) that the women have freely chosen men for their worth as
individuals and as teams. Much as Allison (1994) has described the Japa-
nese nightclubs where businessmen are expected to socialize after hours,
dawe anda provide men with an air of male camaraderie and the thrill of
being desired, even when no sex occurs. In this sense, then, men's "phallic inadequacy," as Tuzin puts it, is assuaged through the *dawe anda*—
without the gender exclusion that Tuzin asserts is necessary (see also
Jenkins 1996). The *dawe anda* is defined as an arena where women are not
speaking subjects (or, more accurately, singing subjects), and, unlike the
men present, women act as individuals rather than as members of teams
or corporate groups. Thus, while the overt eroticism at the *dawe anda*
contradicts normative sexual propriety, the structure and format of the
dawe anda singing rituals actually reinforce normative constructions of
gender, such as the importance of the male corporate group, men's privileged position in shaping events, and the ideology that *"meri nogat tok-
tok"* (literally, women don't have talk; women lack rhetorical skills).

Dawe Anda Women

Many Huli men—educated and not, well traveled and not, salaried and
not—attend *dawe anda.* It is a legitimate (if frowned upon) nighttime

leisure activity for men that does not stigmatize men as individuals. If a young man or the local pastor were to attend, it would surely be a different story, but other men are not branded as "good" or "bad" according to whether or not they attend *dawe anda*. This is not true for women. The cases below provide some idea of what it takes for women to end up at a *dawe anda*.

•   •   •

Pekame's mother was a fourth wife, and the two of them resented their low position in the family hierarchy. Pekame's father wouldn't pay for her to go to school, the other wives' children stole from their gardens, the first wife made sure they received only small and less valuable pieces of pork, and Pekame's mother fought with her father constantly. Pekame claims that when her only brother died, she decided to engage in premarital sex in order to "ruin" herself so that no one would want to marry her, effectively preventing her half-brothers — the sons of her father's other wives — from claiming and distributing her bridewealth. She did not leave home, however; rather, she crept out at night, went to bush discos, and had sex with young men she met there.[6] She was caught doing this twice, and the third time her father successfully demanded that the family of the young man take her as a bride. She pointedly asked her father not to let her half-brothers distribute any of her bridewealth pigs because she didn't want the wealth obtained through her marriage to end up in the hands of the kin of her mother's co-wives.

Her husband continued to attend bush discos after they married, and they often fought about his infidelities and later about her apparent infertility. She accused him of being *"gonolia pulap"* (full of STDs; also see Wardlow 2002c) because of his infidelities, and he retorted that he only consorted with other women because she had not provided him with children. When I interviewed her, she had never been pregnant, and she had once been extremely ill with fever and severe abdominal pain — evidence, she thought, that her husband had transmitted an STD to her.

This was the first *dawe anda* she had come to, she had only been there two weeks, and she did not appear to be happy or comfortable there. Indeed, she said that she was there only because she had no where else to go. After eleven years of a conflict-ridden and infertile marriage, she ran away from her husband and moved in with her mother, who had remarried after Pekame's father died. Approximately a year after Pekame absconded from her marriage, her husband demanded that his bridewealth be returned, and he publicly shamed her by announcing that since his "pay was still in place" (i.e., his bridewealth had not been returned), he could give her away to any of his "brothers" (clan members) who might want her (an idiom also used by Jakili's husband after she ran away and did not return his bridewealth; see chapter 3). She responded that if he thought he could "put my genitals on display like a market item" *(putim tau bilong mi olsem maket)*, then she would do it for him by becoming a *pasinja meri*, which she proceeded to do.

When she tried to move back to her father's land and build herself a house, her half-brothers destroyed it and made it clear that she would not be allowed to live there, saying that since they hadn't distributed her bridewealth, and since she had not raised pigs to help them with bridewealth payments for their own wives, she couldn't live on their land. The one half-brother who was not yet married grudgingly said she could live with him if she agreed to give all her existing pigs to him and raise yet more so that he could marry, but she refused, which angered him so much that he thrust an arrow into her thigh. She retorted that since her half-brothers were forcing her to "be free"—in other words, they were cutting her loose rather than fencing her in—she would go live at a *dawe anda*. She hadn't actually planned on taking this step, but when they did nothing to stop her, she didn't know where else to go. When I spoke with her she expected her relationship with her half-brothers only to worsen since her husband was demanding that they repay the bridewealth given for her, bridewealth that at her request they had not been allowed to distribute to their kin eleven years earlier. In fact, she had just heard that her pigs had been killed—by her husband or by her half-brothers she didn't know—but she was too afraid of their anger to risk leaving the *dawe anda* to look into the situation.

She had thought about running away to Mendi or to Mt. Hagen, relatively large towns about a day away from Tari by bus, but was afraid: she had never traveled and could not speak Tok Pisin confidently. So she instead took refuge in a *dawe anda* after she met a woman who was scouring the roads trying to recruit women for this particular *dawe anda*. Living at the *dawe anda* was safer than being a passenger woman on her own, she said; even in her short stint as a passenger woman she'd been beaten by the wife of a man she'd had sex with.

Since arriving at the *dawe anda* she could remember in detail six men she'd been with, but knew that there had been more because she'd had sex with a different man almost every night. She stated that she didn't like the *dawe anda* because it seemed to be an unstated expectation that she have sex with men who were interested in her. Of course she'd had sex with a number of men before coming to the *dawe anda,* but she'd been living with her mother then, making her own gardens and raising her own pigs, so she only had sex when she wanted and with men to whom she was attracted, often without any exchange of money. Indeed, although she said she'd been a passenger woman for about seven months, most of her relationships had not been on the basis of pay per sexual transaction; she used the term *pasinja meri* to describe herself because she had fled her marriage and had engaged in extramarital sex with many partners.

Although reluctant, she'd decided that she was willing to marry again; her alternatives, she realized, were not easy or appealing. She reasoned that if she found a man at the *dawe anda* who was willing to marry her, then he could pay bridewealth to her husband, easing the pressure on her half-brothers and thus hopefully ameliorating her relationship with them. Indeed, her determination not to ask for money from men at the *dawe anda* was an element of her matrimonial strategy. Admittedly, if they offered her money, she would accept it, and most had, in fact, offered her between 4 and 10 kina (between US$3 and $8 at that time); however, she insisted that she was choosing men based on her attraction to them, and she hoped that by not demanding cash she would be able to cultivate an ongoing relationship with one of them. She was worried, however, about whether she could have children. She had felt semen dribbling out of her after sex, and she worried that this might be a sign of infertility; perhaps her vagina was not strong enough to hold the semen in. (Since the formation of a fetus is thought to require a critical mass of semen, it is perhaps not surprising that she and a few other women I spoke with were concerned about postcoital semen leakage.)

She had only recently learned about condoms, but she didn't think they were necessary except with some *dawe anda* men. Before she had come to the *dawe anda,* she knew most of the other men she'd had sex with and considered them all *"bush kanaka"* (rural, unsophisticated men), by which she meant that they had not traveled outside of Huli territory and were therefore safe. Unfamiliar with most of the men she met at the *dawe anda,* she was open to using condoms, but wouldn't unless her male partner insisted.

· · ·

Gewame's first marriage was arranged to a young man she knew and was happy to marry. She had two other *lawini* (love interests), and she would have preferred to marry one of them, but she was satisfied with her parents' choice. She had two children with her husband, but, as she put it, she always got pregnant "too quickly" for her husband's liking: she would inform him she was pregnant and that they had to stop having sex (because of gestation-related sexual taboos meant to protect mother and fetus), and he would accuse her of infidelity, arguing that they hadn't had enough sex to create a child. She wasn't sure if he really believed that she'd gotten pregnant with another man, if he was just trying to bully her into abandoning her pregnancy-related sexual abstinence, or if he was tired of the marriage and wanted to harass her into demanding a divorce. Whatever his motives, she eventually became so upset by these accusations that she chopped off her index finger, threw it at him, and ran back to her parents. Her kin returned all twenty-two of the bridewealth pigs, but insisted on keeping the two children since she had done nothing wrong and he had declared that they weren't his anyway.

Knowing that she was available, some of her female kin found a man who was interested in taking her as a fourth wife. She left him after a few months because she didn't enjoy having sex with him and hated being a co-wife. Happily for her, her second marriage occurred during the Mt. Kare gold rush (approximately 1988–90), and she herself was able to return much of her own bridewealth in cash by panning for gold. She stayed at Mt. Kare as a *pasinja meri,* sometimes engaging in one-off paid sexual transactions, but more often acting as a man's sexual, domestic, and mining partner for a few weeks at a time. She eventually married a man there who had a job with CRA, the mining company that had rights over Mt. Kare at that time, but their marriage disintegrated because he continually got drunk, shamed her by urinating in front of her kin during his bouts of insobriety, and persisted in having sex with *pasinja meri.* According to her, she won her divorce case at the local village court and did not have to return any bridewealth.

Her fourth husband was also an employee of CRA at Mt. Kare. Theirs was a happy marriage; as she said, "With all that money from panning for gold, there was no reason to get angry." However, according to her, jealous people convinced her husband that she was cheating on him: she always had too much pocket money to be a good woman, they said; she must still be exchanging sex for money to have that much ready cash. One drunken night he attacked her with a bush knife, almost killing her: when I spoke with her she had deep scars on her face, skull, and chest, and one of her arms and her jaw had clearly been broken in the past. She successfully had him thrown in prison, and held on to his job reference letters and bank book, only agreeing to return them under the condition that he give her K3,000 (US$2,000) as compensation for almost killing her. He agreed, but when he escaped from prison, he ran away. She still had these papers, and was angry that he had never compensated her as he had promised.

When I asked her why she had come to the *dawe anda,* she said that she was initially motivated by anger at her husband's failure to pay compensation for almost killing her. She had loved him, she said, and she'd had no desire to cheat on him or leave him, but then he almost killed her, and she knew he had money in his savings account, and she was furious that he refused to compensate her for her injuries. She had continued to attend *dawe anda,* she said, because she was disabled by her previous injuries and was often in too much pain to do agricultural work for long periods of time. Later in the interview, however, she mused that perhaps she continued to attend *dawe anda* because she missed her recently deceased mother and kept hoping to see her mother's face in the various men and women who passed through the *dawe anda.* Or, she sighed, perhaps she simply wanted to forget her anger and grief by laughing and flirting with men every night. She'd first started attending *dawe anda* six months earlier and moved between three different *dawe anda* sites. She estimated that she'd had about five different sex partners per month, but she also had two regular partners whom she thought of as potential husbands because both had given her large pieces of pork in addition to money. They knew about each other, but cooperated in taking turns with her, and she tried to be discreet about her other partners. As a general rule, she was willing to have sex with men to whom she was attracted for K2–5, but would only sleep with men she wasn't interested in if they offered her more than K10—more than K20 if she really had no desire for them.

She had three younger brothers who were appalled by her behavior and physically tried to stop her, but when they beat her she got hysterical. She was the firstborn daughter, she would tearfully remind them—their mother was dead and she was like their mother now; how could they beat her like that? And they'd received bridewealth for her already, and she'd been beaten by men she'd married; how could her own brothers also beat her like that? Her brothers were afraid of these wild outbursts, she said—afraid that her injuries had made her fragile, that her soul would leave her body, and that she might die if she was made too upset. So they had given up coercion; even so, she made a point of attending *dawe anda* far from where her brothers lived, for she didn't want to shame them or risk another angry confrontation. She was quite sad when I interviewed her because she'd spent almost a full day and night with one of her *dawe anda* boyfriends—sharing pork, laughing, playing cards—and she'd felt the time was right to put pressure on him to marry her: she threatened that if he didn't agree she would marry the first *dawe anda* man who made her an offer. And he had replied that was fine with him. He'd made her feel like "a real two-kina bush woman," she said.

• • •

These life histories correspond in many ways to those of the *pasinja meri* discussed in previous chapters. These women also assert anger at husbands or kin as the initial reason they abandoned marriage and embarked on a path associated with shame and stigma: Pekame was angry at her half-brothers and her husband, and she chose to humiliate them and evade their control by hiding out in the *dawe anda;* Gewame was angry at her husband for his failure to acknowledge his violent betrayal of their relationship and the grave physical damage he had inflicted on her. Like the passenger women discussed earlier, these women felt disappointed and betrayed, and they used autonomous and promiscuous sexuality to express their anger. However, these women, and others I interviewed at the *dawe anda,* also differ in significant ways from the *pasinja meri* discussed earlier. Women who end up at *dawe anda* tend to be somewhat older (in general, mid-thirties to early forties, although there is a wide range); they have been through at least one marriage, usually two or three; and they are less educated, less well traveled, and less fluent in Tok Pisin. They come to *dawe anda* as much out of desperation as defiance.

Moreover, they generally do not express the degree of ambivalence toward marriage that other *pasinja meri* do: most *dawe anda* women, if given the chance to become a *dawe anda* man's third or fourth wife, would agree. Many told me that although they thought it was men who ruined marriages, they still enjoyed being married: raising children, making gardens together, strategizing together about the care and distribution of pigs, participating in community life—this was what they wanted. Thus, while eager to shame male kin or to escape particular marriages, they were not eager to be autonomous or to avoid marriage altogether. *Dawe anda* women, then, are like other *pasinja meri,* but their options are more constrained by their circumstances and by prior events in their lives: less worldly, they are more fearful about simply hopping on a bus and taking their chances elsewhere; some have tried to live independently, but were refused land by their kin; many would like to be married, but until they can safely extricate themselves from existing marriages, they have nowhere else to go. And some, like Gewame, seem beaten down by loss, abuse, and disappointment. Since they cannot or will not return to husbands and natal kin, they are easily recruited into *dawe anda*. Thus, while the cultural institution of the *dawe anda* may serve as a "psychic sanctuary" for men, *dawe anda* sites sometimes serve as physical sanctuaries for women.

The positions and prospects of *dawe anda* women are ambiguous. On the one hand, some men do, in fact, marry *dawe anda* women for six or nine pigs—only a fourth to a third of normal bridewealth because of their stigmatized status. On the other hand, *dawe anda* women are often teasingly called "free food"—"free" because although a man usually pays money to have sex with one, he does not have to marry her and take on all the consequent entailments of bridewealth exchange: meeting affinal obligations, building her a house, giving her gardens, supporting her in disputes, and so on. A few kina is nothing, men say, if it means they can interact sexually, romantically, or flirtatiously with a woman with no fear of kinship entanglements and no expectation of bridewealth. And, although men vie to be "chosen" by *dawe anda* women in the context of the nightly ritual, many also dismiss them as foolish and rebellious women who should have stayed put instead of leaving whatever marriage they were in. As one man said, only women from "broken marriages" go to *dawe anda,* not "real women" *(wali ore).*

The ambiguous position of *dawe anda* women is inscribed in the *dawe* songs, which sometimes suggestively play with the idea of marriage, and sometimes remind *dawe anda* women that they are not really marriageable. For example:

> Daughter of Alibi [name of a founding clan ancestor], when they burn
>   down the *pawa* trees at Kuali [Yaguali, Imawi, Yandawi], they go look-
>   ing for men.
> Yes, at Wariama too.
> Yes, when they burn down *pawa* trees at Kaloma, they look for men.

> *Alibi wane naga Kuali [Yaguali, Imawi, Yandawi] pawa dara angi agali hai*
>   *piagaya.*
> *E o Wariama nde.*
> *E o Kaloma pawa dara angi agali taya piagaya.*

In other words, when her people at Kuali (Yaguali, Imawi, etc.) are engaged in a tribal fight and their enemies burn down the *pawa* trees on her land, her kin will be looking for allies, and as a potential husband, he could be one of those allies. This song addresses the woman as a person firmly embedded in a network of kinship and firmly tied to place—she is descended from Alibi and is presumed to care about the *pawa* trees marking her clan's land at Kuali. And the singer suggests that he too could be loyal to such a place. A more direct example is:

> You come over here, and we'll find out whether it is a matter of pigs that can be eaten or a matter of bridewealth pigs.

> *O ayali, nogo [ibuna, apora, awaia] tabe wariabu tabe ogoria tapabiya ibube.*
> *E o, parila nde.*
> *E o, paiyoga tape wariabu tabe ogoria tapa biya ibu.*

This verse tells the woman to come to him and identify her lineage so he can find out whether they are related or not. If it is "a matter of bridewealth pigs" this means that he has received bridewealth for her or someone related to her, and so she is a classificatory sister and they cannot marry. If, however, it is "a matter of pigs that can be eaten," then he has not received bridewealth for her (bridewealth pigs may not be eaten by a woman's brothers), meaning they are not related and can marry.

The above verses suggest that the woman being sung to is a potential marriage partner; however, men can also use *dawe* songs to remind women that they are *pasinja meri*, that they have "white hair" (are getting old), and that they "steal" money from men (i.e., expect money just for providing sex). (These latter themes are usually sung to women only when they refuse to choose a man—that is, when they refuse to fulfill their proper *dawe anda* role of exercising "female choice.") One cruel and clever verse of this nature translates as: "Now you women only have to look for firewood, but later you will be looking for wood to build a house," which implies that as women living at a *dawe anda*, they are cared for by the *papa bilong pati* (the father of the party; that is, the *dawe anda* owner) and the men who give them money, so all they really have to do is fetch firewood. However, when they grow older and less attractive, they will have no one to build them houses because they have chosen to cut themselves off from women's expected sources of security. (Not surprisingly, men's songs rarely acknowledge that *dawe anda* women are, in a sense, already homeless and are at the *dawe anda* because they have found other alternatives to be untenable.) Similarly, another verse asserts,

> Oh no! This piece of pig from Baro [Babali, Endoli, Gambali] that you are now eating you will not eat in the future.

Aya ayali Baro [Babali, Endoli, Gambali] nogo koraga nereligo tege na nole bere.
E o, Erego nde.
E o, Andigi nogo koraga naraligo tege na nole bere.

Here the singer is asserting that the women only eat pork at the *dawe anda* because men give them money to do so, but since they are social outcasts there will be no pork forthcoming when they are older. Along the same lines, some verses assert that *dawe anda* women will not have children to care for them when they get old, invoking the belief that *dawe anda* women cannot become pregnant—not necessarily because they are infertile through *gonolia,* but because they do not have enough sex with any one man for a fetus to be formed.[7]

"The *dawe anda* is our church"

Though people discouraged me for months from going to a *dawe anda* site and insisted that I would only be learning about "dirty" practices from people who were *"rabis"* (rubbish) and *"gonolia pulap"* (full of STDs), once I was there, the men in attendance proudly asserted that I was learning about the only remaining genuine Huli ritual. They were proud of the inventive songs, proud that men still gathered and competed in this way, and proud that going to the *dawe anda* was still a male prerogative. Indeed, a number of *dawe anda* participants—primarily men, but also some women—mischievously, but earnestly, declared to me that "the *dawe anda* is our church," suggesting an institutionalized ritual arena in and through which specific kinds of subjectivity are formed and maintained. They suggested that these two "churches"—the Christian church and the *dawe anda*—were mutually exclusive; one could not participate in both. Either one chose to subject oneself to God and all the constraints and humiliations that being a Huli Christian entailed—being rebuked by pastors every Sunday, having to give money to the church, sitting docilely during sermons, participating in rituals that have yet to fulfill their implicit promise of eventual wealth and power, and (for men) sitting on the floor alongside women and children—or, one can choose the uproarious exuberance and esprit de corps of the *dawe anda*. One can dully accept the admonishments not to gossip, steal, covet, and fight, or one can feel the thrill and chagrin of desire. One can repeatedly sing *"Jisas i namba wan"* (Jesus is number one), or one can sing about the cirrus clouds hovering over the place of one's beloved.

The choice between church and *dawe anda* is not framed by most participants as a choice between modernity and tradition. While some people see the Christian church as a modern institution, others assert that it is merely the current incarnation of a body of moral thought that has long been adhered to by the Huli. And, as discussed earlier, some see current *dawe anda* practices as traditional, and some see them as modern. Rather, the choice is between a subjectivity that is constituted through, and regulated by, church and state institutions, or a subjectivity that is not.[8] For men in particular (although also some strong-minded women), the *dawe anda* is a space free from what are seen as the increasing incursions of the state. Thus, *dawe anda* participants strongly resent—indeed, are baffled by—interference on the part of the police and the local hospital. As long as no crime has been committed, they see no reason why these organizations feel entitled to burn down *dawe anda* sites or haul *dawe anda* women (and only the women) off to jail. Why on earth should the government care if men are getting together to sing and perhaps have sex with women who do not belong to anyone? Since they do not see the *dawe anda* as a public health or moral threat, they interpret occasional police raids as the state's desire to eradicate indigenous practice. Thus some men asserted that the police and the hospital staff were out to *"daunim ol grassroots"* (subjugate the rural, unemployed classes) in part through eradicating *dawe anda*.[9]

"Haus guap gonolia pulap"
(Houses for fucking are full of STDs)

Men's anger about what they see as meddling in *dawe anda* by state institutions also emerged loudly and clearly in their discussions about treatment for sexually transmitted diseases; in particular, they resented having to be examined and treated at the STD clinic, which at that time was spatially set apart from other services at Tari Hospital. They complained bitterly about the shame they experienced at being observed by other patients who could see which door they were entering and who would, men said, immediately conclude that they were *gonolia pulap* (full of *gonolia*) and had been having sex with *pasinja meri*. While much of the international health literature suggests that it is typically more shameful and stigmatizing for women to be seen at STD clinics (and that this stigma deters treatment seeking), among the Huli I believe this shame may be particularly acute for men, who, according to dominant constructions of masculinity, should be morally self-disciplined and pure and who are associated with the public realm and with display because they are thought to radiate a kind of physical charisma cultivated through their moral self-discipline and purity. That the state's spatial organization of medical services put them on display when they felt they were at their most morally compromised was a bitter pill for many men.

Male *dawe anda* participants were equally angry at the gatekeeping role hospital staff play in accessing STD medication, at having to talk about their bodies with female nurses, and at having their names written into government record books. They argued that the *papa bilong pati* (fathers of the party; *dawe anda* owners) should be supplied with stocks of STD medication that could be administered to *dawe anda* participants when necessary. They saw no compelling reason why the hospital should have sole control over this medication or why their bodies should be inscribed into monthly reports. Their opposition was motivated in part by the anxiety that wives might get hold of such documents and use them in a village court setting to humiliate men or even demand compensation from them (Wardlow 2002c). Wanting to keep knowledge about STD infections safely inside the *dawe anda* community, some men were perturbed when I informed them that they could transmit STDs to their wives and then be reinfected by them if their wives were not also treated.

However, men's resistance to hospital STD records went beyond a fear of possible marital repercussions. They also resented the state's ability, through control over curative resources, to secure patient compliance in matters that had little to do with treatment, such as participating in the keeping of government records and monthly reports. Many men suggested that they were at a complex impasse: they appreciated and even felt entitled to government health services; however, they did not see why their names and identifying characteristics (clan territory, marital status, approximation of age) should be recorded. What exactly they feared might happen remained murky; they had difficulty articulating possible concrete negative consequences of participating in this kind of epidemiological "surveillance." However, I suggest that what men are resisting in this instance is an expanding regime of sexuality, in Foucault's sense, in which control is exerted over populations in part through institutional discourses and practices that categorize them as "cases" of various diseases and disorders. Their instinctive opposition to being counted, classified, and recorded—as well as the stigma of being seen at the STD clinic—contributed to men's delay in seeking treatment for STDs. A study conducted in 1990 showed that 15% of Huli men who tested positive for any STD presented within a week of experiencing symptoms, 35% within six months, and 30% said they had experienced symptoms for over two years before seeking help (Hughes 1991a;

see also NSRRT and Jenkins 1994; Passey 1996). Similarly, nine men I interviewed in 1997 at the *dawe anda* said they were currently suffering from symptoms of STDs, such as genital lesions and pain on urination, but none of them had sought treatment at Tari Hospital.

To make matters worse, condoms are not readily available in Tari. For a brief period they were available in some stores in Tari town, but community outrage was so vociferous that these stores quickly stopped supplying them. There are no independent pharmacies in Tari, and at the time of my research condoms were only available upon request at the Tari Hospital STD clinic and family planning clinic, again making men feel like they were under surveillance by (female) agents of the state who might record such requests in a government report or gossip to other women in the community. Some men managed to obtain condoms from male rural Aid Post Orderlies (APOs), but most men asserted that the primary source of condoms was male kin and friends who had traveled outside of Tari and brought them back. Thus, while most men I interviewed at the *dawe anda* stated that they would use condoms (admittedly, not a reliable indicator of actual use), access was a fundamental stumbling block. Again, many men expressed anger that access to condoms was mediated by hospital staff, and they only agreed to be interviewed in exchange for condoms and answers to their questions about STDs.

The *dawe anda* is a site of contradiction. The women there are potential wives, but they are also "free food." Female participants are highly stigmatized, even by men who happily attend *dawe anda,* but it is also a space where male dominance seems less overt and the one place where you can see men and women affectionately holding hands and leaning against each other. Many men proudly claim it as a site of resistance to church and state; and yet participation in it can lead to health conditions that can only be remedied by putting oneself under the microscope, as it were, of the state. Moreover, it is a site where the exchange of sex for money is most highly institutionalized—a characteristic many might associate with modernity—and yet men claim that it is the one current practice that is "traditional" and "authentically Huli." Indeed, male participants' resistance to the potential commercialization or de-ritualization of erotic practice at the *dawe anda* can be seen in some of their song verses:

> Some men from Timba [Timbalu, Itupe, Erebo] are killing pigs in secret
> and so we have our bows ready.

> *Nogo ndime barago naga Timba [Timbalu, Itupe, Erebo] danda bebena pibiya.*

This verse reveals that the singers are aware of the fact that some men, reluctant to join in the ritualized competition of *dawe anda,* have paid women in advance so that the women will choose them or will simply leave the *dawe anda* space altogether to go have sex. In other words, the singers are warning the interlopers against attempting to use the *dawe anda* as a brothel—a place to pay women for sex. If one comes to the *dawe anda,* one must play by the rules: be part of a male team, learn the meanings of the various *dawe* metaphors, do one's homework about the place-names of individual women, and wait—at least a little while—for the ritual of female choice to play itself out. To do otherwise, it is implied, is to contribute to the erosion of Huli masculinity and tradition. (Women express mixed opinions about this issue: some appreciate men's competitive singing, while others would prefer simply to talk and play cards with potential male partners.) Thus, while the sexual transactions at the *dawe anda* are "commercialized," they are equally ritualized. Indeed, the *dawe anda* can be seen as a unique space where certain aspects of modernity are indigenized through male ritual work: the songs transport men to a liminal space outside of the bridewealth system where they can experiment with a more individualized sexual and romantic self, but at the same time can situate this sexuality in a "sanctuary" of male camaraderie, competition, and artistic expression.

However, this ritualized experimentation with and "domestication" of new, less socially embedded modes of male sexuality depends, to some extent, on women's seeking safe haven at *dawe anda* sites. It is their rejection of the bridewealth system, their consequent repudiation by kin, and their lack of alternatives that often propel women to the *dawe anda* and make them more amenable to men's desires and authority within the *dawe anda.* This is not to say that all women who come to *dawe anda* sites have nowhere else to go or are there only because of a kind of structural coercion. Some women do have access to land for gardening, have been invited back into the fold by their kin, or are unafraid of hopping on public buses and making their own way elsewhere—yet choose to stay at *dawe anda* anyway because they enjoy the rituals, appreciate the existence of a relatively safe space for an alternative way of life, and want to stay within Huli territory. Nevertheless, many women who arrive at the *dawe anda* seem worn down by violence, disappointment, and their own anger and defiance; thus, this "modern male sanctuary" is largely constructed through women's stigmatization and marginalization.

Conclusion

In light of the foregoing discussion, many readers may be wondering about the status of HIV/AIDS in Papua New Guinea. At the end of 2004, almost 10,000 HIV+ cases had been reported. This number may seem small in comparison to the millions of cases in sub-Saharan Africa and Asia, but it likely does not reflect the epidemiological reality in Papua New Guinea. At the time of my research in the mid-1990s very little research on HIV incidence had been done, and even in the early 2000s most epidemiological research was being conducted in the capital city, with the reporting of cases by hospitals and STD clinics being the only source of information for most areas of the country.[1] By 2004, newspaper articles and health authorities regularly asserted that for every reported case there were at least ten undetected cases, and recent research undertaken by the Papua New Guinea National AIDS Council Secretariat (NACS), as well as past epidemiological research on other STDs, suggests that rates of HIV infection will rapidly become quite high—in rural as well as urban areas, in the general population as well as in people who are conventionally (if problematically) categorized as being at greater risk.[2]

Tari Hospital only began testing for HIV antibodies in 1995, during the period of my research, and at that time tested only those patients who had previously been diagnosed with syphilis or gonorrhea, and whom the STD clinic staff subjectively decided were at risk for HIV.[3] Of five tests done that year, all were negative; of thirty-five tests done in 1996, one was positive. By 2004, Tari Hospital had documented eighty HIV+

or AIDS cases in the area. Some of these were people who had been diagnosed while living in Port Moresby and had come home to be cared for by family. A few of the others were newly married couples who had been unwell themselves and whose first baby had sickened and died soon after birth; bewildered, many numbly agreed to be tested and were shocked to learn they were both HIV+. The hospital staff suspected that they were finding only a small fraction of cases in the Tari area, and then only people who did not suspect that they might be HIV+. Anyone who thought that they might be HIV+, hospital staff said, went to Mendi, Mt. Hagen, or even Port Moresby to be tested, hoping both for more anonymity and a shorter wait for test results at hospitals located in larger urban areas.

If little was known about the incidence of HIV/AIDS at the time of my research, equally little was known by the Tari community about the nature of *"sik AIDS,"* as it was called. While some men and a small number of women knew this term, few people were familiar with the progression of the syndrome, symptoms, prevention methods, means of transmission, lack of cure, or the likelihood that medication would not be available to them should they become ill. During the Christmas holidays of my second year of research, some young male Huli university students conducted public educational talks about AIDS, announcing over a loudspeaker that it was a "disease of the blood" and that it was due to "young girls writing love letters to high school boys." Taboos on speaking explicitly about sex in public (Goldman 1983) hampered their efforts, but everyone understood that sex was implied in this model of causality. Drawing on longstanding gendered anxieties about pollution, the talk also constructed young men as vulnerable to, and potentially victimized by, aggressive and modern young women who lured young men into inappropriate relationships while also derailing their educational careers.

Although discourse about *sik AIDS* was minimal at that time, discourse about *gonolia* (sexually transmitted diseases as the Huli construct them) was elaborate and pervasive (Wardlow 2002c; Hughes 1991a, 1991b; Clark and Hughes 1995). *Gonolia* was spoken of as the manifestation of improper desire, bodies mobilized outside of social reproduction, wealth consumed rather than distributed, genealogical history fragmented and cut short. As many women told me, *pasinja meri* contract *gonolia,* and consequently become infertile, because no one has received bridewealth for them; that is, it is their own selfish use of their sexuality that renders their bodies vulnerable to this particularly modern kind of pollution. (Likewise, but more rarely, women asserted that men contracted *gonolia* from passenger women because they hadn't given bridewealth for them.) Clearly, in this etiology, disease is not conceptualized as resulting from a microbe that is transmitted mechanically from one body to another; rather, moral practice is deeply implicated in disease, and moral practice is defined, at least in part, as acting as a relational person properly connected to others through bridewealth.[4] Thus, the deployment of one's reproductive energies—or the consumption of another's reproductive energies—outside of the web of generative relationality potentially results in both corporeal corruption and barrenness. Female negative agency is cast as especially pernicious in this model: *gonolia* is thought to be the just comeuppance for a woman who "breaks the fence," as well as for the men who seek out the sterile pleasures to be had from her. Thus, while *gonolia* is understood as a disease for which one should go to the health center to receive biomedical treatment, it is also seen as a kind of stigma—that is, a mark of opprobrium, a materialization of one's duly discredited moral state.

Getting Back Inside the Fence

And it is largely because of stigma, and its other very material manifestations—abandonment by male kin, being violently attacked by the wives of sexual partners, the threat of gang rape for being *bighed,* anxiety about future economic security—that many passenger women attempt to retrieve their "encompassed" position. When I met Megeme, Ogai, and Tarali, they were all struggling to give up the *pasinja meri* way of life and to reintegrate themselves into their families and communities. I say "struggling" because this, as one might imagine, was not an easy feat. Not only did they have to surmount pronounced stigma, they also had to overcome the taste they had acquired for a high degree of autonomy—whether this autonomy was expressed through a liberality of language (swearing at others in public), a sense of entitlement to coming and going as they pleased, or the occasional sexual dalliance. In other words, they had to convince others—husbands, natal families—to take them back inside the familial circle, and then they had to discipline themselves to stay within that socio-moral fence. All of them chafed under the restrictions they had decided to reimpose upon themselves, but all of them wanted to relinquish their former way of life for the security of being known as a *wali ore* (although, as chapter 2 amply demonstrates, being a proper, married woman is hardly a guarantee of physical safety). As Sherry Ortner

(1995) has suggested, the practices actors engage in potentially change not only the social structures around them, but also the actors themselves; in these three cases, having *"kalapim banis"* (jumped over the fence), the women found it difficult to renounce a sense of entitlement to self-determination in some arenas.

The ways in which they went about reinventing themselves as *wali ore* differed somewhat, but marriage was key to all of their strategies. Tarali remarried, but still occasionally resorted to the exchange of sex for money when her husband was absent. She was one of the only *pasinja meri* who told me that she was economically motivated to sell sex; however, her explication of this was not what one might expect: she stated that her relationships with her husband and his mother (who lived with them) always fared better if she had her own source of money, and so she covertly sold sex in order to salvage her volatile marriage. Her mother-in-law constantly berated her for her previous life as a *pasinja meri* and for her apparent infertility, and her husband—too easily influenced by his mother's words, she said—would beat her. Being able to provide the household with the occasional chicken and some store-bought rice enabled Tarali to reduce these tensions.

Ogai, for her part, simply began working in her husband's fields again, and when he found her there, she asked him to take her back. He had his own reasons for accepting this proposition: he had lost his job at the mining company and needed help working his land. Moreover, Ogai had deposited their two children with her kin when she ran away from him, arguing that he never sent money home and that her kin were already investing more in "making" their children than he was. She flatly told him that if he didn't take her back she would leave their children with her kin and do her best to make sure he never received any of his own daughter's bridewealth. (Indeed, Ogai was worried that her kin might not permit her to take her children back to her husband's land. Her siblings—having cared for the children during the six years that Ogai lived as a passenger woman—were now "greedy," as Ogai put it, about future rights to her daughter's bridewealth.)

According to Ogai, her husband forgave her for her philandering (although he didn't know the half of it, she said, and might have had second thoughts if he had known the full extent of her sexual escapades) and declared that he himself was one of the *tene* (ultimate causes) of her decision to become a passenger woman: he had *"kalapim"* (jumped over; disrespected) her through his own sexual indiscretions, he had failed to support her when she was raped, and she was right that he had not adequately cared for his children. (I couldn't confirm this account with Ogai's husband or anyone else, and while I have no doubt that Ogai's husband did take her back—she made a special visit just to tell me, and the delight was written all over her face—I am somewhat skeptical of her husband's purportedly abject apology; this may be an example of the "triumphalist agency" Huli women often ascribe to themselves). All seemed to be progressing smoothly, and Ogai had decided to move her children back onto her husband's land, when, embarrassingly, she and her husband caught each other at a local bush disco. This led to a public and violent confrontation, and when I left Tari, Ogai and her children were back living with her kin.

Megeme too had remarried, although she did not live with her husband and avoided him whenever possible.[5] Even though she had given up exchanging sex for money, she was too *"bighed"* for her husband, she declared; that she went wherever she pleased and spoke with whomever she wanted infuriated him. Megeme's other strategy for reestablishing her reputation was to paint herself as devoutly religious; she often claimed that she was a better Christian than those who disparaged her because she did not lie about or hide her sins. Although Megeme never spoke about her *pasinja meri* life in a way that even approached the remorseful or confessional, she asserted that her candor with me was evidence of her proper Christian spirit. "God is *witness trutru* [the real or ultimate witness]," she often told me, "He sees everything." And, she once added, "The people here didn't create you. God created you. Everything you do, you do before his eyes. You are sitting on the earth as if it was denuded of everything. Everything is in the open! You are living like that, and you act in the world. So if you don't speak out about what you do, you are committing a sin. You must speak out! For example, 'this man, he's my lover' or 'that man, he sleeps around, he told me we should go have sex.' I speak out! I don't hide things." To Megeme, hypocrisy was the worst sin. Married women who had affairs, churchgoers who stole, women who sat next to each other in prayer and then viciously dug up each other's gardens—that such people vilified her as a *pasinja meri* made her seethe. Her newfound Christian candor was also quite expedient: she claimed that whenever previous sexual partners approached her, she would loudly and publicly announce that she had just been propositioned, which would shame the men into not asking again.

Certainly not all passenger women are able to find men willing to marry them or have husbands willing to take them back. There are many men who view the possibility of marrying a passenger woman with con-

FIGURE 15. Woman inside the *anda* (the domestic sphere). Families who cannot afford kerosene lamps make them out of empty beer bottles, using rags as wicks.

tempt, sneering, "Passenger women don't know how to work—what would she give me to eat, her vagina?" That *gonolia* is associated with passenger women also deters some men from marrying them, although more because of assumptions about passenger women's infertility than because of fears about disease transmission. Nevertheless, this path seemed more feasible than I expected. While passenger women are typically characterized as lazy, selfish, disloyal, and disobedient, they are also associated with romantic, companionate, and erotic relationships. Thus, some men are willing to take them as second or third wives, particularly since their bridewealth is typically quite low, often less than what a man might usually pay as *tauwa*. (Of course some passenger women use their low bridewealth to escape from such marriages when they go sour, asserting that what was given for them was not *tapu* [bridewealth], but *tauwa*—in other words, that they were never actually married at all.) Thus, if a man can get over her sexual past, marrying a passenger woman is a relatively cheap means for him to obtain an additional wife, who (in the best of all possible worlds) will not only continue to be an amenable sexual companion, but will also work in his fields, bear him children, and care for his pigs.

Structure and Agency

In the course of this book I have discussed the "structures" that propel some women to act in ways that result in them being labeled "passenger women," a label that many come to embrace (albeit with a range of different attitudes, from pride to irony to resignation). The monetization of bridewealth and women's uneasy sense that they have become *"olsem maket"* (like market goods); men's incipient individualism in the context of wage labor and women's perceptions that men are failing to carry out their social obligations; and an organization of gender that channels female agency into a "negative" mode—these are some of the more important factors. In a sense, one can see passenger women's refusal to be "encompassed" by "local" structures (such as bridewealth marriage) as stemming ultimately from the fact that Huli society as a whole is being "encompassed" by the structures of the state and the global economy.

From a practice theory perspective it is also important to ask whether and how passenger women's actions work to reproduce or change the structures around them. Dominant Huli discourses assert that passenger women have no agency: "they are passengers, not the driver," people say, meaning that they have no ability to initiate social, transactional plans and no ability to encompass the endeavors of others in a legible—that is, relational—way. And passenger women themselves, like other women, speak most happily about the opportunities they have had to exercise what might be called "positive agency"—that is, the ability to initiate, contribute to, take credit for, and shape transactional, relational endeavors. They boast of the times when they were able to "go forward, like men" by contributing money or pigs "in their own names" to bridewealth or homicide compensation payments, helping to influence the sociopolitical field in ways that are publicly visible and acclaimed. Thus, like other women, passenger women tend to think of transactional or relational agency as both superior to other forms of agency and innately masculine. Nevertheless, despite dominant discourses to the contrary, passenger women's negative agency can be seen to impact the structures that they inhabit, particularly in the domains of bridewealth and sexuality.

BRIDEWEALTH

In Bourdieu's analysis of marriage he is primarily concerned with how individuals' marriage strategies work to "spontaneously" reproduce the social system:

The constraints that surround every matrimonial choice are so numerous and appear in such complex combinations that the individuals involved cannot possibly deal with all of them consciously . . . Far from being simple procedures . . . these strategies are the product of *habitus,* meaning the practical mastery of a small number of implicit principles that have spawned an infinite number of practices and follow their own pattern . . . Predicated upon a "spontaneous" compliance with the established order and with the will of the guardians of that order . . . *habitus* is the principle that will generate the different solutions . . . which individuals, depending on their position in the social hierarchy, their place in the family's order of birth, their sex, and so forth, can bring to the practical dilemmas. (1976: 141)

That *habitus*—the internalization and embodiment of social structures—seems to lead almost inevitably to the "spontaneous" reproduction of social structures has been one of the primary critiques of Bourdieu's work: if objective structures are so seamlessly internalized as *habitus,* is agency illusory? *Pasinja meri* make an interesting intervention into this predicament: like other Huli women, they have "mastered" the "implicit principle" that bridewealth marriage is what makes women *wali ore,* but at certain critical junctures their compliance is no longer spontaneous, and in fact they choose to stop participating in this "established order" altogether. This would suggest that although external structures are internalized, and indeed fundamentally mold subjectivity and the imaginable possibilities for action, room for other practices exists, and actors can choose to act otherwise even while operating within the dominant categories that make social life meaningful. That is, Huli women who act as *pasinja meri* know and believe that bridewealth is "what women are for," and that is exactly why they choose the path they do. Although they often narrate their initial sexually transgressive acts as impulsive, unplanned, and driven by anger, they are very aware that it is the refusal to be "for" marriage and bridewealth that will most enrage, humiliate, and materially injure their kin or husbands. In other words, although their refusals, disruptions, and transgressions are discursively framed as illegible and "Other" (not *wali ore,* literally, not "real women"), in fact their actions are quite legible to those around them in that they simultaneously stem from, display, and defy aspects of normative femininity. Thus, Huli women's agency—including that of *pasinja meri*—is not a seamless reproduction, a performance of objective social structures, or something alien or foreign to these structures; it responds to these structures and enacts ideologies that define women as able to influence the social field through bodily disorder.

Passenger women's transgressive sexual acts can thus be seen as attempts to disrupt social reproduction. If bridewealth marriage is the principal means by which normative gender roles, corporate clan-based sociality, and genealogical temporality are reproduced, then passenger women's repudiation of marriage is a refusal to contribute to social reproduction. Indeed, passenger women can be seen as refusing to participate in the "trafficking of women" as Gayle Rubin first theorized it—that is, the exchange of women that occurs through and enables the reproduction of kinship systems. In "The Traffic in Women: Notes on the 'Political Economy' of Sex," Rubin (1975) argued that "sex/gender systems are not ahistorical emanations of the human mind; they are products of historical human activity . . . There is an economics and a politics to sex/gender systems" (204). Putting both Marxist and Lacanian spins on Levi-Strauss's analysis of marriage as the exchange of women, Rubin argued that gender—at least in pre-state societies—is a product of kinship systems: "[There is] a taboo against the sameness of men and women, a taboo dividing the sexes into two mutually exclusive categories, a taboo which exacerbates the biological differences between the sexes and thereby creates gender . . . Furthermore, individuals are engendered in order that marriage be guaranteed" (178–80). More specifically, female gender must result in persons who are psychologically amenable to being exchanged; thus, Rubin concluded that "we are not only oppressed as women, we are oppressed by having to be women" (204).

In an interview with Judith Butler, Rubin suggested that "it might be possible to get beyond gender identity if one could do something like overthrow kinship" (1997: 72), and in a sense, that is exactly what passenger women are doing in partial, fragmented, and atomistic ways. They are taking aim at their kin—particularly their male kin—precisely where women can hurt them most: through disrupting the kinship-based trafficking in women, appropriating their own sexuality, selling it, and keeping the resources acquired for themselves. Of course, whether passenger women intend through their practices to "get beyond gender identity" is another question. They are certainly aware that many of their acquired behaviors contravene proper femininity, and they themselves associate some of their actions—mobility, commodity consumption, the open display of one's powers of attraction—with masculinity. Nevertheless, an awareness of the transgressive nature of one's behavior does not necessarily imply a conscious attempt to "get beyond gender." What is undoubtedly intended by many women, however, is the humiliation and economic punishment of their kin.

Whether the cumulative actions of individual passenger women have an impact on the bridewealth system itself is a complex issue. Certainly some people worry that they might: on a few occasions, men I interviewed or spoke with became swept up in a kind of rhapsody of moral panic, envisioning an era in which more and more women become *pasinja meri,* no bridewealth is exchanged, there is thus no real marriage, children therefore have no real fathers, no one knows who belongs to what clans, and "everyone is a passenger" (meaning everyone is socially disconnected and without meaningful purpose). However, anxiety about how the future might look if bridewealth exchanges were to cease does not mean that the actions of passenger women are actually having this kind of structural effect. The fact that the category "passenger woman" is stigmatized and is explicitly contrasted with the category *wali ore* (good women) potentially reinforces the importance of bridewealth marriage as the structure by which proper adult women are constituted. Negative agency may thus actually serve to bolster hegemonic structures. In other words, when one's personhood is constructed as "naturally" encompassed by or subsumed under others, the refusal to be subsumed may be so contrary to the social order that one's very status as a person is thrown into question, thus fortifying the dominant structures that define personhood. Indeed, one of the worst things a Huli man can declare when he discovers that his sister has "become" a passenger woman is that if she is killed, he will neither seek revenge nor demand homicide compensation. This is the ultimate statement of repudiation: to refuse to avenge the murder of one's sister is to deny that she is one's sister, which, by implication, is to deny that she is a person.

On the other hand, it is also the case that *pasinja meri* tend to be more reflective and critical about bridewealth marriage than other women, at moments questioning its hegemonic status. In other words, negative agency may have a gradual impact by putting actors in subject positions where they are predisposed to a more critical consciousness of the structures that have shaped their actions. To reiterate Ortner's (1995) point, the practices actors engage in potentially change the actors themselves; thus, a more critical orientation may emerge after one has already acted in ways that look like resistance. Stepping—or being thrust—outside of dominant structures may enable one to view them as less natural and less necessary. Thus, Ogai, for example, argued long and hard with her relatives that her younger sister should not be made to marry. She was too headstrong and temperamental, Ogai claimed, and she would only end up being killed by her husband, committing suicide, or running off to become a *pasinja meri*. Convinced of her position, she argued that she and her other sisters had already provided sufficient bridewealth for their family and that her kin should therefore stop being so "greedy." Then she threatened to take her own children back to her husband, intimating that she would deny her kin any share of her daughter's future bridewealth.

In this threat, of course, Ogai inhabits a contradictory political position: she attempts to get her sister out of the bridewealth system by using the leverage of her own daughter's future bridewealth, thus simultaneously challenging and complying with the structure at hand. Indeed, it is her daughter's future bridewealth that seems to give her the most social leverage: she exercises influence over both husband and natal kin by threatening each with its loss. Bridewealth becomes both an oppressive structure against which she struggles and the weapon she wields in this struggle. Thus, negative agency, in this case, does not result in wholesale repudiation of the structure at hand. Of course, it is important to bear in mind that "the bridewealth system," as I call it, is not the only structure enmeshing women in relations of inequality; rather, it is the imbrication of bridewealth with the organization of wage labor, with the monetization of the economy, and with state policies and institutions that increasingly molds the contemporary dynamics of marriage. Thus, wholesale repudiation of bridewealth may not be in Ogai's, or other women's, best interests.

SEXUAL "TRAFFICKING" AND EROTIC AGENCY

By stepping outside of the bridewealth system, it is possible that passenger women may unwittingly be exchanging one form of "trafficking" (the reproduction of kinship through the exchange of women) for another (the trafficking of women in commercialized sex work). Arguably their practices most importantly shape "structure" by contributing to the institutionalization of prostitution as a socioeconomic niche. However, at this point in time there is much that distinguishes the practices of Huli passenger women from sex work, survival sex, or transactional sex as these are typically described and theorized in the academic literature (Wardlow 2004). First, "initiation" into this subject position often occurs as an act of resistance, or what I prefer to conceptualize as negative agency; thus, at least for passenger women themselves, selling sex is not the fundamental truth of their identity—or is so only to the extent that the sale of sex is an act of spite against husband and/or natal family. Relatedly, passenger women's sexual liaisons are rarely conceptualized by them as motivated by economic need. Undeniably, the means by which women can obtain cash are few, and no doubt passenger women appreciate the financial benefits of selling sex; nevertheless, the unrelenting structural violence so marked in many contemporary analyses of prostitution and transactional sex (Farmer et al. 1996; Schoepf 1992, 1993) is less acute in this context (at least at this time).[6]

If their sexuality is initially a clan resource or relational potency wrested and alienated from their kin, it eventually becomes for some passenger women a form of individualized erotic agency—that is, the power and delight of being desired, desired so much that a man is willing to part with cash, no less. Huli male corporeality has long been constructed as embodying potential erotic agency; a man's moral status, charisma, and social potency are said to show on the skin and can attract women to him. The female body is not thought of as compelling in this way, and thus women must sometimes resort to *hubi bi* (love magic) to attract male interest. This is not to say that men have no use for exogenous technologies to enhance their attractiveness; certainly they do. However, men's spells, rituals, and technologies tend to work through the male body— purifying it, masculinizing it, or in some way augmenting its power (Biersack 2001). Huli women's love magic, in contrast, does not enhance the female body; rather, it works by subordinating male will, occluding male intentions and supplanting female ones in their place. Thus, while women often think of their bodies as powerful in a generative, nurturing, or even physically aggressive way, they don't often speak of their bodies as erotically powerful. Many passenger women do, however.

Thus, one way that the practices of passenger women change existing structures is through their embodiment and enactment of an individually possessed, erotically powerful female sexuality. It is important not to mistake this erotic agency for some kind of emancipatory practice through which passenger women "discover" their sexuality. For one, the costs for women of possessive sexual individualism can be quite high: repudiation by family, gang rape, and the stigma attached to any children born as *"nogat papa"* (not having a father) or as *"mix mix"* (having too many fathers, as it were)—both of which further imply the lack of a paternal clan identity. That is, a passenger woman's child is not a *tene* (agnate) of any clan, a situation that presents many potential difficulties, particularly for boys. Moreover, many passenger women express as much disgust and anxiety about sexual fluids—their own and their male partners'—as other women do. Nevertheless, passenger women do embody a kind of sexual "self-propriety" (Jolly 2001a) and do often speak with a kind of pride about their abilities to elicit desire. They also talk more openly and less ambivalently than other women about what they see as their abilities to use erotic agency to accomplish other things, such as achieving alternative kinds of relationships with men or traveling to other parts of Papua New Guinea. Finally, self-identified passenger women often discursively connect their sexual self-assertion with other forms of assertiveness—speaking loudly in public forums, daring to approach government officials that other women might not, feeling bold enough to ask what various unfamiliar products are for in urban stores, and so on.[7]

From "Alliance" to "Sexuality"

Changes are taking place in the meanings and practices of bodily desire among the Huli (Clark 1997; Clark and Hughes 1995), and these changes can be construed as indicating a shift from something that looks like what Foucault (1990a) calls "the deployment of alliance" toward something like "the deployment of sexuality," with its attendant emphasis on individualism, productivity, consumption, and self-monitoring. This assertion is not meant to suggest a teleological scheme in which passenger women are the sentinel subjects of a predetermined "stage" or "regime" of modern sexuality. Rather, it is to point out that it can be instructive to attempt the translation of Foucault's genealogical concepts into contexts with other cultural, economic, and colonial histories, both in order to analyze substantive changes occurring in sexual discourse and practice and to problematize Foucauldian concepts (Knauft 1996). Thus, in the Huli case, it is clear that this is not precisely the regime of sexuality as Foucault describes it, nor are quite the same factors at work. For example, Foucault focuses on governmental institutions and the scientific disciplines that legitimize and receive legitimation from them. According to Foucault's history of the West, subjects are increasingly produced and controlled through "standards of normality which are disseminated by a range of assessing, diagnostic, prognostic and normative knowledges such as criminology, medicine, psychology and psychiatry" (Armstrong 2003: 3). In contrast, monetization, wage labor, migration, Christian missionization, and even imported pornographic media may be more important in constituting new kinds of modern sexual subjects among the Huli. In other words, there are a range of factors that are constitutive of sexual subjects in Papua New Guinea, and some of these factors overlap with those that constituted modern sexuality in Europe (the rise of pastoral power), while others are unique to the history of colonialism and globalization in the region.

Perhaps more troublingly, it would seem that some characteristics that are central to Foucault's conceptualization of the modern subject apply equally well to the Huli "premodern" context: arguably discourses and practices concerning the powers and dangers of the female body have long worked to instill in Huli women a state of "conscious and permanent visibility" (Foucault 1979: 201), as well as practices of self-surveillance. This observation raises the possibility that not only is Foucault deaf to the differences that female gender makes—a charge many feminist scholars have made (Morris 1988; Soper 1993)—but also that gender may condition the epistemic nature of modernity (and other historical concatenations of power and knowledge, for that matter) (Felski 1995; Wardlow 2002b). In other words, the nature of the relationship between power and knowledge, so central to Foucault's analysis, may differ by gender, making broad generalizations about how this relationship operates during various historical periods and how "the subject" is produced by this relationship, more problematic (Deveaux 1996; Plaza 1981).

Scholars, and particularly feminist scholars, have been drawn to Foucault's work because of his attention to the micropolitics of the body and his analyses of the way in which disciplinary power operates outside of the formal political realm and reaches into the most intimate and "private" of domains (Bartky 1988; Bordo 1993). At the same time, however, they have been wary (Bartky 1995), or even condemnatory (Hartsock 1990), about his theorization of "the subject" as a "discursive effect" (but see Butler 1990 for an alternative view). Thus, Bartky (1995) compares the "good Foucault," who asserts that resistance is not only possible but is always present, with the "bad Foucault," who suggests that our assumption that we have primary and stable identities capable of agency is an illusion continually produced through the discourses in which we are enmeshed and through the disciplinary practices to which we willingly and regularly "subject" ourselves. Thus, according to the latter model, we experience ourselves as individuals who possess a sexual nature that contains the truth of our identities because modern discourses have produced this embodied conviction within us.

Again, passenger women make an interesting intervention into this theorization of modern sexuality as discursive effect. Passenger women are not first and foremost an effect of a modern medico-religious discourse; rather, they are a refusal of the "deployment of alliance": they repudiate their encompassed positions within the bridewealth system by amputating their sexual capacities from it. Thus, in the first instance, passenger women are an agentive act of disruption, neither fully determined by existing Huli discourses about *wali ore* nor fully subjected by the dividing and typologizing discourses and practices described by Foucault. It may be, particularly with the globalization of both international health and religious apparatuses directed at combating HIV/AIDS, that such discourses will soon catch up to passenger women and more firmly fix them to the "truth" of their identity. However, at the moment they demonstrate the possibility of agency within and between competing discursive regimes.

Given their liminal positionality, passenger women are, in a sense, not full "subjects," which may help to explain their figurative and polysemous role in the following narrative. I conclude this book with the story of Waripa, a woman imprisoned for the murder of her brother-in-law. This story, like the story of Pugume Mangobe's murder that opened this book, had taken on mythic qualities in the public imagination, vividly dramatizing the gendered tensions of modernity. I heard about Waripa long before I ever met her, for people loved to tell of how she had avenged her sister's murder by publicly stabbing her sister's husband. People spoke of her with approval, and some women admiringly asserted that she had "gone forward, like a man" when her own male kin refused to do their duty of revenge. Even the prison warden intimated that he was of the opinion that she shouldn't be in prison for what she had done. I finally met Waripa during my last month of fieldwork when I interviewed the three female inmates at Hawa prison. I had wanted to learn more about female violence, and I hypothesized that most of the women in prison would be there for violent crimes since I rarely heard of women being arrested for theft. (In fact, the prison had very few female inmates, and according to the prison records, most of them had been there for failing to pay fines for absconding from their marriages, for public fighting, or for other minor infractions.)

· · ·

Waripa was the second child of six and had never attended school because her parents decided she was needed at home for agricultural work. She was not angry about this: she was proud of her gardening and pig-raising skills, and through her labors she was able pay the school fees for her youngest sister, who she said was like a daughter to her. Their parents died before this youngest sister married, and, highly religious, Waripa objected to her sister's choice of husband because he already had two wives. However, the men in the family supported the match because the husband-to-be had rights to land on which a few of the power pylons between the Hides power station and the Porgera gold mine were located, and therefore received annual "occupation fees." Waripa, as her sister's primary caretaker, was designated to distribute the pigs that their mother would have distributed, but she claims that she was so opposed to the marriage that she refused to do so for days, hoping that her sister would change her mind and that the bridewealth could be returned.

But her sister did not change her mind, and in fact the marriage seemed relatively harmonious. However, about a year into the marriage, a tribal fight broke out between their two clans. A female member of Waripa's clan—a woman Waripa didn't actually know well and whom she scathingly described as "a *pasinja meri* who had AIDS in her side"—was, according to Waripa, fatally kicked in that side by someone from her sister's husband's clan. Her sister's husband's clan refused to pay homicide compensation, and in retaliation some of Waripa's kin burned down some houses and stores belonging to her sister's husband. In further retaliation, Waripa claimed, her sister's husband hired some men to kill his wife, Waripa's sister. It is important to remember that no AIDS cases were diagnosed in the Tari area until 1996—a number of years after these events took place—and thus it is highly unlikely that the woman described by Waripa as a *pasinja meri* actually had AIDS. I believe that Waripa characterized her in this way to indicate that her sister had become a pawn in interclan hostilities Waripa found pointless (her tone of voice during this part of her narrative was contemptuous). By asserting the worthlessness of the woman whose death precipitated the series of retaliatory events, she was condemning the conflict as a whole, and thus suggesting that her sister's death had been wholly unnecessary. (Also of interest is that Waripa's version of events departs dramatically from other people's. Waripa's sister died after falling out of her husband's open-back truck while he was driving, and many people said that he was at fault and should pay compensation for her death because he had failed to maintain his vehicle, even after being warned by the authorities that his vehicle was a hazard [Geoff Hiatt, personal communication]. Only Waripa asserted the importance of the history of conflict between their clans, and only she claimed that her sister's husband had both refused to allow her sister to ride inside the cab of his vehicle and had persuaded his male kin to push her out of the vehicle.)

Whether this was a case of negligent homicide or something more malevolent, Waripa's sister's husband refused to pay any compensation for his wife's death, and Waripa's male kin did not pursue a tribal fight against him. Perhaps his clan was too strong, or perhaps they felt that they were in a precarious position, unable to prove that he was to blame. After her sister's death, Waripa repeatedly saw her brother-in-law in town. She would go to the Tari market to sell cigarettes, and he would deliberately choose her out of the dozens of women to buy from. This was a flagrant violation of Huli *mana,* which says that a murderer should not consume food produced by the clan of his victim. On three occasions he approached her with a huge wad of cash, chortled that he had just won at a game of "Lucky," a popular card game, and tried to pay for a few cigarettes with a 50K note. She interpreted his behavior as an attempt to insult and provoke her: in essence, he was boasting that he was "lucky" in more ways than one since he could win card games *and* get away with her sister's murder. Moreover, he was showing her that he had money, loads of it, to pay compensation for her sister's death, but would not. The third time he demanded change for a large bill she responded by growling that she would give him his change and then some. When he turned around to leave the market place, she followed him and attacked him from behind. Upon grabbing him, she realized that he was carrying a knife inside his clothes, and she seized it and stabbed him.

Waripa claimed that on the day she killed him her ghost sister appeared to her in the form of a *pasinja meri* and promised to help her take revenge. As Waripa followed her brother-in-law out of the marketplace, she almost lost him in the crowd, but her sister, still in the form of a passenger woman, caught his attention, flirted with him, and held him by the shoulder, thereby allowing Waripa to catch up to him. She said that it was her sister's apparition as an enticing passenger woman that urged her forward and helped her to avenge her murder.

· · ·

The figure of the *pasinja meri* is mobilized in this narrative in contradictory ways that show the polysemous and multivalent position passenger women occupy in the Huli public imagination. Waripa uses the stigma attached to passenger women to indicate the worthlessness of one woman—the woman whose death precipitated clan conflict—but uses the erotic agency associated with passenger women to indicate their power over men. As Waripa said, it was only her sister's appearance as a *pasinja meri* that gave her the courage, sense of efficacy, and presence of mind to physically accost her sister's husband. And it was her sister's guise as a passenger woman that held her husband in place, enabling Waripa to grab hold of him. Thus, despite being stigmatized and sneered at, *pasinja meri* occupy an important symbolic space in the popular imaginary, a space that joins sexuality, death, and transformation; a space which offers all the desires and anxieties of modernity.

Notes

Introduction

1. All names used in this monograph are pseudonyms, and care has been taken to obscure place-names and other identifying features.

2. In this ethnography I usually use the word "gardens" instead of "fields" and the word "gardening" instead of "agricultural work." In Papua New Guinea people use the Tok Pisin terms *"gaden"* (garden) and *"wokim gaden"* (literally, work garden; agricultural work) to refer to any area under cultivation, large or small.

3. While earlier ethnographies of the Huli suggest that such rigidly defined gender roles have long been the case (Glasse 1968; Goldman 1983), it is also possible that certain "traditional" aspects of femaleness have become more pronounced in the contemporary context; that is, insistence on the "traditional" and "authentic" nature of rigid gender roles can be a strategy for maintaining cultural continuity in the face of forces perceived to be eroding cultural identity (Wardlow 2002b).

4. As many anthropologists have pointed out, the deployment of such discourses can be contextual and strategic; that is to say, such statements are cultural resources that may be articulated for certain reasons at certain times and are not necessarily monolithic. Thus, I should note that while denigrating discourses about women are prominent, they are not mobilized in all contexts all of the time, and there are other (more muted) discourses that characterize women as emotionally nurturing, self-sacrificing, brave, loyal, insightful, and capable of motivating men to proper, moral action when men themselves have become lax or selfish.

5. This is certainly not always the case in other world areas: the Aba Women's War in colonial Nigeria, and Igbo women's organizations more generally, are

perhaps the most well known ethnographic examples we have of female collective agency (Amadiume 1987; Van Allen 1972).

6. Papua New Guinea has, of course, inherited such discourses—if not psychiatry, then certainly the Christian confession and institutions related to medicine and public health. Nevertheless, at the time of my fieldwork these discourses had not made great inroads into public imaginings of why passenger women act as they do.

7. The film *Advertising Missionaries* is a wonderful depiction of how such theater groups act as mobile, embodied commercials.

8. Marilyn Strathern (1972) describes Hagen women as "in between" their natal families and their affinal families; that is, important social, political, and economic links between men are forged through the ties of marriage, and women can gain prestige as the agentive embodiments of these links or "roads" (another idiom used by Hagen people). At the same time, "Brothers-in-law may assert their own joint interests against the wife/sister, for between them they control the woman, who is powerless to act on her own accord . . . what prestige she has derives from her dependence on males. By herself she is nothing" (ix). Marriage similarly positions Huli women as potentially important actors between their brothers and husbands; however, in the contemporary context, many women suggest that this role—and its concomitant power—are eroding as men become less dependent on affinal relationships and more dependent on ties forged through school, work, church, and other modern institutions, such as "youth groups."

9. In all I hired four field assistants over the course of my fieldwork, two men and two women. Only one, Henry Hariki, persevered with me throughout the fieldwork period, and I owe him a tremendous debt of thanks for his hard work, resourcefulness, intellectual acuity, and willingness to speak with me about gendered issues that were often embarrassing or irritating to him. When I speak of "my field assistant" in this book, I am almost always referring to him.

10. My testimony only confirmed the mediators' suspicions that Alembo had beaten Yerime, but since I was the only adult witness to the case, it is possible that the outcome would have been different had I chosen not to testify. Not surprisingly, Alembo was very angry with me for testifying against him, and since Yerime was leaving the household until he could pay compensation for injuring her, it was impossible for me to stay there. Alembo implied, however, that he would not take it well should I attempt to move to another household in the area. Finding myself in an untenable and unsafe position, I had my field assistants walk me to town the next day, and I only returned later (with the authorities) to retrieve my belongings.

1. "Tari is a *jelas* place"

1. Many women—particularly those whose husbands are absent or, ironically, those whose husbands are traditionalists who prefer to live apart from their wives—gamble for high stakes in the privacy of women's houses at night. Even

the little boys I knew gambled; when they didn't have any toiea they wagered other valuable items such as shoes or pencils.

2. Since I observed occupation fee distributions only once and in only one location, I do not know if this was common practice. It cannot be assumed that community leaders in other areas advocated for women or had as much influence. On the other hand, Huli women, as agnates, may own land "in their own names," as Huli people say, so it is possible that elsewhere they have been included in compensation payments for land.

3. For example, when my field assistant and his younger brother decided to live on contiguous areas of their father's land, they felt that this was an unprecedented and potentially precarious undertaking: they were not establishing ties to other pieces of land—their mother's father's land, for example—and they might find that with such close proximity they could not get along. They asserted that an important component of their endeavor was to generate new *mana* that would enable them to live next to each other.

4. The "system" is actually more negotiable than the sketch I have just provided. For example, over many generations, descendants of *yamuwini* may be designated as *tene* if they have consistently lived on the land and acted like *tene*—that is, if they have helped the clan during times of warfare and with financial obligations. However, there are no hard and fast rules about this, and the decision to designate someone as *tene* is usually strategic. For example, one woman I knew had lived in town for a number of years and was therefore worried that her daughters would have no secure claims to land for gardening. She thus strategized to have her daughters made *tene* of a clan to which she herself had only a *yamuwini* relationship. She explained that her request was granted, but only because she had no sons and all her daughters were in school. In other words, the clan granting her request took a calculated risk by figuring that all the daughters would probably marry out and only want to maintain small gardens on the clan's land. If the young women were given *tene* status, the clan, or, more accurately, some members of the clan, might have claims on the bridewealth of these daughters; and since they were women, all their children would once again only have *yamuwini* status. Thus, both parties felt like they benefited from this shift in kinship status.

5. And, according to the Tari Hospital injury records, this does occasionally happen. Moreover, throwing oneself into these trenches is a method some women use in their attempts to abort unwanted pregnancies, medically assisted abortion being illegal in Papua New Guinea.

2. "To finish my anger"

1. One version of this myth I recorded was: When he called out "Mother of Life" this woman was silent. When he called out "Mother of Death," she answered. Did she cause us to go with that which is good (or go with Payapaya/Jesus)? No! She said no, and so now it is go with headaches, go with diarrhea, go with fever. So now this is the way things are. Go with death she said.

Now we should reflect on this. *(Ai wali piagome "Habe Ainya-o" layagola tembola ho wuwa. "Homabe Ainya" layagola, "yia" layago. O piagoni payapaya la pube lole piyago ndo. Wahalu I hagua la pube, ti bele la pube, homama la pube layago. Ayu kabagonigo homa la pube layagoni. Ayu ogoni manda puwa habe.)*

2. Calling a woman "mother of [child's name]" is the normative form of address among the Huli, but it is also a constant reminder to adult women of their reproductive status. Married women who have not yet had children are usually called "mother of [the name of one of their pigs]"—e.g., I was called Nogo Mali Ainya (mother of the pig named Mali), after a pig that had been given to me. Married women without children tend to be very sensitive to this form of address and eager to have children.

3. The myth does not explicitly say that sexual reproduction substitutes for bodily renewal, but this is its implicit logic. Whether or not sexual reproduction would have been precluded by the consumption of First Man's special water is debated by the Huli themselves. My field assistant once argued that it was a good thing that this woman refused to respond to the call "Mother of Life" because it was clear that overpopulation was becoming a problem among the Huli. Imagine, he said, what it would be like if all the people who had ever been born were still alive. No, his older interlocutors responded, for if she had responded to the name Mother of Life, then no would one die and there would be no need for sexual reproduction.

4. One of the names given to men who participated in bachelor cults was Iba Ngiya—literally, water given—which could perhaps refer to the bespelled water that First Man was never able to give to his child.

5. In her book on hate speech, Judith Butler explores what it means to be "called a name": "To be called a name is one of the first forms of linguistic injury that one learns . . . Being called a name is also one of the conditions by which a subject is constituted in language . . . In being called an injurious name, one is derogated and demeaned. But the name holds out another possibility as well: by being called a name, one is also, paradoxically, given a certain possibility for social existence . . . Thus the injurious address . . . may also produce an unexpected and enabling response" (Butler 1997: 2). It is exactly this kind of philosophy of language that is at work in the myth. The male protagonist attempts to constitute the identity of the woman, and their child, by hailing her as the Mother of Life. She refuses to respond, and angered, as Huli men often are by women's refusal to cooperate, First Man calls her a name, Mother of Death, and constitutes her in this way, thereby producing an "unexpected" subject who sarcastically embraces this label and thus destines humanity to mortality, an agentive act if there ever was one.

6. Apparently some women did participate in tribal fights during the early colonial period by running onto the battlefield to collect arrows that had missed their mark, cheering on their own warriors, and jeering at enemy warriors (Ron Hiatt, personal communication).

7. Important exceptions to this are women's dirges, which are often said to motivate men to seek revenge.

8. Huli men's attention to their bodily appearance and moral state is reminis-

cent of Foucault's discussion of Greek men's "care of the self" (1990b). But, as Bristow points out, "Foucault's discussion of the 'care of the self' is strangely unaware of how the male citizen's ethical development might involve interaction with women, notably the wives whose voices remain surprisingly muted" (1997:191). Similarly, Soper notes, "Foucault defines the ethical so as to make it appear a very private—and masculine—affair" (1993: 41). Huli women, in contrast, feel strongly implicated in the maintenance of the healthy and ethical male body.

9. It is said that a man who uses cooking firewood that a woman has stepped over may be injured by her sexual substances as he inhales the smoke.

10. This act might seem to be an example of "positive agency" (not negative agency) in that a woman is taking steps to harness her husband's energies for her own purposes. However, it is still the case that she is refusing to manage her body properly, potentially endangering not only her husband, but also other persons and things (other men, children, ritual objects, pigs, weapons, etc.) that might inadvertently come into contact with her uncontrolled substances. Moreover, many of the stories I heard about women who had done this may have been apocryphal, and they were almost always told as cautionary tales—that is, they were all about women being caught and beaten for attempting to subordinate their husbands in this way.

11. Barss (1991) used a demographic database maintained by the Tari Research Unit (TRU), a branch of the Papua New Guinea Institute of Medical Research. Due to lack of funds, this project ended in 1995. For twenty-five years, however, TRU followed the births, deaths, and migration of approximately 30,000 people in the Tari Basin through a system of verbal reporting in which Huli men were hired to keep track of 500–1,000 people on their own clan territories and report all demographic events monthly. This enabled researchers to study the fertility and mortality rates for a highly dispersed rural population that would not have otherwise reported its births and deaths. Barss himself was particularly interested in the "verbal autopsy" data: when a "demographic reporter" learned that someone in the population assigned to him had died, he would conduct a detailed verbal autopsy to ascertain the cause of death.

When I spoke with women at the Tari District Women's Association about the high rate of female suicide indicated by Barss's analysis, they were suspicious of the data and asserted that some apparent suicides were actually murders in which a husband killed his wife and then strung her up to make it look like she had hanged herself. Moreover, they asserted that since all the demographic reporters used for the study were men and members of the clans for which they were gathering information, they would have been motivated to protect their fellow male clan members and would therefore have been motivated to ascribe a woman's death to suicide rather than murder.

12. Although Goldman does not discuss the use of the word *"ba"* in children's socialization for physical aggression, it can be seen in some of the Huli texts he analyzes for other purposes (Goldman 1987: 453). The hitting games Rutherford (2003: 49) describes for the Biak also sound very similar those of the Huli.

13. Local dispute mediators are elderly male community leaders who are ap-

pointed by the government to settle conflicts as best they can and thereby stem the tide of cases flooding the government offices in Tari town. These mediators have no powers of enforcement, and the decisions they make through village court cases can be appealed at the district court office in Tari town. Where I worked the local dispute mediators were highly respected and very few of their decisions were appealed to a higher level of authority.

14. Centers of Distance Education are a popular educational strategy in Papua New Guinea, allowing people to attain high school diplomas and other credentials without having to score high enough on national exams to get into boarding high schools and without having to pay to attend these schools.

15. Only recently, in such popular visual media as *Terminator 2, G.I. Jane,* or *Buffy the Vampire Slayer,* has female physical aggression been represented as rationally motivated and effective (and even cosmologically mandated in Buffy's case).

16. When asked why women do not injure or murder people as frequently as men, men will give a variety of reasons, but an innate constitutional lack of aggression is not one of them; according to both men and women, women have the same propensity as men for physical aggression. What women lack, men say, is the ability to discern the proper moments and motivations for violence.

17. A number of researchers have raised the question of whether violence against women has increased or decreased relative to the past (Jolly 1996, n.d.). Without adequate data, it is difficult to compare pre- and postcolonial rates of gendered violence; however, the ethnographic literature about the Huli suggests that women have long been subject to male disciplinary violence. Glasse (1968), for example, alludes to men burning wives' genitals as punishment for adultery, and one of the earliest colonial patrol reports for the area where I conducted my research discusses an incident in which a man struck his wife with an axe for accepting cabbage from another man. His clan members then shot and killed her with their bows and arrows, and a tribal fight subsequently erupted over her murder, during which four men were killed (Jinks 1959). While it is important to examine colonial reports with a critical eye, they do suggest that male violence against women was extreme in the precolonial period.

However, there is also much evidence that violence against women in Melanesia more generally has increased in the postcontact era (Toft 1985; Counts 1992, 1993). Bradley (1988) notes that the fact of bridewealth is used to justify men's right to make increasing demands of wives and then to beat them when they are perceived as "failing in their duties." Jolly similarly attributes this apparent increase to "the novel pressures of marriage—how the cash economy creates a new dependency between spouses, how bridewealth has become inflated and commoditized as bride-price, how the family has become more nucleated (and thus other kin are less likely to intervene), and how the old ideas of a husband's domination have been amplified by the ways in which both state and church construct him as the head of the household" (n.d.: 13–14).

18. Tribal fight injuries were excluded because I wanted to focus on fights that were motivated by interpersonal, not political, conflicts, although admittedly

these categories are not always distinct. The numbers in this table do not include mortality figures. I considered doing a similar analysis of the morgue records at the hospital, but decided this was somewhat pointless: people do not bring bodies to the morgue unless they are unsure of the cause of death.

19. When I finally realized just how important physical aggression was to female identity and friendship, I resolved that the next time I was with a friend when a fight broke out I would join in. However, by that time I was living in my own flat in town where I was not as exposed to interpersonal altercations.

20. As the story went, Liname's husband caught her selling cigarettes outside of a *dawe anda*. He was angry that she was anywhere in the vicinity of a *dawe anda*. Further, he was embarrassed because she saw that he was a *dawe anda* participant himself, something he had tried to hide from her. Men's and women's stories about what happened next diverge at this point. Men say that he was trying to chastise her by hitting her with the flat of his bush knife, and it was only because she threw her arm up to deflect the blow that she was injured by the blade. Women tended to assert that he was trying to cut her throat and it was only because she threw her arm up to deflect the blade that she wasn't dead.

21. There may be some "selection bias" at work in my representation. The interviews I conducted were opportunistic, not "random"—that is, I interviewed those women who were willing to be interviewed, often allowing curious strangers to approach me in town or using women I had already interviewed to recruit their friends and kin. It is therefore possible that my sample is somewhat weighted toward women whose lives were more than usually conflict ridden and who wanted to air their resentments by speaking with an interviewer.

22. Knauft, writing more generally of the gendered tensions of modernity in Melanesia, has argued that "as women become more desirous of trade goods, but are constrained in their extra-domestic activities, they may act by demanding more commodities from men" (1997: 241). From Huli women's perspectives, however, their requests often have little to do with striving to be more "modern," and more to do with demanding what women see as men's fair share in child rearing. Huli women complained more often about men's negligence in providing soap or food for children than about their negligence in providing trade store goods for the women themselves.

23. Traditional mana also says that a man should only have sex with his wife on four consecutive days following the end of her menstrual period and that once she is pregnant he should abstain from sex with her until the child is approximately three years old. Some women expressed particular frustration about men's failure to abide by postpartum taboos and the consequent decrease in child spacing.

3. "I am not the daughter of a pig!"

1. See Glasse (1959) for an explication of Huli homicide compensation.

2. I interviewed a few young women whose young husbands were unable to

give bridewealth in full at the time of the marriage and whose families solved the problem by having the young couple live on the woman's natal territory until the young man's family could complete the bridewealth payment. Such a situation served to remind everyone that the young woman's productive capacities had not yet been fully transferred to her affinal family, and it also served as a kind of de facto bride service, with the young husband assisting the young woman's family in various productive tasks until the bridewealth was given in full.

3. Sturzenhofecker (1998) found that newly married Duna couples are expected to raise pigs to pay back those kin who contributed to the wife's bridewealth, thus effectively demanding that a woman pay for her own bridewealth. Huli women who had lived with or married into Duna families reviled this practice.

4. Though Breton emphasizes the material aspect of bridewealth, he also shows that participation in this process of collective investment is not only an economic undertaking, but also a bodily one. When an outsider moves in with a clan and participates in the clan's bridewealth compensations, for instance, he is transformed: "Contributing to the purchase of shares of his new brothers' wives enables an immigrant to receive a portion in return for the payment of their sisters—a payment he 'eats' and which transforms his identity. His social reaffiliation—described as a body transformation—is the consequence of his monetary contributions" (1999: 566).

5. This case also shows how men are better able to manipulate the bureaucratic structures of the nation-state and to escape the relational logic of bridewealth when it benefits them to do so. Igibe successfully invoked relatively new rules about what counts as "evidence" in village court cases, knowing full well that Wangale did not have an X-ray in hand and thus deftly getting around the fact that his son had, in fact, beaten Wangale.

6. Time is often of the essence in Huli marriages, and young men express much anxiety about their ability to assemble the necessary cash and pigs for bridewealth payments, worrying that the women they have chosen will be married to other men who are able to mobilize these payments more quickly. Sexual assault, then, is usually a reliable means of preventing other possible marriages: a young man may feel that his only guaranteed recourse is to "steal" his beloved's sexuality—sometimes through force—thus putting her kin in the position of demanding that the marriage take place (see also Wardlow in press).

7. The image of shit is often used to signify the repudiation of reciprocity and relationship (Clark 1995; Weiner 1994).

8. This law also contributes to the increasing construction of women as wives and mothers, as opposed to sisters and clan agnates—a construction that may contribute to women's economic dependence and subordination (Sacks 1979; Dureau 1998).

9. The records for these shorter (one- to three-month) prison stays were poorly kept and I was not permitted to examine them thoroughly; thus, even a simple numerical comparison of women's various crimes proved impossible.

10. Here, then, is a case in which the human labor put into a commodity does not increase its value at all. Or perhaps more accurately, transforming a pig from a transactional item into a consumable commodity reduces its value.

11. I do not claim that these numbers are representative. My sample was not random, and toward the end of my fieldwork I made a point of interviewing women who attend *dawe anda*. Most women who attend *dawe anda* are separated from their husbands.

4. "You, I don't even count you"

1. Megeme's phrasing ("I supplied . . .") of the distribution of these compensation pigs is a rhetorical device. Pigs were distributed among both her mother's and her father's kin on both occasions.

2. Huli women rarely wear shirts or blouses that expose their shoulders, so Megeme stood out for wearing tank tops. What Megeme proudly called her "Bruce Lee" shoes were black cotton shoes generally called Chinese slippers. Very few women wear flip-flops, let alone shoes, and the tacit expectation is that only women whose jobs require it, such as nurses or teachers, should wear shoes. Other women who do so risk being called "show-off *meri*" or *"bighed meri"*—labels that imply a willfulness and vanity that can invite the disapproval and resentment of others.

3. As discussed earlier, Huli use the Tok Pisin word *"repim"* to refer to any pre- or extramarital sex, consensual or not. Thus, Ogai herself did not know whether her assailant was asserting that he had raped white women or had consensual sex with them.

4. Because the exchange of sex for money in Tari is so decentralized, and because passenger women are extremely reluctant to be identified, it is very difficult to get a sense of, let alone document, the proportion of women who sell sex. Indeed, obtaining interviews with self-identified *pasinja meri* was extremely difficult. Many did not want to draw attention to themselves by being seen walking into my flat, which was on the hospital compound, where other residents sometimes kept track of who came and went. Moreover, initially many of the women assumed that I would disapprove of them and that they would be forced into the position of either lying about their lives, which they did not want to do, or revealing the truth about their lives and thus risking my condemnation. Also, some *pasinja meri* stay up late gambling and sleep during the day. Thus, almost every interview entailed at least two no-show appointments before the interview actually took place. In all I conducted interviews with eighteen self-identified passenger women, and had informal conversations with many more who declined a more formal interview.

5. People do on occasion use the term *"pasinja man." Pasinja man* similarly implies mobility and lack of social connectedness and purpose, but these meanings are not sexualized as they are in the case of *pasinja meri*.

6. The Tok Pisin word *"sikarap"* means itch or scratch, but is also used to convey eagerness or restlessness.

7. A number of scholars have argued that the female body is a site through which the struggles of colonialism and racism take place, noting that differently racialized bodies have different meanings and values (Fanon 1967; JanMohamed

1992; Fuss 1994; Sharpe 1991). For example, Bergner, commenting on Fanon's *Black Skin, White Masks,* argues, "If women function as commodities mediating social and symbolic relationships among men, then colonialism may be contested largely through the ability of black men and white men to control the exchange of 'their' women. For example, white men succeed in colonizing black men to the extent that they are not subject to black men's dictates regarding 'their' (black men's) women (i.e., black women)" (1995: 81). Similarly, in his interpretation of the rape and murder of a black woman by a black man in Richard Wright's novel, *Native Son,* JanMohamed asserts that Wright proceeds from the perspective of "a protagonist so profoundly castrated that he experiences himself as an already 'feminized' black male who needs to (re)assert his 'manhood' through rape and murder. The fundamental premise . . . is that the protagonist can [through rape and murder] overcome the racialization of his subjectivity . . . [The novel] demonstrates in fact that the phallocratic order can . . . position some black males in such a way that they are incapable of asserting their 'manhood' against racism except by replicating phallocratic violence against women . . . Within this highly charged matrix, Wright characterizes sexuality in general and rape in particular as the paradigm of all modes of crossing the racial boundary" (1992: 108).

In these examples and their exegeses, the black woman's subjective experience of sexual appropriation and devaluation is effaced; indeed, in Wright's narrative she ceases to exist (i.e., she is murdered). Ogai's rape—and the construction of her identity as un-rapeable—is another example of black women's devaluation in the context of (post)colonial relations; however, Ogai's subjectivity was not effaced by this experience. Indeed, Ogai, and other women who eventually decide to become passenger women, are interesting in part because they refuse to be effaced, and they work hard to articulate their experiences of rape, despite the failure of the local representational system to provide a meaningful way to do so.

8. No man would take a *pasinja meri* as a first or even a second wife. For one, a man's kin would refuse to help him with bridewealth payments for such an ignominious match. Moreover, since *pasinja meri* are said to be lazy and infertile, most young men—set to embark on building families and pig herds—would perceive such a match as too risky. However, once a man has successfully achieved these markers of full adult masculinity, he may be willing to take a reputed *pasinja meri* as a third or fourth wife.

9. The husband that Megeme fights with in this incident is different from the husband she claims to have almost killed in my opening vignette about her.

5. "Eating her own vagina"

1. The "commoditization" of sex in this conceptualization is, then, actually a double theft: the "theft" of a woman's sexuality from her kin by her male sexual partner, and the theft by the woman herself of the compensation owed to her kin for the first theft.

2. The corporeal consequences of being a passenger woman resemble those at-

tributed to witchcraft—another female figure of perverse consumption—but in this case passenger women seem to play the roles of both witch and victim, both consumer and consumed. Passenger women are said to become infertile, to age quickly, and to rot from the inside out. Witches are said to eat the internal organs of their victims, also causing them to rot from the inside out. I am reluctant to make too much of this symbolic resonance, however, since Huli people themselves do not draw explicit parallels between witches and passenger women.

3. As it was explained to me, selling garden produce is arduous and risky: you have to carry heavy string-bags full of sweet potatoes or greens all the way to market, and then, if they go unsold, you have to carry them back home, and by then they may be starting to dry out or rot. Thus, for many women, the goal is to save enough money selling produce to buy lightweight wholesale goods—such as instant noodle soups, soap, or cigarettes—which one then sells per piece at a price just below those of local trade stores but still high enough above the wholesale price to make a small profit. Such items are easier to carry and can be stored for long periods of time if they do not sell quickly. The one drawback to this strategy is that civil servants working in Tari frown upon the sale of store goods at market; "village women should sell village produce," many town inhabitants maintain. Indeed, there have been efforts by some town women, such as nurses, to implement a ban on the sale of store goods at market. Nevertheless, once a woman has saved up enough money selling such goods, the next step is to buy a bundle of used clothing, which tends to sell better than items like soap or cigarettes because there is less competition.

4. While I was careful about my reputation, I was frank about my own sex/love life when talking to some passenger women. I hoped that candid discussions of my own sexuality would indicate that I was not going to be judgmental about theirs. Moreover, in essence we engaged in what I came to think of as a mutual exchange of risk: I could potentially gossip about them and damage their reputations; they could potentially gossip about me and thus put me at much greater risk for sexual violence.

5. I hesitate to label these sexual practices "untraditional" since there is little information about what Huli couples actually did sexually during the precolonial period. And, as anthropologists have often discovered, actual practice can depart dramatically from what is asserted as normative or ideal. Nevertheless, it is accurate to say that newly married Huli men have long been schooled in the dangers of female sexual fluids and in ways to minimize exposure to them (Frankel 1986), and there does not ever seem to have been any schooling of young men or women in sexual techniques for pleasing marital partners.

6. Implicit in many studies of prostitution, and in Western constructions of (hetero)sexuality more generally, is a pseudobiological assumption that men are the sexual desirers and women the desirables: of course it is women who sell sex, withhold sex, and variously bargain with the one chip they automatically have regardless of other conditions. However, sexual desire is not everywhere constructed in this particular way. A number of critics of naturalized or biologized notions of prostitution have asserted that prostitution has little to do with desire,

and everything to do with power, the implication being that if women were the ones with economic and political power, they just might find themselves paying men for sex.

7. According to my observations in four households, more care is taken to make sure that little boys are washed with soap, have oil rubbed on their skin, and are dressed in nice clothing. However, I never witnessed any preferential feeding of boys over girls, any neglect of girls, or any evidence that boys have better access to health care than girls, or anything that would suggest more emotional nurturance of boys. There is, however, preferential schooling of boys.

8. The Huli conceptualization of desirability as a source of power may sound reminiscent of the work of Camille Paglia and other like-minded theorists, what critics have sometimes called "Babe Feminism" (Quindlen 1996). However, even Huli passenger women, who often assert that their ability to attract male desire gives them some influence over men's money, would not argue that this compensates for the fact that women have less control over land, less control over dispute settlement, less access to wage labor, less access to education, etc.

9. In quite different ethnographic areas, Mayfair Yang (1999) and Lila Abu-Lughod (1998) also discuss the shifting terrain of gender as women are increasingly seen, and come to see themselves, as objects of male desire. As Yang says of a young Chinese woman, "She feels a certain guilt about replacing her proletarian masculinity and defecting to the bourgeois feminine side. Once she has gotten used to her new persona, she begins to enjoy the male desire and admiration she can elicit. In this new identity as a beautiful woman, a different gender structure emerges in her . . . her subjectivity is gauged by the pleasure she can produce in the male. This new construction of woman has a definite material dimension, as it is both product as well as driving force of the new market economy" (49–50). Abu-Lughod similarly notes, "Young Bedouin women in Egypt try to resist their elders and the kin-based forms of domination they represent by embracing aspects of a commodified sexuality—buying makeup and negligees—that carry with them both new forms of control and new freedoms" (1998: 13). Both Yang and Abu-Lughod emphasize the way in which commodity penetration affords young women the means to resist certain forms of subordination (by the state, by the gerontocratic patriarchal family), but also makes them vulnerable to new forms, such as the commoditization of the eroticized female body. The penetration of commodities in Papua New Guinea has not (yet) had an impact on Huli passenger women's visual appearance, and, in fact, most are indistinguishable from other Huli women. Although some would certainly like to experiment with products that are thought to enhance and modernize a woman's appearance, most are too afraid of violent male reprisal to do so.

10. "*Tene*" refers to the root or first cause of something. In genealogies, the *tene* are the agnates of clans; in myths, *tene* are those substances or events that created important ritual objects or features of the landscape; and in court cases, *tene* are the persons or actions that instigated a conflict. As Goldman asserts, the Huli have a "predilection for explanations in terms of 'first causes' *(tene)* . . . *tene* is used to attribute causation, ownership, and responsibility" (1983: 78).

11. At an earlier time I might not have written "(yet)" in this sentence. However, since my doctoral research in 1995–97, the Papua New Guinea currency has been devalued significantly, and health and economic services have declined from already poor levels. I do therefore wonder whether the nature and meaning of women's monetized sexual exchanges will change and become shaped more by "structural violence" (Farmer et al. 1996).

12. In point of fact, men also use *hubi bi,* and some of it is directed at attracting women, but often its purpose is to attain women without having to pay bridewealth.

13. Although women sometimes complain that *hubi bi* doesn't work or isn't real, more often they worry that it works too well. I had a few friends who had used love magic to ensure that their husbands would be devoted to them, and they complained that they ended up with men who followed them around like puppy dogs. Their *"hongo"* seemed completely vitiated; they were no longer like men. On the other hand, other women claimed that *hubi bi* had worked so well that their husbands had become fiercely jealous and abusive at the slightest hint that their interest had waned or migrated elsewhere. "Be careful what you wish for" was the *hubi bi* caveat; the devotion of the beloved can be a two-edged sword.

14. Tari Hospital staff, familiar with this belief, denied that they'd ever had to remove a condom from a woman's vagina and expressed impatience at the persistence of this belief. It is possible that women attribute pelvic inflammatory disease, quite common according to Tari Hospital records, to "stuck" condoms.

6. "When the pig and the bamboo knife are ready"

1. *"Dawe anda"* literally means courtship house — that is, the place where the ritualized team singing takes place. However, the term is also used by Huli speakers to refer to the activity of ritualized singing at *dawe anda.* Therefore, in this chapter I use the term *"dawe anda"* to refer to both place and activity/ritual.

2. The way "sex seekers" and "sex providers" come together varies. One of the more well-known *pasinja meri* in Tari had young men act as messengers for her; for example, if a wealthy looking businessman stepped off the plane, they would inform her so that she could go try to entice him. She usually gave the young men a small share of whatever she received for helping to arrange these liaisons. In contrast, both Megeme and Ogai said they were briefly members of *pasinja meri* groups that were led by a *"boss meri"* (boss woman) with whom men could negotiate. Megeme described these groups as quite organized, while Ogai suggested they were more contingent, only coming together upon specific requests by men. More commonly, passenger women said that they acted individually, and that men would approach them at market, video houses, bush discos, or on the road.

3. It is important to note that while disapproving of *dawe anda,* hospital staff were also open to STD prevention strategies other than *dawe anda* eradication. For example, they supported the idea of condom distribution and STD education at *dawe anda* sites, and were even willing to discuss the administration of STD

medication at *dawe anda* based on men's reports of their symptoms to me. I engaged in condom distribution and STD education at a *dawe anda* on an ad hoc basis during the last month of my fieldwork: men were willing to be interviewed if I gave them condoms and answered their questions about STDs/HIV. The administration of STD medication at *dawe anda*—which I was already uneasy about for reasons of sustainability and lack of a plan for including men's wives—never took place because a murder in Tari led to the closure of the *dawe anda* I had been attending.

4. To some extent the *dawe* genre is the male equivalent of women's mourning songs. The two genres use a similar melodic pattern, and both draw heavily on people's knowledge of the place-names associated with specific persons—the dead, in the case of mourning songs, and the beloved, in the case of *dawe* songs (Goldman 1983). Once when I heard a man singing in the distance and asked Lirime what it was, she impatiently answered, *"disco song o daiman song, mi no save. Longwe na tupela wankain, yia"* (Is it a "disco" [i.e., *dawe anda*] song or a "dead man" [i.e., mourning] song, I don't know. It's far away and the two sound the same).

5. Laurence Goldman (personal communication) notes that the first half of this phrase could also be translated as, "When the birds fly from the trees . . ." My male informants who attended this particular *dawe anda* provided the translation used here. In general, *dawe* songs are quite difficult to translate in the abstract. Everyday words can take on different meanings at *dawe anda;* abstruse, esoteric vocabulary is often used; and the erotic implications of specific verses sometimes only emerge contextually in relation to the specific women being sung to. In other words, an accurate, fully developed translation can only really be provided by someone who attended the *dawe anda* in question and who remembers the specific participants and the emotional dynamics of that evening.

6. Both bush discos and *dawe anda* take place after dark, involve music, are considered illicit, and occasionally occur side by side; that is, the male organizer will mark off two different spaces—one for a *dawe anda* and one for a bush disco—and participants can move from one to the other as they desire. However, the two are different: bush discos are a relatively recent innovation in which a local "string band" plays and men and women dance together.

7. While it is likely that women who attend *dawe anda* experience higher rates of infertility than women who do not, in fact two of the women I interviewed had been pregnant, according to my female field assistant (although they themselves did not mention these pregnancies during the interviews). She did not know what had happened to the infants, but mentioned a number of possibilities: they had been given to kin to raise; they had been given to the nurses at Tari Hospital, who would find families for them; or they had been "dumped down a pit latrine," the option that most appealed to her sense of *pasinja meri* as "Other." Those women who did speak candidly about becoming pregnant while at the *dawe anda* asserted that their children *"nogat papa"* (had no father) or were *"mix mix,"* were formed from the semen of too many men. They felt that they could make no claims on a father, since they didn't know who the father was, and most

of them believed their natal kin would also reject the child as "fatherless"—that is, without real identity since the clan of the child's father was unknown.

8. I realize here that I am eliding church and state, institutions that are, in fact, separate in Papua New Guinea. (The Preamble to the Papua New Guinea Constitution does vow "to guard and pass on to those who come after us . . . the Christian principles that are ours now." However, this is the only part of the constitution that mentions Christianity, and the constitution itself guarantees religious freedom; indeed the Baha'i faith has long been present in Papua New Guinea, and there are now between 1,000 and 2,000 Muslims in the country.) However, Huli people themselves—men who attend *dawe anda,* in particular— elide church and state in their discourse, sometimes (although certainly not always) characterizing them as entities that seek to erode cultural traditions and to constrain and discipline Huli people. Moreover, many public services in Tari (and elsewhere in Papua New Guinea) are, in fact, administered by various Christian churches. Most of the nurses at Tari Hospital, for example, were educated at nursing schools run by either the Catholic or Lutheran churches, and the information and education they provide to patients often reflects a religious and sometimes moralistic orientation.

9. Indeed, the politician mentioned above deliberately tried to court the "grassroots" by attending a number of *dawe anda,* buying all the participants tea and biscuits and showing that he was a credible inventor and performer of *dawe* songs. He was not, he implied, someone who had become too worldly or too Christian to appreciate *dawe anda.* Most of the people I spoke with spotted right off that this was a strategy to appeal to a rural male constituency that feels alienated from both government and church, but they also appreciated it as an insightful and clever strategy.

Conclusion

1. HIV positive cases have been reported in all provinces. One recent analysis of reported cases showed that only 60% specified age, 20% occupation, and 33% province of origin; thus, it is difficult to make generalizations about distribution or transmission patterns (AusAID 2002). However, almost 95% of the cases reported gender, and it is fairly certain that HIV is distributed equally between men and women.

2. One study in Eastern Highlands Province found, for example, that 26% of women tested positive for chlamydia, 46% for trichomoniasis, 1.5% for gonorrhea, and 4% for syphilis (Tiwara et al. 1996; Passey 1996). Since trichomonal infections increase the risk of transmission of HIV by a factor of 2.7, and chlamydial infection increases the risk by 4.5 (Fleming and Wasserheit 1999), there is good reason to worry that HIV will rapidly spread, even in rural areas of Papua New Guinea.

3. In 1987, attendance at the Tari Hospital STD clinic totaled 428; by 1989 the figure was 905 (Hughes 1991a), and in 1995, 985 patients tested positive for an

STD (although one monthly report was missing, so the figure is probably closer to 1,085). During my research, Tari Hospital regularly ran out of materials needed for laboratory diagnosis and thus many diagnoses were based solely on clinical examination, an inadequate method since women are often asymptomatic for gonorrhea and chlamydia. This information suggests an increase in STDs since 1987 (or at least an increase in people attending the STD clinic), but it also shows the inadequacies of relying on case reports as a source of epidemiological data.

4. Also prominent in moral etiologies of *gonolia* was the conviction—particularly among women, who, with less access to formal education and radios, tend to be less knowledgeable about biomedical notions of disease transmission—that it is only one's own sexual transgressions that can cause *gonolia*. In other words, many women I interviewed asserted that it was not possible for a wife to be infected by her husband because it was only her own sexual transgressions that caused disease. This notion is not universal, however: some women also say, for example, that anyone can contract *gonolia* from sharing clothes or cigarettes with passenger women, and a few women I interviewed objected to their husbands' taking a passenger woman as an additional wife in part because of the fear of contracting *gonolia*. Nevertheless, awareness about the possibility of marital transmission was not high at that time, and even some men I interviewed were shocked at the possibility that they could infect their wives with *gonolia*, potentially causing their infertility.

5. More than most of the other self-identified passenger women I knew, Megeme had engaged in many long-term romantic relationships in addition to her more commercial exchanges. However, she was quite clear about which of her long-term relationships were marriages and which were not. She'd had four husbands—distinguished from her other relationships by the fact that they had all given at least a nominal amount of bridewealth to her kin. Those men with whom she had lived for a few months but who had never given any gifts or money to her family, she did not consider husbands.

6. It is important to note, however, that many of the factors that do tend to push women into such desperate positions—less access to education and employment, marital separation because of the organization of labor, currency devaluation, stringent structural adjustment programs, a national economy centered on the export of natural resources—are present in Papua New Guinea and have shaped the sexual economy elsewhere (Hammar 1996a, 1996b). Moreover, "structural violence" may express itself somewhat differently in this context; for example, when men violently punish *pasinja meri* for making class differences between men more visible by choosing men who can pay more.

7. Feminist scholars have shown the slippery nature of what I am calling erotic agency (Quindlen 1996). Both Lila Abu-Lughod (1998) and Mayfair Yang (1999), for example, have examined the ways in which women's newfound "erotic agency" quickly and easily becomes enmeshed in capitalist commodity relations, thus binding them into new structures of inequality.

References

Abu-Lughod, Lila

1990 The Romance of Resistance: Tracing Transformations of Power through Bedouin Women. *American Ethnologist* 17: 41–55.

1998 Introduction: Feminist Longings and Postcolonial Conditions. In L. Abu-Lughod (ed.), *Remaking Women: Feminism and Modernity in the Middle East*, pp. 3–31. Princeton: Princeton University Press.

Ahearn, Laura

2001 Language and Agency. *Annual Review of Anthropology* 30: 109–37.

Akin, David, and Joel Robbins (eds.)

1999 *Money and Modernity: State and Local Currencies in Melanesia*. Pittsburgh: University of Pittsburgh Press.

Allison, Anne

1994 *Nightwork: Sexuality, Pleasure, and Corporate Masculinity in a Tokyo Hostess Club*. Chicago: University of Chicago Press.

Allen, Bryant.

1995 At Your Peril: Studying Huli Residence. In A. Biersack (ed.), *Papuan Borderlands: Huli, Duna, and Ipili Perspectives on the Papua New Guinea Highlands*, pp. 141–71. Ann Arbor: University of Michigan Press.

Amadiume, Ifi

1987 *Male Daughters, Female Husbands: Gender and Sex in an African Society*. London: Zed Books.

Armstrong, Aurelia

2003 Foucault and Feminism. In *The Internet Encyclopedia of Philosophy* (www.iep.utm.edu/f/foucfem.htm).

AusAID
2002 Potential Economic Impact of an HIV/AIDS Epidemic in Papua New Guinea. Report prepared for AusAID by the Centre for International Economics.

Baier, Annette
1985 *Postures of the Mind: Essays on Mind and Morals.* Minneapolis: University of Minnesota Press.

Ballard, Chris
1994 The Centre Cannot Hold: Trade Networks and Sacred Geography in the Papua New Guinea Highlands. *Archeology Oceania* 29: 130–48.

1995 The Death of a Great Land: Ritual History and Subsistence Revolution in the Southern Highlands of Papua New Guinea. PhD dissertation, the Australian National University.

2002 A History of Huli Society and Settlement in the Tari Region. *Papua New Guinea Medical Journal* 45(1–2): 8–14.

Barss, Peter Geoffrey
1991 Health Impact of Injuries in the Highlands of Papua New Guinea: A Verbal Autopsy Study. PhD dissertation, Johns Hopkins University, School of Public Health.

Bartky, Sandra Lee
1988 Foucault, Femininity, and the Modernization of Patriarchal Power. In I. Diamond and L. Quinby (eds.), *Feminism and Foucault: Reflections on Resistance,* pp. 61–86. Boston: Northeastern University Press.

1995 Agency: What's the Problem? In J. Gardiner (ed.), *Provoking Agents: Gender and Agency in Theory and Practice,* pp. 178–93. Urbana: University of Illinois Press.

Beck, Ulrich, and Elisabeth Beck-Gernsheim
1995 *The Normal Chaos of Love.* Cambridge: Polity Press.

Behar, Ruth
1993 *Translated Woman: Crossing the Border with Esperanza's Story.* Boston: Beacon Press.

Bergner, Gwen
1995 Who Is That Masked Woman? Or, the Role of Gender in Fanon's *Black Skin, White Masks. PMLA* 110(1): 75–88.

Biersack, Aletta
1987 Moonlight: Negative Images of Transcendence in Paiela Pollution. *Oceania* 57: 178–94.

1991 Thinking Difference: A Review of Marilyn Strathern's *The Gender of the Gift. Oceania* 62: 147–54.

1992 Short-fuse Mining Politics in the Jet Age: From Stone to Gold at Mt. Kare and Porgera. Paper presented at the annual meeting of the American Anthropological Association. San Francisco, December 5.

1995a Introduction: The Huli, Duna, and Ipili Peoples Yesterday and Today. In A. Biersack (ed.), *Papuan Borderlands: Huli, Duna, and Ipili Perspectives on the Papua New Guinea Highlands,* pp. 1–54. Ann Arbor: University of Michigan Press.

1995b Heterosexual Meanings: Society, Economy, and Gender among Ipilis. In A. Biersack (ed.), *Papuan Borderlands: Huli, Duna, and Ipili Perspectives on the Papua New Guinea Highlands,* pp. 231–63. Ann Arbor: University of Michigan Press.

1998 Horticulture and Hierarchy: The Youthful Beautification of the Body in the Paiela and Porgera Valleys. In G. Herdt and S. Leavitt (eds.), *Adolescence in Pacific Island Societies,* pp. 71–91. Pittsburgh: University of Pittsburgh Press.

1999 The Mount Kare Python and his Gold: Totemism and Ecology in the Papua New Guinea Highlands. *American Anthropologist* 101(1): 68–87.

2001 Reproducing Inequality: The Gender Politics of Male Cults in the Papua New Guinea Highlands and Amazonia. In T. Gregor and D. Tuzin (eds.), *Gender in Amazonia and Melanesia: An Exploration of the Comparative Method,* pp. 69–90. Berkeley: University of California Press.

Bordo, Susan

1993 *Unbearable Weight: Feminism, Western Culture, and the Body.* Berkeley: University of California Press.

Bourdieu, Pierre

1976 Marriage Strategies as Strategies of Social Reproduction. In R. Forster and O. Ranum (eds.), *Family and Society: Selections from the Annales,* pp. 117–44. Baltimore: Johns Hopkins University Press.

1977 *Outline of a Theory of Practice.* Cambridge: Cambridge University Press.

Bourdieu, Pierre, and Loic J. D. Wacquant

1992 *An Invitation to Reflexive Sociology.* Chicago: University of Chicago Press.

Bradley, Christine

1988 Wife-Beating in Papua New Guinea—Is It a Problem? *Papua New Guinea Medical Journal* 31: 257–68.

Breton, Stéphane

1999 Social Body and Icon of the Person: A Symbolic Analysis of Shell Money among the Wodani, Western Highlands of Irian Jaya. *American Ethnologist* 26(3): 558–82.

Bristow, Joseph

1997 *Sexuality.* London: Routledge.

Burbank, Victoria

1994 *Fighting Women: Anger and Aggression in Aboriginal Australia/Victoria.* Berkeley: University of California Press.

Busby, Cecilia

1997 Permeable and Partible Persons: A Comparative Analysis of Gender and Body in South India and Melanesia. *Journal of the Royal Anthropological Institute* 3(2): 261–78.

Butler, Judith

1990 *Gender Trouble: Feminism and the Subversion of Identity.* New York: Routledge.

1997 *Excitable Speech: A Politics of the Performative.* New York: Routledge.

Carrier, James

1992 Occidentalism: the World Turned Upside-Down. *American Ethnologist* 19: 195–212.

Clark, Jeffrey

1993 Gold, Sex, and Pollution: Male Illness and Myth at Mt. Kare, Papua New Guinea. *American Ethnologist* 20(4): 742–57.

1995 Shit Beautiful: Tambu and Kina Revisited. *Oceania* 65(3): 195–211.

1997 State of Desire: Transformations in Huli Sexuality. In L. Manderson and M. Jolly (eds.), *Sites of Desire/Economies of Pleasure: Sexualities in Asia and the Pacific,* pp. 191–211. Chicago: University of Chicago Press.

Clark, Jeffrey, and Jenny Hughes

1995 A History of Sexuality and Gender in Tari. In A. Biersack (ed.), *Papuan Borderlands: Huli, Duna, and Ipili Perspectives on the Papua New Guinea Highlands,* pp. 315–40. Ann Arbor: University of Michigan Press.

Code, Lorraine

1991 *What Can She Know? Feminist Theory and the Construction of Knowledge.* Ithaca: Cornell University Press.

Counts, Dorothy

1992 "All Men Do It": Wife-Beating in Kaliai, Papua New Guinea. In D. Counts, J. Brown, and J. Campbell (eds.), *Sanctions and Sanctuary: Cultural Perspectives on the Beating of Wives,* pp. 63–76. Boulder: Westview Press.

1993 The Fist, the Stick, and the Bottle of Bleach: Wife Bashing and Suicide in a Papua New Guinea society. In V. S. Lockwood, T. Harding, and B. Wallace (eds.), *Contemporary Pacific Societies: Studies in Development and Change,* pp. 249–55. Englewood Cliffs, NJ: Prentice-Hall.

Dasgupta, Shamita Das, and Sayantani Dasgupta

1996 Public Face, Private Space: Asian Indian Women and Sexuality. In N. Maglin and D. Perry (eds.), *Bad Girls/Good Girls: Women, Sex, and Power in the Nineties,* pp. 226–47. New Brunswick: Rutgers University Press.

Deveaux, Monique

1996 Feminism and Empowerment: A Critical Reading of Foucault. In S. Hekman (ed.), *Feminist Interpretations of Michel Foucault,* pp. 211–38. University Park: Pennsylvania State University Press.

de Zalduondo, Barbara

1991 Prostitution Viewed Cross-Culturally: Toward Recontextualizing Sex Work in AIDS Intervention Research. *The Journal of Sex Research* 28(2): 223–48.

Dirks, Nicholas, Geoff Eley, and Sherry Ortner
1994 Introduction. In N. Dirks, G. Eley, and S. Ortner (eds.), *Culture/Power/History: A Reader in Contemporary Social Theory,* pp. 3–48. Princeton: Princeton University Press.

Dureau, Christine
1998 From Sister to Wives? Changing Contexts of Maternity on Simbo, Western Solomon Islands. In K. Ram and M. Jolly (eds.), *Modernities and Maternities: Colonial and Postcolonial Experiences in Asia and the Pacific,* pp. 239–74. Cambridge: Cambridge University Press.

Errington, Frederick, and Deborah Gewertz
1998 On Humiliation and Class in Contemporary Papua New Guinea. Paper presented at the annual meeting of the American Anthropological Association. Philadelphia.

Ewing, Katherine
1990 The Illusion of Wholeness: Culture, Self, and the Experience of Inconsistency. *Ethos* 18(3): 251–78.

Fanon, Frantz
1967 *Black Skin, White Masks.* Translated by Charles Markmann. New York: Grove.

Farmer, Paul, M. Connors, and J. Simmons (eds.)
1996 *Women, Poverty and AIDS: Sex, Drugs and Structural Violence.* Monroe, Maine: Common Courage Press.

Felski, Rita
1995 *The Gender of Modernity.* Cambridge: Harvard University Press.

Filer, Colin
1985 What Is This Thing Called "Brideprice"? *Mankind* 15(2): 163–83.

Fleming, D. T., and J. N. Wasserheit
1999 From Epidemiological Synergy to Public Health Practice: The Contribution of Other Sexually Transmitted Disease to Sexual Transmission of HIV Infection. *Sexually Transmitted Infections* 75(1): 3–17.

Foster, Robert
1995 *Social Reproduction and History in Melanesia.* Cambridge: Cambridge University Press.

2002 *Materializing the Nation: Commodities, Consumption, and Media in Papua New Guinea.* Bloomington: Indiana University Press.

Foucault, Michel
1979 *Discipline and Punish: The Birth of the Prison.* New York: Vintage/Random House.

1990a *The History of Sexuality. An Introduction: Volume 1.* New York: Vintage Books.

1990b *The Use of Pleasure. The History of Sexuality, Volume 2.* New York: Vintage Books.

Frankel, Stephen

1980 "I Am Dying of Man." *Culture, Medicine, and Psychiatry* 4: 95–117.

1986 *The Huli Response to Illness.* Cambridge: Cambridge University Press.

Fuss, Diane

1994 Interior Colonies: Frantz Fanon and the Politics of Identification. *Diacritics* 24(2–3): 20–42.

Gardner, Donald S.

1984 A Note on the Androgynous Qualities of the Cassowary: Or Why the Mianmin Say It Is Not a Bird. *Oceania* 55(2): 137–45.

Geertz, Clifford

1984 From the Native's Point of View: On the Nature of Anthropological Understanding. In R. Shweder and R. LeVine (eds.), *Culture Theory,* pp. 123–136. Cambridge: Cambridge University Press.

Gewertz, Deborah, and Frederick Errington

1996 On PepsiCo and Piety in a Papua New Guinea "Modernity." *American Ethnologist* 23(3): 476–93.

1998 Sleights of Hand and the Construction of Desire in a Papua New Guinea Modernity. *The Contemporary Pacific* 10(2): 345–68.

Giddens, Anthony

1984 *The Constitution of Society: Outline of the Theory of Structuration.* Berkeley: University of California Press.

Glasse, Robert M.

1959 Revenge and Redress among the Huli: A Preliminary Account. *Mankind* 5(7): 273–89.

1968 *Huli of Papua: A Cognatic Descent System.* Paris: Mouton.

1974 Le Masque de la Volupté: Symbolisme et Antagonisme Sexuels sur les Hauts Plateaux de Nouvelle-Guinée. *L'Homme* 14(2): 79–86.

1995 Time Belong Mbingi: Religious Syncretism and the Pacification of the Huli. In A. Biersack (ed.), *Papuan Borderlands: Huli, Duna, and Ipili Perspectives on the New Guinea Highlands,* pp. 57–86. Ann Arbor: University of Michigan Press.

Goldman, Laurence

1981 Compensation and Disputes in Huli. In R. Scaglion (ed.), *Homicide Compensation in Papua New Guinea: Problems and Prospects,* pp. 56–69. Law Reform Commission of Papua New Guinea, Monograph No. 1.

1983 *Talk Never Dies: The Language of Huli Disputes.* London: Tavistock.

1986 The Presentational Style of Women in Huli Disputes. *Papers in New Guinea Linguistics* 24: 213–89.

1987 Ethnographic Interpretations of Parent-Child Discourse in Huli. *Journal of Child Language* 14(3): 447–66.

1988 *Premarital Sex Cases among the Huli: A Comparison between Traditional and Village Court Styles.* Sydney: University of Sydney Press.

1998 *Child's Play: Myth, Mimesis and Make-Believe.* Oxford: Berg.

Gregg, Jessica
2003 *Virtually Virgins: Sexual Strategies and Cervical Cancer in Recife, Brazil.* Stanford: Stanford University Press.

Gregor, Thomas
1990 Male Dominance and Sexual Coercion. In J. Stigler, R. Shweder, and G. Herdt (eds.), *Cultural Psychology: Essays on Comparative Human Development,* pp. 447–95. Cambridge: Cambridge University Press.

Grindstaff, Laura, and Martha McCaughey
1996 Re-Membering John Bobbitt: Castration Anxiety, Male Hysteria, and the Phallus. In A. Myers and S. Wright (eds.), *No Angels: Women Who Commit Violence,* pp. 142–60. San Francisco: Pandora.

Guyer, Jane
1995 The Value of Beti Bridewealth. In J. Guyer (ed.), *Money Matters: Instability, Values and Social Payments in the Modern History of West African Communities,* pp. 113–32. Portsmouth, NH: Heinemann.

Hammar, Lawrence
1992 Sexual Transactions on Daru: With Some Observations on the Ethnographic Enterprise. *Research in Melanesia* 16: 21–54.

1996a Brothels, Bamu, and Tu Kina Bus in South Coast New Guinea: Human Rights Issues and Global Responsibilities. *Anthropology and Humanism* 21(2): 140–58.

1996b Bad Canoes and *Bafalo:* The Political Economy of Sex on Daru Island, Western Province, Papua New Guinea. *Genders* 23: 212–43.

Hansen, Karen Tranberg
2000 *Salaula: The World of Secondhand Clothing and Zambia.* Chicago: University of Chicago Press.

Harris, G. T.
1972 Labor Supply and Economic Development in the Southern Highlands. *Oceania* 43(2): 123–39.

Hartsock, Nancy
1990 Foucault on Power: A Theory for Women? In L. Nicholson (ed.), *Feminism/Postmodernism,* pp. 157–75. New York: Routledge.

Heller, Thomas, Morton Sosna, and David Wellbery (eds.)
1986 *Reconstructing Individualism: Autonomy, Individuality, and the Self in Western Thought.* Stanford: Stanford University Press.

Herdt, Gilbert
1999 *Sambia Sexual Culture: Essays from the Field.* Chicago: University of Chicago Press.

Herdt, Gilbert, and Fitz John P. Poole
  1982 "Sexual Antagonism": The Intellectual History of a Concept in New
    Guinea Anthropology. In F. J. Poole and G. Herdt (eds.), *Sexual Antago-
    nism, Gender, and Social Change in Papua New Guinea. Special Issue of Social
    Analysis* 12: 3–28.

Herdt, Gilbert, and Robert J. Stoller
  1990 *Intimate Communications: Erotics and the Study of Culture.* New York:
    Columbia University Press.

Hughes, Jenny
  1991a STD in the Tari Basin: A Medical Anthropological Study. Research re-
    port prepared for the Papua New Guinea Institute of Medical Research,
    Tari Research Unit.

  1991b Impurity and Danger: The Need for New Barriers and Bridges in the
    Prevention of Sexually-Transmitted Disease in the Tari Basin, Papua New
    Guinea. *Health Transition Review* 1(2): 131–41.

  1997 A History of Sexually Transmitted Diseases in Papua New Guinea. In M.
    Lewis et al. (eds.), *Sex, Disease, and Society: A Comparative History of Sexu-
    ally Transmitted Diseases and HIV/AIDS in Asia and the Pacific,* pp. 231–48.
    Westport, CT: Greenwood Press.

Hunt, Lynn
  1992 Foucault's Subject in *The History of Sexuality.* In D. Stanton (ed.), *Dis-
    courses of Sexuality: From Aristotle to AIDS,* pp. 78–93. Ann Arbor: Univer-
    sity of Michigan Press.

Jacobson-Widding, Anita
  1990 The Shadow as an Expression of Individuality in Congolese Conceptions
    of Personhood. In M. Jackson and I. Karp (eds.), *Personhood and Agency:
    The Experience of Self and Other in African Cultures,* pp. 31–58. Washington,
    DC: Smithsonian Institution Press.

JanMohamed, Abdul R.
  1992 Sexuality on/of the Racial Border: Foucault, Wright, and the Articulation
    of "Racialized Sexuality." In D. Stanton (ed.), *Discourses of Sexuality: From
    Aristotle to AIDS,* pp. 94–116. Ann Arbor: University of Michigan Press.

Jenkins, Carol
  1996 The Homosexual Context of Heterosexual Practice in Papua New
    Guinea. In P. Aggleton (ed.), *Bisexualities and AIDS: International Per-
    spectives,* pp. 191–206. London: Taylor and Francis.

Jinks, B.
  1959 Patrol Report No. 6 on Puyero, Kau'i, and Iumu, Tari district, Southern
    Highlands. Papua New Guinea National Archives.

Johnson, Patricia
  1981 When Dying Is Better than Living: Female Suicide among the Gainj of
    Papua New Guinea. *Ethnology* 20(4): 325–34.

Jolly, Margaret

1992 Partible Persons and Multiple Authors: Review of Marilyn Strathern's *The Gender of the Gift. Pacific Studies* 15(1): 137–49.

1994 *Women of the Place: Kastom, Colonialism and Gender in Vanuatu.* Camberwell, Australia: Harwood Academic Publishers.

1996 *Woman ikat raet long human raet o no?* Women's Rights, Human Rights and Domestic Violence in Vanuatu. In A. Curthoys, H. Irving, and J. Martin (eds.), *The World Upside Down: Feminisms in the Antipodes. Special Issue of Feminist Review* 52: 169–90.

2001a Embodied States: Familial and National Genealogies in Asia and the Pacific. In M. Jolly and K. Ram (eds.), *Borders of Being: Citizenship, Fertility, and Sexuality in Asia and the Pacific,* pp. 1–35. Ann Arbor: University of Michigan Press.

2001b Damming the Rivers of Milk? Fertility, Sexuality, and Modernity in Melanesia and Amazonia. In T. Gregor and D. Tuzin (eds.), *Gender in Amazonia and Melanesia: An Exploration of the Comparative Method,* pp. 175–206. Berkeley: University of California Press.

n.d. Domestic Violence in Vanuatu: A View from Australia. Unpublished manuscript.

Jorgensen, Dan

1993 Money and Marriage in Telefolmin: From Sister Exchange to Daughter as Trade Store. In R. Marksbury (ed.), *The Business of Marriage: Transformations in Oceanic Matrimony,* pp. 57–82. Pittsburgh: University of Pittsburgh Press.

Josephides, Lisette

1991 Metaphors, Metathemes, and the Construction of Sociality: A Critique of the New Melanesian Ethnography. *Man* 26: 145–61.

Karp, Ivan

1986 Agency and Social Theory: A Review of Anthony Giddens. *American Ethnologist* 13(1): 131–37.

Keesing, Roger

1985 Kwaio Women Speak: The Micropolitics of Autobiography in a Solomon Island Society. *American Anthropologist* 87(1): 27–39.

Kempadoo, Kamala

1998 Introduction: Globalizing Sex Workers' Rights. In Kamala Kempadoo and Jo Doezema (eds.), *Global Sex Workers: Rights, Resistance, and Redefinition,* pp. 1–28. New York: Routledge.

Knauft, Bruce

1989 Bodily Images in Melanesia: Cultural Substances and Natural Metaphors. In M. Feher, R. Nadaff, and N. Tazi (eds.), *Fragments for a History of the Human Body, Part Three,* pp. 198–279. New York: Urzone.

1996 *Genealogies for the Present in Cultural Anthropology.* New York: Routledge.

1997 Gender Identity, Political Economy, and Modernity in Melanesia and Amazonia. *Journal of the Royal Anthropological Institute* 3: 233–59.

1999 *From Primitive to Postcolonial in Melanesia and Anthropology.* Ann Arbor: University of Michigan.

Kratz, Corinne A.

2000 Forging Unions and Negotiating Ambivalence: Personhood and Complex Agency in Okiek Marriage Arrangement. In D. Masolo and I. Karp (eds.), *African Philosophy as Cultural Inquiry,* pp. 136–71. Bloomington: Indiana University Press.

Kulick, Donald

1992 Anger, Gender, Language Shift and the Politics of Revelation in a Papua New Guinea Village. *Pragmatics* 2(3): 281–96.

1993 Speaking as a Woman: Structure and Gender in Domestic Arguments in a New Guinea Village. *Cultural Anthropology* 8(4): 510–41.

Kyakas, Alome, and Polly Wiessner

1992 *From Inside the Women's House: Enga Women's Lives and Traditions.* Buranda, Australia: Robert Brown.

Law, Lisa

1997 A Matter of "Choice": Discourses on Prostitution in the Philippines. In L. Manderson and M. Jolly (eds.), *Sites of Desire, Economies of Pleasure: Sexualities in Asia and the Pacific,* pp. 233–61. Chicago: University of Chicago Press.

Law Reform Commission of Papua New Guinea

1989 The Law of Maintenance in Papua New Guinea. Working Paper no. 23.

Leavitt, Stephen

1998 The *Bikhet* Mystique: Masculine Identity and Patterns of Rebellion among Bumbita Adolescent Males. In G. Herdt and S. Leavitt (eds.), *Adolescence in Pacific Island Societies,* pp. 173–94. Pittsburgh: University of Pittsburgh Press.

Lederman, Rena

1984 Who Speaks Here? Formality and the Politics of Gender in Mendi, Highland Papua New Guinea. In D. Brenneis and F. Myers (eds.), *Dangerous Words: Language and Politics in the Pacific,* pp. 85–107. New York: New York University Press.

Lehman, Deborah

2002 Demography and Causes of Death among the Huli in the Tari Basin. *Papua New Guinea Medical Journal* 45(1–2): 51–62.

Lehman, Deborah, John Vail, Peter Vail, Joe Crocker, Helen Pickering, Michael Alpers, and the Tari Demographic Surveillance Team

1997 Demographic Surveillance in Tari, Southern Highlands Province, Papua New Guinea: Methodology and Trends in Fertility and Mortality between 1979 and 1993. Goroka, Papua New Guinea: Papua New Guinea Institute of Medical Research.

Lindenbaum, Shirley

1979 *Kuru Sorcery: Disease and Danger in the New Guinea Highlands*. Mountain View, CA: Mayfield.

LiPuma, Edward

1998 Modernity and Forms of Personhood in Melanesia. In M. Lambek and A. Strathern (eds.), *Bodies and Persons: Comparative Perspectives from Africa and Melanesia*, pp. 53–79. Cambridge: Cambridge University Press.

1999 The Meaning of Money in the Age of Modernity. In D. Akin and J. Robbins (eds.), *Money and Modernity: State and Local Currencies in Melanesia*, pp. 192–213. Pittsburgh: University of Pittsburgh Press.

Macintyre, Martha

1995 Violent Bodies and Vicious Exchanges: Personification and Objectification in the Massim. *Social Analysis* 37: 29–43.

Mackenzie, Catriona, and Natalie Stoljar

2000 Introduction: Autonomy Refigured. In C. Mackenzie and N. Stoljar (eds.), *Relational Autonomy: Feminist Perspectives on Autonomy, Agency, and the Social Self*, pp. 3–31. Oxford: Oxford University Press.

MacLeod, Arlene E.

1992 Hegemonic Relations and Gender Resistance: The New Veiling as Accommodating Protest in Cairo. *Signs* 17(3): 533–57.

MacPherson, C. B.

1962 *The Political Theory of Possessive Individualism: Hobbes to Locke*. Oxford: Oxford University Press.

Maggi, Wynne

2001 *Our Women Are Free: Gender and Ethnicity in the Hindukush*. Ann Arbor: University of Michigan Press.

Mallett, Shelley

2003 *Conceiving Cultures: Reproducing People and Places on Nuakata, Papua New Guinea*. Ann Arbor: University of Michigan Press.

Marksbury, R. (ed.)

1993 *The Business of Marriage: Transformations in Oceanic Matrimony*. Pittsburgh: University of Pittsburgh Press.

McCaughey, Martha

1997 *Real Knockouts: The Physical Feminism of Women's Self-Defense*. New York: New York University Press.

McDowell, N.

1992 Household Violence in a Yuat River Village. In D. Counts, J. Brown, and J. Campbell (eds.), *Sanctions and Sanctuary: Cultural Perspectives on the Beating of Wives*, pp. 87–99. Boulder: Westview Press.

McElhinny, Bonnie

1998 Genealogies of Gender Theory: Practice Theory and Feminism in Sociocultural and Linguistic Anthropology. *Social Analysis* 42(3): 164–89.

McNay, Lois
> 2000 *Gender and Agency: Reconfiguring the Subject in Feminist and Social Theory.* Cambridge: Polity Press.

Meggitt, Mervin J.
> 1964 Male-Female Relationships in the Highlands of Australian New Guinea. *American Anthropologist* 66: 204–24.

Meigs, Anna
> 1990 Multiple Gender Ideologies and Statuses. In P. R. Sanday and R. G. Goodenough (eds.), *Beyond the Second Sex: New Directions in the Anthropology of Gender,* pp. 98–112. Philadelphia: University of Pennsylvania Press.

Mines, Mattison
> 1988 Conceptualizing the Person: Hierarchical Society and Individual Autonomy in India. *American Anthropologist* 90(3): 568–79.

Modjeska, Nicholas
> 1982 Production and Inequality: Perspectives from Central New Guinea. In A. Strathern (ed.), *Inequality in New Guinea Highlands Societies,* 50–108. Cambridge: Cambridge University Press.

Moore, Henrietta
> 1994 *A Passion for Difference: Essays in Anthropology and Gender.* Cambridge: Polity Press.
> 1999 Whatever Happened to Women and Men? Gender and Other Crises in Anthropology. In H. Moore (ed.), *Anthropological Theory Today,* pp. 151–71. Cambridge: Polity Press.

Morris, Meaghan
> 1988 The Pirate's Fiancée: Feminists and Philosophers, or Maybe Tonight It'll Happen. In I. Diamond and L. Quinby (eds.), *Feminism and Foucault: Reflections on Resistance,* pp. 21–42. Boston: Northeastern University Press.

National Sex and Reproduction Research Team (NSRRT) and Carol Jenkins
> 1994 Sexual and Reproductive Knowledge and Behaviour in Papua New Guinea. Papua New Guinea Institute of Medical Research Monograph no. 10. Goroka: Papua New Guinea Institute of Medical Research.

Nihill, Michael
> 1994 New Women and Wild Men: "Development," Changing Sexual Practice and Gender in Highland Papua New Guinea. *Canberra Anthropology* 17(2): 48–72.

O'Hanlon, Michael
> 1989 *Reading the Skin: Adornment, Display and Society among the Wahgi.* Bathurst, Australia: Crawford House Press.

Ortner, Sherry
> 1974 Is Female to Male as Nature Is to Culture? In M. Rosaldo and L. Lamphere (eds.), *Woman, Culture, and Society,* pp. 67–87. Stanford: Stanford University Press.

1984 Theory in Anthropology since the Sixties. *Comparative Studies in Society and History* 26: 126–66.

1989 *High Religion: A Cultural and Political History of Sherpa Buddhism*. Princeton: Princeton University Press.

1995 Resistance and the Problem of Ethnographic Refusal. *Comparative Studies in Society and History* 37(1): 173–93.

1996 *Making Gender: The Politics and Erotics of Culture*. Boston: Beacon Press.

Passey, Megan
1996 Issues in the Management of Sexually Transmitted Diseases in Papua New Guinea. *Papua New Guinea Medical Journal* 39: 252–60.

Pheterson, Gail
1993 "The Whore Stigma: Female Dishonor and Male Unworthiness." *Social Text* 37: 39–64.

Plaza, Monique
1981 Our Damages and Their Compensation—Rape: The "Will Not to Know" of Michel Foucault. *Feminist Issues* 1: 25–35.

Quindlen, Anna
1996 And Now, Babe Feminism. In N. Maglin and D. Perry (eds.), *Bad Girls/Good Girls: Women, Sex and Power in the Nineties*, pp. 3–6. New Brunswick: Rutgers University Press.

Robbins, Joel
1998 Becoming Sinners: Christianity and Desire among the Urapmin of Papua New Guinea. *Ethnology* 37(4): 299–316.

2002 My Wife Can't Break off Part of Her Belief and Give It to Me: Apocalyptic Interrogations of Christian Individualism among the Urapmin of Papua New Guinea. *Paideuma* 48: 189–206.

Rubin, Gayle
1975 The Traffic in Women: Notes on the 'Political Economy' of Sex. In R. Reiter (eds.), *Toward and Anthropology of Women*, pp. 157–210. New York: Monthly Review Press.

1997 Sexual Traffic. Interview with Judith Butler. In E. Weed and N. Schor (eds.), *Feminism Meets Queer Theory*, pp. 6–108. Bloomington: Indiana University Press.

Rutherford, Danilyn
2003 *Raiding the Land of the Foreigners: The Limits of the Nation on an Indonesian Frontier*. Princeton: Princeton University Press.

Ryan, Peter
1991 *Black Bonanza: A Landslide of Gold*. South Yara, Australia: Hyland House Press.

Sacks, Karen
1979 *Sisters and Wives: The Past and Future of Sexual Equality*. Westport, CT: Greenwood Press.

Sahlins, Marshall

1981 *Historical Metaphors and Mythical Realities: Structure in the Early History of the Sandwich Islands Kingdoms.* Ann Arbor: University of Michigan Press.

Sanday, Peggy R.

1981 *Female Power and Male Dominance: On the Origins of Sexual Inequality.* Cambridge: Cambridge University Press.

Schoepf, Brooke

1992 Women at Risk: Case Studies from Zaire. In G. Herdt and S. Lindenbaum (eds.), *The Time of AIDS: Social Analysis, Theory, and Method,* pp. 259–86. Newbury Park: Sage.

1993 Gender, Development, and AIDS: A Political Economy and Culture Framework. In R. Gallin, A. Ferguson, and J. Harper (eds.), *The Women and International Development Annual.* Vol. 3, pp. 53–85. Boulder: Westview Press.

Shanahan, Daniel

1992 *Toward a Genealogy of Individualism.* Amherst: University of Massachusetts Press.

Sharpe, Jenny

1991 The Unspeakable Limits of Rape: Colonial Violence and Counter-Insurgency. *Genders* 10: 25–46.

Shaw, Rosalind

2000 "Tok Af, Lef Af": A Political Economy of Temne Techniques of Secrecy and Self. In I. Karp and D. A. Masolo (eds.), *African Philosophy as Cultural Enquiry,* pp. 25–49. Bloomington: Indiana University Press.

Shweder, Richard, and Edmund Bourne

1984 Does the Concept of the Person Vary Cross-Culturally? In R. Shweder and R. LeVine (eds.), *Culture Theory,* pp. 158–99. Cambridge: Cambridge University Press.

Simmel, Georg

1990 *The Philosophy of Money.* 2nd ed. London: Routledge.

Sökefeld, Martin

1999 Debating Self, Identity, and Culture in Anthropology. *Current Anthropology* 40(4): 417–31.

Soper, Kate

1993 Productive Contradictions. In C. Ramazanoglu (ed.), *Up against Foucault: Explorations of Some Tensions between Foucault and Feminism,* pp. 29–50. London: Routledge.

Stewart, Pamela J., and Andrew Strathern

1998 Money, Politics, and Persons in Papua New Guinea. *Social Analysis* 42(2): 132–49.

2000a Introduction: Narratives Speak. In P. Stewart and A. Strathern (eds.), *Identity Work: Constructing Pacific Lives,* pp. 1–26. Pittsburgh: University of Pittsburgh Press.

2000b Fragmented Selfhood: Contradiction, Anomaly, and Violence in Female Life Histories. In P. Stewart and A. Strathern (eds.), *Identity Work: Constructing Pacific Lives,* pp. 44–57. Pittsburgh: University of Pittsburgh Press.

Stewart, Randall G.

1992 *Coffee: The Political Economy of an Export Industry in Papua New Guinea.* Boulder: Westview Press.

Strathern, Andrew

1977 Why Is Shame on the Skin? In J. Blacking (ed.), *The Anthropology of the Body,* pp. 99–110. London: Academic Press.

1979 Gender, Ideology and Money in Mount Hagen. *Man* 14: 530–48.

1985 Rape in Hagen. In S. Toft (ed.), *Domestic Violence in Papua New Guinea,* pp. 134–40. Port Moresby: Law Reform Commission of Papua New Guinea.

Strathern, Andrew, and Pamela J. Stewart

1999 Objects, Relationships, and Meanings: Historical Switches in Currencies in Mount Hagen, Papua New Guinea. In D. Akin and J. Robbins (eds.), *Money and Modernity: State and Local Currencies in Melanesia,* pp. 164–91. Pittsburgh: University of Pittsburgh Press.

Strathern, Marilyn

1972 *Women in Between: Female Roles in a Male World: Mount Hagen, New Guinea.* London: Seminar Press.

1979 The Self in Self-Decoration. *Oceania* 59: 241–57.

1984 Domesticity and the Denigration of Women. In D. O'Brien and S. Tiffany (eds.), *Rethinking Women's Roles: Perspectives from the Pacific,* pp. 13–31. Berkeley: University of California Press.

1987 No Nature, No Culture: The Hagen Case. In C. MacCormack and M. Strathern (eds.), *Nature, Culture and Gender,* pp. 174–222. Cambridge: Cambridge University Press.

1988 *The Gender of the Gift: Problems with Women and Problems with Society in Melanesia.* Berkeley: University of California Press.

1996 Cutting the Network. *Journal of the Royal Anthropological Institute* 2(3): 517–35.

Sturzenhofecker, Gabriele

1994 Visions of a Landscape: Duna Pre-Meditations on Ecological Change. *Canberra Anthropology* 17(2): 27–47.

1998 *Times Enmeshed: Gender, Space, and History among the Duna of Papua New Guinea.* Stanford: Stanford University Press.

Thomas, Nicholas

1991 *Entangled Objects: Exchange, Material Cultural and Colonialism in the Pacific.* Cambridge: Harvard University Press.

Tiwara, Steven, et al.

1996 High Prevalence of Trichomonal Vaginitis and Chlamydial Cervicitis among a Rural Population in the Highlands of Papua New Guinea. *Papua New Guinea Medical Journal* 39: 234–38.

Toft, Susan (ed.)

1985 *Domestic Violence in Papua New Guinea. Monograph No. 3,* Law Reform Commission of Papua New Guinea.

Turner, Victor

1969 The Ritual Process: Structure and Anti-Structure. Chicago: University of Chicago Press.

Tuzin, Donald

1997 *The Cassowary's Revenge: The Life and Death of Masculinity in a New Guinea Society.* Chicago: University of Chicago Press.

Vail, John

1995 All That Glitters: The Mt. Kare Gold Rush and Its Aftermath. In A. Biersack (ed.), *Papuan Borderlands: Huli, Duna, and Ipili Perspectives on the Papua New Guinea Highlands,* pp. 343–74. Ann Arbor: University of Michigan Press.

2002 Social and Economic Conditions at Tari. *Papua New Guinea Medical Journal* 45(1–2): 113–27.

Valeri, Valerio

1994 Buying Women but Not Selling Them: Gift and Commodity Exchange in Huaulu Alliance. *Man* 29: 1–26.

Van Allen, Judith

1972 Sitting on a Man: Colonialism and the Lost Political Institutions of Igbo Women. *Canadian Journal of African Studies* 6(2): 168–81.

Wardlow, Holly

1993 "Women Are Our Coffee": Historical Factors and Current Variables in Smallholder Coffee Production in Papua New Guinea. Unpublished manuscript.

1996 Bobby Teardrops: A Turkish Video in Papua New Guinea. Reflections on Cultural Studies, Feminism, and the Anthropology of Mass Media. *Visual Anthropology Review* 12(1): 30–46.

2001 The Mt. Kare Python: Huli Myths and Gendered Fantasies of Agency. In A. Rumsey and J. Weiner (eds.), *Mining and Indigenous Life Worlds in Australia and Papua New Guinea,* pp. 31–67. Adelaide, Australia: Crawford House Press.

2002a Headless Ghosts and Roving Women: Specters of Modernity in Papua New Guinea. *American Ethnologist* 29(1): 5–32.

2002b "Hands-Up"ing Buses and Harvesting Cheese-Pops: Gendered Mediation of Modern Disjuncture in Melanesia. In B. Knauft (ed.), *Critically Modern: Alternatives, Alterities, Anthropologies,* pp. 144–72. Bloomington: Indiana University Press.

2002c Giving Birth to *Gonolia:* "Culture" and Sexually Transmitted Disease among the Huli of Papua New Guinea. *Medical Anthropology Quarterly* 16(2): 151–75.

2004 Anger, Economy, and Female Agency: Problematizing "Prostitution" and "Sex Work" in Papua New Guinea. *Signs: Journal of Women in Culture and Society* 29(4): 1017–40.

In press All's Fair When Love Is War: Romantic Passion and Companionate Marriage among the Huli of Papua New Guinea. In J. Hirsch and H. Wardlow (eds.), *Modern Loves: The New Anthropology of Romantic Love and Companionate Marriage.* Ann Arbor: University of Michigan Press.

Watson, J. B.
1977 Pigs, Fodder and the Jones Effect in Postipomoean New Guinea. *Ethnology* 16(1): 57–70.

Weiner, Annette
1992 *Inalienable Possessions: The Paradox of Keeping-While-Giving.* Berkeley: University of California Press.

Weiner, James
1994 The Origin of Petroleum at Lake Kutubu. *Cultural Anthropology* 9: 37–57.

1999 Psychoanalysis and Anthropology: On the Temporality of Analysis. In H. Moore (ed.), *Anthropological Theory Today,* pp. 234–61. Cambridge: Polity Press.

Wikan, Unni
1989 *Managing Turbulent Hearts: A Balinese Formula for Living.* Chicago: Chicago University Press.

Williams, Raymond
1977 *Marxism and Literature.* London: Oxford University Press.

Wood, Andrew W.
1984 Land for Tomorrow: Subsistence Agriculture, Soil Fertility, and Ecosystem Stability. PhD dissertation, University of Papua New Guinea.

Wood, John
1999 *When Men Are Women: Manhood among the Gabra Nomads of East Africa.* Madison: University of Wisconsin Press.

Yang, Mayfair
1999 From Gender Erasure to Gender Difference: State Feminism, Consumer Sexuality, and Women's Public Sphere in China. In M. Yang (ed.), *Spaces of Their Own: Women's Public Sphere in Transnational China,* pp. 35–67. Minneapolis: University of Minnesota Press.

Zimmer-Tamakoshi, Laura
1993a Bachelors, Spinsters, and *Pamuk Meris.* In R. Marksbury (ed.), *The Business of Marriage: Transformations in Oceanic Matrimony,* pp. 83–104. Pittsburgh: University of Pittsburgh Press.

1993b Nationalism and Sexuality in Papua New Guinea. *Pacific Studies* 16(4): 61–97.

1997 "Wild Pigs and Dog Men": Rape and Domestic Violence as "Women's Issues" in Papua New Guinea. In C. Brettell and C. Sargent (eds.), *Gender in Cross-Cultural Perspective,* pp. 538–53. Dallas: Southern Methodist University Press.

Index

Text: 10/13 Galliard
Display: Galliard
Compositor: Binghamton Valley Composition, LLC

CPSIA information can be obtained
at www.ICGtesting.com
Printed in the USA
LVOW12s0635071217
558966LV00002B/353/P